CONSUMER
BOYCOTTS

CONSUMER BOYCOTTS

EFFECTING CHANGE THROUGH THE MARKETPLACE AND THE MEDIA

MONROE FRIEDMAN

ROUTLEDGE
New York and London

Published in 1999 by
Routledge
29 West 35th Street
New York, NY 10001

Published in Great Britain in 1999 by
Routledge
11 New Fetter Lane
London EC4P 4EE

Printed in the United States of America on acid-free paper
Design and composition: Jack Donner

Library of Congress Cataloging-in-Publication Data

Friedman, Monroe.
    Consumer boycotts : effecting change through the marketplace
and the media / by Monroe Friedman.
        p.   cm.
    Includes bibliographical references and index.
    ISBN 0–415–92456–1 (hbk.). — ISBN 0–415–92457–X (pbk.)
    1. Consumer behavior. 2. Boycotts. 3. Consumer satisfaction.
4. Consumer complaints. I. Title.
HF5415.32.F75   1999
381.'3—dc21   99–18522
                                                                CIP

To the memory of
Esther Peterson (1906–1997),
a warm and wonderful
"woman warrior" who
devoted the last third
of a remarkably rich and
productive life to the leadership
of national and international
efforts to protect and empower
consumers. It was my
privilege to have known
and worked with
this extraordinary human being.

CONTENTS

ACKNOWLEDGMENTS

I am indebted to many people who have contributed generously to this scholarly effort. First and foremost are a dozen or so graduate and undergraduate students who have gathered and coded boycott data over the years. Heidi Zimmer has been very helpful here, and no one has devoted more hours to data collection and organization than Jim Cranford.

I am also indebted to many colleagues who have read and commented upon earlier versions of the chapters in the book. They include Ann Bettencourt, Steve Brobeck, Daryl Hafter, Bob Herrmann, Michael Homel, Rob Mayer, Doug Mackenzie-Mohr, Folke Ölander, Stuart Oskamp, Ivan Ross, Howard Schutz, and Michele Wittig. Moreover, Harry Briggs saw the value of a book devoted to consumer boycotts, and I am grateful to him for his encouragement.

I am grateful too to about a dozen typists over these years who struggled to make sense of my longhand scribble. While many contributed to this effort at the University of Leuven in Belgium (where I spent a year as a visiting professor) and at Eastern Michigan University, no one did more than Carolyn Rickelmann, who has had a hand in the typing and retyping of each and every chapter. I owe her a special acknowledgment of thanks.

I would also like to thank the Graduate School of Eastern Michigan University for faculty fellowship grants over the years; these grants provided me with the time and money to complete the boycott research included in this book.

And finally, I would like to thank my wife, Rita, for her emotional, spiritual, and intellectual support over the years of writing and rewriting this book. Her advice and encouragement over these years and, indeed, over the course of my professional career, have never failed to be a source of strength and inspiration.

PREFACE

I caught the boycott bug in 1966 and have never been able to get it out of my system. And like many scholars with a career-long love-hate fascination with a topic or problem, I'm not sure I want to. In the introductory remarks that follow, I start by tracing the history of my academic involvement with boycotts and tell how this involvement led to the writing of this book. I talk next about the content of the book, with emphasis on its origins and organization.

In 1966 I had the good fortune to be awarded a Congressional Fellowship by the American Political Science Association. The Congressional Fellowship program, which is funded by the Ford Foundation, brings young academics and journalists to Washington each year for a nine-month period split into two equal work assignments, one in the office of a senator and the other in the office of a representative. Since I had three free months before the program began, I found a position as a consultant to Esther Peterson, who at that time was working for President Lyndon Johnson as the first Special Assistant to the President for Consumer Affairs. It now appears that these few months were critical ones for Peterson in that a consumer boycott occurred during this period that may have cost her her job. I should add parenthetically that they also got me going, as a young academic, on the topic of boycotts.

What happened to Peterson started in Colorado in the fall of 1966 when a Denver homemaker, outraged at the rapidly increasing prices at her local supermarket and convinced that retail marketing practices were adding to the cost of groceries, called for a local boycott. Like a shot heard 'round the world, the boycott soon spread to some 100 cities across the nation.

Esther Peterson was pleased with this groundswell of boycott activity; indeed, one of her goals in her new White House position was to raise national consciousness of consumer problems, and the nationwide boycott seemed to be just the kind of grassroots initiative she could welcome and support. So off she went to Denver to embrace the boycott, and she expressed her support by posing for a photo with her arm around the boycott leaders. When this graphic depiction of Peterson's solidarity with the boycotters appeared the next day in newspapers across the nation, it triggered reactions of anger and frustration in the corporate boardrooms of major American producers and retailers. They could not believe that the White House, through its new special assistant, was encouraging the American people not to buy groceries in their local supermarkets. The corporate message to the White House was loud and clear: Peterson must go. Shortly thereafter she left her post, and many years later she publicly shared the reasons for her departure in her memoirs: "In the end, I was kicked out of the White House because I was too much of a zealot" (Peterson, 1995, p. 135).

Several months after the Peterson resignation I was working as a Congressional Fellow in the office of Rep. Lester Wolff, D-NY. I was attracted to Wolff's office because he shared my interest in consumer protection, and I thought working with him and his staff would help me understand how behavioral science research on consumer-protection issues affects federal consumer legislation. Having just completed behavioral research studies on two "hot" consumer legislative bills (truth-in-packaging and truth-in-lending), I wanted to find out how such research is used by Congress.

One of Wolff's key concerns was trading stamps, a marketing device that translated into "free gifts" for shoppers but at a cost of about 2 cents for each consumer dollar spent in the supermarket. In the 1960s trading stamps were a major industry; they had created a new form of private currency with booklets for attaching the stamps one had earned, gift catalogs to peruse, and even free-standing redemption centers to spend the currency one had saved. Consumer advocates criticized the marketing device, arguing that it pressured shoppers into participating in the private economy of trading stamps because to not do so meant losing money to the markups that supported trading stamps. Wolff had proposed giving consumers a choice: either trading stamps or a 2 percent reduction on one's supermarket bill at the checkout stand.

When I told Wolff about my recent experience in Peterson's office he quite naturally wondered aloud what role, if any, consumer dissatisfaction with trading stamps had had in the consumer boycott. Wolff's comment got me thinking that it might be helpful to go beyond the news media coverage of the boycott to look at some larger questions. I decided to undertake a survey study of the consumer protest, focusing on protest leaders in 64 communities across the nation. A write-up of this study (Friedman, 1971) appears in abbreviated form in Appendix A in this book.

Several of the study findings were noteworthy from a social science perspective. First, all 64 leaders were women, and almost all were middle-class homemakers whose pocketbooks had been pinched by higher supermarket prices. Frustrated by these circumstances, they devoted hundreds of hours to energizing and directing thousands of people like themselves to participate in the protest. Second, while they used a multipronged approach to their problem, the leaders felt the boycott had been their most effective tactic. And third, their efforts did pay off in price reductions, but only over the short run; the long-term effects on prices, according to the leaders, were far more modest.

The findings were also noteworthy from a humanistic perspective. The consumer protest had unleashed passion in women across the land who found themselves frustrated by circumstances that seemed beyond their control. Inspired by feelings of empowerment perhaps associated with the fledgling women's movement of the 1960s, these women decided in David-versus-Goliath fashion to take on the supermarket industry as well as the producers and processors that supplied it with goods. Adding support and encouragement to their campaign was the unexpected appearance on the scene of a guardian angel in the form of a White House proponent of the consumer interest, Peterson. It seemed at first that they were winning the battle, but a short time later the consumer conflict ran its course with the protesters losing the war.

Boycotts as high drama? Often it seems that they are imbued with this quality, and the more I read about them the more I found that I had been bitten (some would say smitten!) by the boycott bug. I began assembling materials on boycotts, in time amassing a small library of articles and books on the topic. With these materials in hand I did a study of 90 boycotts that occurred in the 1970s (Friedman, 1985). I also developed a conceptual framework and research agenda for boycotts (Friedman, 1991) and looked in depth at boycotts relating to consumer economic concerns (Friedman, 1995a). This was followed by a major study of 24 boycotts concerned with ecological issues (Friedman, 1995b) and a look at how consumer boycotts may be viewed historically as grassroots efforts to confront the corporation (Friedman, 1996a). Next I examined the "buycott" as an alternative to the boycott (Friedman, 1996b), and most recently I have tried to tackle ethical issues relating to boycotts (Friedman, in press).

Much of what appears in this book draws upon these articles. Other major academic sources on consumer protests I have drawn upon include Garrett (1986, 1987) Herrmann (1970, 1991), Mayer (1989), Smith (1990), and many of the entries in the pioneering *Encyclopedia of the Consumer Movement* (Brobeck, 1997). Two early economists contributed comprehensive doctoral dissertations on boycotts, which have also proved to be very helpful (Laidler, 1913; Wolman, 1914). Many of Laidler's and Wolman's observations still appear to be relevant some 80 years beyond their time.

In addition to these academic sources, this book draws upon the works of several contemporary boycott proponents who have served as editors of boycott newspapers and magazines. Like a shooting star, each of these publications has burned brightly for a short time before disappearing from view. Fortunately for their readers, the "short times" have each been about five to seven years, and during these periods the publications' editors provided the latest information on who's boycotting whom, including details of the protest activities.

Todd Putnam deserves special mention for getting the ball rolling in the mid-1980s with his *National Boycott News*, an often-cited tabloid-size newspaper that he published from his home in Seattle for about seven years, first quarterly and then far less frequently. Anne Zorc of Co-op America followed in Washington, D.C., with *Boycott Action News*, which was published for about five years as a self-contained unit of Co-op America's publication, the *Co-op Quarterly*. At about the time of the *National Boycott News*' demise, Zachary Lyons, a Seattle colleague of Putnam's, started a magazine called *Boycott Quarterly*. Lyons had worked with Putnam on *National Boycott News* and had provided a one-page flier called *Boycott Monthly* for several years to interested consumer food cooperatives around the country; each issue provided a thumbnail sketch of an ongoing boycott. The *Boycott Quarterly*, like the *National Boycott News* that preceded it, was a labor of love, a largely one-person operation with input and support from a host of volunteers. However, unlike its predecessors, this magazine had a professional appearance with an attractively designed cover that made creative use of graphics, and its content went beyond boycotts to include stories about economic democracy. The magazine's success at fulfilling its mission was signaled by its being nominated a few years ago by the *Utne Reader* as one of the best new entries of the alternative press.

Unfortunately, this bright star faded when in 1998 a combination of financial pressures and old-fashioned burnout led Lyons to discontinue publication. As this is written in the summer of 1998 there is no national newspaper or magazine to cover boycotts on a regular basis, although Co-op America has contracted with Lyons to prepare, on a continuing basis, a brief overview of ongoing boycotts, which appears on a single page of the *Co-op Quarterly*.

Having met and worked with all of these editors of boycott publications, I can attest to their intelligence, their youthful enthusiasm (all, I believe, were in their 20s or early 30s at the time of their editorships), and their dedication to boycotts as an instrument of change. They have all contributed tremendous amounts of time and energy to provide the latest news on ongoing boycotts as well as additional background stories relating to boycotts; and they did this with little or no thought to their own personal economic welfare, often using their own limited personal funds, or those of their families, to get their publications out to their readers. Collectively, these editors have succeeded in providing their readers with a remarkably rich source of boycott information over the course of the last decade.

All this is not to suggest that these boycott periodicals were free of problems. The most common is endemic to low-budget publications of this kind in that their boycott updates derive from reports voluntarily provided by boycotting groups and the business firms that they target; the quality of the stories appearing in the publications is thus critically dependent on the quality of these reports. Needless to say, both boycotters and businesses boycotted want to present their best sides to the publications' readers. And the bare-bones budgets of the boycott periodicals make it difficult if not impossible for them to check out each side's story. Thus a boycott that has become almost completely inactive might be termed "active" by the boycott representative contacting the boycott publication. Or a target of a successful boycott might not wish to admit this success publicly, so the target representative may feign surprise when asked about the boycott, claiming, "That's the first I've heard of it."

Still another problem with the boycott periodicals is that their coverage favors national boycotts over local boycotts. For a boycott organizer to contact a boycott periodical to provide a summary of recent developments, he or she would have to know about the existence of the periodical and take the time to write up and submit a report. This makes sense for a well-funded national boycott with savvy supporting staff, especially when one considers that the story that appears in the boycott periodical could help to mobilize support for the national boycott. It makes far less sense for a local boycott with a small volunteer staff with little free time and far less to gain from having their boycott publicized in a national periodical. As a result, local boycotts are underrepresented in the boycott periodicals.

Despite these problems the young editors of the boycott publications provided a real service to their readers. Their periodicals will be missed both by boycott scholars and boycott activists.

In addition to my contacts with the academic literature on boycotts and with the various boycott periodicals, I have had frequent personal contact over the years with the representatives of boycotting groups and boycotted targets. I met some of them through my academic publications on boycotts and others during the data-collection phase of my study on ecological boycotts. The study, which is published in chapter 8 in this book, consists of a telephone survey of boycotters and their targets for 24 cases of ecological boycotts.

This book begins with two foundational chapters. The introductory chapter, in which boycotts are defined and categorized by type, is followed by a chapter that applies to the taxonomy of the first chapter some theoretical developments in organizational psychology, and the result is an elaborate set of research hypotheses to guide scholarly study of consumer boycotts. With that framework in place, the book then explores substantive types of consumer boycotts. Labor boycotts receive full-chapter attention, as do consumer economic boycotts, since these two boycott types represent the two sides of the economic coin, namely, production and consumption. Minority group boycotts are considered next with a whole chapter devoted to African American boycotts, including the historic Montgomery bus boycott led by Martin Luther King Jr. A second chapter on minority boycotts examines boycotts dealing with the rights of American Jews, Italian Americans, Chinese Americans, Mexican Americans, and Native Americans. Also included in this chapter are boycotts concerned with women's rights and gay rights.

Following this chapter is one that examines concerns of religious groups on both sides of the political spectrum. While boycotts on the right have dealt primarily with media depictions of sex and violence, boycotts on the left have been largely concerned with human rights issues, and especially the rights of various disadvantaged and neglected populations around the world.

The chapter devoted to ecological boycotts includes environmental boycotts as well as animal rights boycotts. This chapter is unique in that it reports an empirical study, updated in 1998 for this book, of a sample of these boycotts.

Also of interest is the penultimate chapter, which looks exclusively at "consumer buycotts," the flip side of consumer boycotts. These are actions that encourage selective buying of "good guys' wares" as opposed to the boycott of "bad guys' wares."

The last chapter looks at some key boycott concepts and how they relate to boycott actions and consequences over the years. This chapter also examines some important ethical questions relating to consumer boycotts.

Finally, two appendices are attached. Appendix A provides a write-up of my study of the 1966 consumer boycott of supermarkets. Appendix B provides a sample of notable boycott descriptions and opinions spanning more than 100 years of history. Taken together, the Appendix B comments reveal the variety of views people have had of boycotts along with the emotional reactions that sometimes accompany these views.

While the book's chapter structuring of the universe of consumer boycotts has a logic behind it, it may not be the best approach for all readers. Readers with a historical perspective may have preferred a partitioning by time period beginning, say, at the start of the 20th century and proceeding, perhaps by decade or historical period, to the present time. Readers with a business background may have preferred a breakdown by type or size of corporate boycott target. Still others of a humanistic bent may have preferred to see a focus on the various personalities participating in boycotts with stress placed on how they affected and were affected by the boycott struggles.

While the content breakdown employed herein does not adopt these various approaches, it does touch upon the noted concerns within the individual chapters. It is my hope that this structuring of the boycott universe is useful to the general reader as well as to boycott scholars and participants.

Before closing this preface I would like to say a few words about two major limitations of the examination of boycotts in this book. First, its coverage is incomplete in that many consumer boycotts are not treated at all, and others are treated only in part. This incompleteness results from two practical considerations: lack of information about the boycotts and lack of space to tell their stories. To compensate, I have tried to give the reader a sense of what boycotts are about by presenting examples of significant initiatives under each of the various major categories of boycott actions. A second limitation has to do with approach. The approach taken in this book is primarily descriptive rather than prescriptive, with the focus on what prompted the boycotts to begin, how the boycotters carried out their actions, and what consequences resulted from these initiatives. The book is not a practical guide for boycotters (or targets) on how to successfully carry out (or avoid) a consumer boycott, although many of the descriptive findings have implications for boycott practice.

◆ 1 ◆

CONSUMER BOYCOTT BASICS

To buy or not to buy? This behavioral question, while lacking the momentous, life-or-death quality of the Shakespearean original, is nonetheless apparently becoming a vexing one for many American consumers. On the one hand, consumers are exposed to hundreds of advertisements every day, and the result, some believe, is a new focus on shopping as a recreational activity that, in the extreme, has led to the emergence of shopping junkies (O'Guinn and Faber, 1989) and a new subject for bumper-sticker humor (e.g., "Shop 'til you drop," "I shop therefore I am," "Gone shopping," and "When the going gets tough, the tough go shopping"). On the other hand, these same consumers are besieged by requests from organizations representing almost every imaginable point on the political spectrum asking that they refrain from buying certain products or services in order to help the organizations further their goals. Although precise numbers are not known, Todd Putnam, founding editor of *National Boycott Newsletter*, has claimed that boycotts have increased markedly in number from the 1960s and 1970s, with more than 100 national efforts under way in the early 1990s as well as scores of local activities (Putnam, 1993).

This book seeks to advance understanding of consumer boycotts. We begin in this chapter by defining and classifying consumer boycotts and by establishing the historical roots for the

boycott term. The analytical framework employed is multidisci-
plinary, drawing upon theoretical work in the behavioral and
social sciences (e.g., Friedman, 1991, 1996b; Hirschman, 1970;
Vroom, 1964) and empirical studies conducted by the author and
others (e.g., Friedman, 1985, 1995b, 1996b; Garrett, 1987;
Pruitt and Friedman, 1986; Vogel, 1970). These studies reveal
that consumer boycotts have involved a wide range of protest
groups, target organizations, and social concerns in all regions of
the United States. And, as already indicated, they also appear to
be increasing in frequency.

The concerns addressed herein should be of interest to many
scholars, practitioners, and laypersons. Two audiences that may
be especially attentive are students of social change as well as
consumer affairs specialists, and particularly those specialists
who deal with consumer protection. Since 1980 there has been a
dramatic drop in government support for consumer protection
programs, and, in light of existing political and economic realities, it seems unlikely that government support will increase
markedly in the near future (Brobeck, 1997). As a result, consumers may have to look to themselves for help in advancing
their own interests. Since the boycott is a technique that has long
been used in support of consumer protection efforts, learning
more about it, from both academic and practitioner perspectives,
would seem especially important.

Of likely interest to students of social change is the use of the
boycott instrument to serve not only consumer economic objectives, such as lower prices, but also the political objectives of various special interest groups outside the consumer movement.
Included here are groups representing animal welfare and environmental protection, as well as the rights of women, gays,
African Americans, Mexican Americans, Chinese Americans,
Jewish Americans, and various labor organizations. At one time
or another since 1970 all of these groups have called for boycotts
of consumer products and services in an effort to help realize
their organizational objectives. The book will consider these
political boycotts as well as consumer economic boycotts.

Before proceeding with our analysis it is necessary to say a few
words of rationale about the choice of the boycott as *the consumer strategy* to subject to intensive scholarly examination in

this book. While other candidates (e.g., class action suits, letter-writing campaigns, and lobbying) are also worthy of research attention (Herrmann et al., 1988), the boycott appears to have two qualities that give it a special status. First, it has been perceived as more effective than other techniques by business leaders, the group whose organizations are usually the target of boycotts. A nationwide survey of senior business managers found that it was on the top of their list of "most effective techniques for the consumer movement to use" (Sentry Insurance Co., 1977). Indeed, 51 percent of the sample assigned this description to the boycott, while the next most popular choice on a list of 12 items garnered only 24 percent of the votes.

A second reason for the focus on boycotts concerns their important social justice role in American history. Since the Revolutionary War it can be argued that the boycott has been used more than any other organizational technique to promote and protect the rights of the powerless and disenfranchised segments of society. Indeed, Scott (1985), in a penetrating historical analysis of the efforts of peasants to resist oppression, referred to the boycott as a "weapon of the weak."

Some highly publicized examples from the postwar era are the United Farm Worker boycotts of grapes and lettuce led by Cesar Chavez from the late 1960s through the 1990s and the Montgomery, Alabama, bus boycott led by Martin Luther King Jr. in the 1950s. Historically significant earlier efforts include the anti-Nazi boycott of German goods called by the American Jewish community in the 1930s and early 1940s and the turn-of-the-century initiatives of the Knights of Labor and other fledgling members of the trade union movement of that time. Moreover, the period of the American Revolution witnessed boycotts of British goods in Boston, New York, and Philadelphia following the passage of the Stamp Act in 1765.

The boycotts occurring during the American Revolutionary period are especially important historically; indeed, they have been cited by protesters to justify the often-heard claim that boycotts are "as American as apple pie." Moreover, the boycotts initiated during this early period were very effective. Britain's Parliament supposedly enacted the Stamp Act to enable the British government to recover the costs of "defending, protecting and securing the British Colonies and plantations in America." The new law required the colonists to purchase stamps varying in price from a few pence to a few pounds for a whole host of legal documents including mortgages and deeds, as well as law and liquor licenses. The American colonists were outraged, and various groups, such as the Daughters of Liberty and the Sons of Liberty, protested by initiating boycotts.

> The day before the Act was to go into effect, two hundred New York merchants signed an agreement to import nothing more from Great Britain until the Stamp Act should be repealed. The Philadelphia merchants and retailers subscribed similar agreements the next week, and the Boston merchants in December, to be followed by those of Salem, Marblehead, Plymouth and Newbury. (Morgan and Morgan, 1962, p. 331)

Parliament repealed the Stamp Act a year later after being pressed to do so by British merchants whose businesses had been hurt by the boycott.

Eight years later, in 1774, the American colonists once again turned to the boycott as a weapon against the British. As Stencel (1991) has noted in an overview of boycotts and their influence, the First Continental Congress, upon finding that colonial grievances were not being redressed by the king's government, passed a formal resolution stopping the importation of British goods. This resolution, which was in violation of British law, also established local committees to help with the execution of the boycott. Did the boycott work? History does not provide an answer; before the effectiveness of this boycott initiative could be assessed, the Revolutionary War was under way.

A Definition of Consumer Boycotts

Before attempting to analyze consumer boycotts it is necessary to define the term. A working definition used by the author in an earlier study spoke of a consumer boycott as "an attempt by one or more parties to achieve certain objectives by urging individual consumers to refrain from making selected purchases in the marketplace" (Friedman, 1986, p. 97).[1]

The reader should note three characteristics of this definition. The first is the focus on individual consumers rather than organizational entities such as professional associations, business firms, or government agencies, even though organizations of these various types have often been urged to participate in boycotts.

A second characteristic of the definition concerns the goals of boycotts. For the purposes of this book consumer boycotts are viewed as attempts to use marketplace means to secure what may or may not be marketplace ends. There is good reason for not limiting boycott ends or goals to those of the marketplace. For, as we have already seen, in addition to such common marketplace concerns of consumer boycotts as lower prices and higher quality goods, a multitude of considerations external to the marketplace, such as environmental quality and labor union recognition, have assumed significant roles in boycott actions.

A third characteristic of the definition is its emphasis on urging consumers to withdraw selectively from participation in the marketplace. As we shall see presently, this urging or lobbying effort may be direct and immediate, as when retail stores are picketed by boycott groups, or it may be indirect and gradual, as when boycotters focus on creating dramatic demonstrations to attract the attention of the news media in the hopes that the resulting news coverage will alert consumers to the problem being addressed by the boycotters.[2]

Origins of the Boycott Term

Although the boycott tactic goes back almost to the dawn of history, the term itself is of relatively recent origin. The story behind the term, which derives from the name of a British estate manager, begins more than a 100 years ago in Ireland.[3] The details have been carefully recorded by a key participant, the American journalist James Redpath, in an article appearing in the *Magazine of Western History*. According to Redpath,

> I was dining with Father John O'Malley and he asked me why I was not eating. I said that I was bothered about a word. "What is it?" asked Father John. "Well," I said "when a people

ostracize a landgrabber we call it excommunication, but we ought to have an entirely different word to signify ostracism applied to a landlord or land agent like Boycott. Ostracism won't do. The peasantry would not know the meaning of the word, and I can't think of anything." "No," Father John said, "ostracism wouldn't do." He looked downward, tapped his forehead, and then out it came. "How would it do to call it 'to boycott him?'" (1881, pp. 214–215)

Redpath expressed delight at the idea; he agreed to use the word in his writings and asked O'Malley to do likewise so that "between us we will make it famous." Months later, after reflecting upon the success of their efforts, Redpath paid a tribute to O'Malley and himself by noting, "He was the first man who uttered the word, and I was the first man who wrote it" (1881, pp. 214–215).

According to Laidler (1913), the circumstances that triggered this historic conversation are especially noteworthy. For many years Irish peasants had been very poorly treated by the British landlord class. The peasants' land had been taken, their homes destroyed, and their wages reduced to starvation levels. These inhumane actions were not taken by the British landlords but by their agents. Among the most notorious was a retired British army captain, Charles Cunningham Boycott, who had been the estate manager for Lord Erne in County Mayo since 1873.

In the summer of 1880, after several years of extremely dire living conditions for the Irish peasants, Boycott sent his tenant farmers into the fields to harvest crops at only a fraction of the regular wage. When they refused, Boycott and his family attempted to bring in the crops themselves; however, they had to give up, completely exhausted, after a few hours of work. Boycott's wife pleaded with the tenants to go back to work, which they did; however, on rent day they were summarily served with eviction papers by constables under orders from Boycott.

The outraged tenants called a mass meeting at which they persuaded Boycott's employees (his servants, drivers, and animal herders) to desert him and his family. Three days after this declaration of social and economic ostracism the term "boycott" was coined by O'Malley.

That the term was understood and supported by the Irish peasantry became clear in the next few years. In the opinion of the *London Times* in 1885,

> It means that a peaceful subject of the Queen is denied food and drink, and that he is run down in his business; that his cattle are unsalable at fairs; that the smith will not shoe his horse nor the carpenter mend his cart; that old friends pass him by on the other side of the street, making the sign of the cross; that his children are hooted at the village school; that he sits apart, like an outcast, in his usual place of worship, all for doing nothing but that the law says that he has a perfect right to do. (Laidler, 1913, p. 26)

Needless to say, the boycott weapon was quickly condemned by the British landlord class. According to Laidler (1913), not only was the boycott effective, but "it called the attention of the people of England and Ireland as perhaps did no other weapon to many grave injustices" (p. 26).

While the story of the origins of the boycott term is not without considerable drama, it should be noted that the definition given by O'Malley and Redpath is somewhat broader than the one commonly used today. In particular, more often than not, the term denotes an act of social isolation *or* an act of economic disengagement, but rarely both acts at the same time. Thus one boycotts a social group by not attending its meetings, or one boycotts a neighborhood store by not buying the goods on sale there. But rarely does one participate in both types of boycott with regard to the same retail entity, perhaps in part because modern-day America, with its large and often impersonal shopping centers, does not particularly encourage consumers to have strong social relationships with the producers, processors, or retailers of the goods they purchase. More typically, it seems, consumers relate not to owners and managers but to clerks and cashiers.

Moreover, not only are the social and economic rarely combined in today's boycott actions, but those that are publicized are more likely to be economic than social. In the many literature searches of computerized and manual reference sources con-

ducted in the preparation for this book, the large majority of cita-
tions were to economic boycotts, and the most common variety
was the consumer boycott as defined earlier in this chapter.

A Taxonomy of Consumer Boycotts

We turn now to a consideration of boycott types and dimensions.

Place and Time Considerations

Boycotts differ with regard to their intended geographic scope. As
we shall see, national boycotts appear to be the most common,
followed by local boycotts; occurring far less frequently are international, state, and regional boycotts (Friedman, 1985). Interestingly, international boycotts appear to have shown the most
growth in the last few years. As social and environmental issues
become increasingly international in character, the volunteer
groups that address them have looked more and more to global-
izing their activities. This is especially true of the environmental
and animal rights movements since their issues transcend
national and regional boundaries.

Time durations of boycotts also vary. *Long-term boycotts*
extend beyond two years, while *medium-term boycotts* go on for
periods ranging between one and two years. Finally, *short-term
boycotts* end within a year of the time they are announced. In
practice these temporal distinctions are often difficult to maintain
because boycotts' beginnings and endings are not always clear.
This is especially true for end points and particularly for those
boycotts that fall short of their leaders' expectations. In these
instances announcing an end to a boycott may be tantamount to
admitting the failure of one's effort, and it is not hard to understand why such disclosures infrequently occur. For this reason,
among others, many boycotts are of unknown duration.

Boycotts also vary on a second temporal dimension. While
almost all are called as full-time activities, some, like the nationwide meat boycott of 1973, are called as a part-time effort (in this
instance, Tuesday and Thursday of each week over the course of
the boycott period).

Still a third time-related characteristic of boycotts is associated with actions that attempt to punish the target of a consumer boycott. In these instances the boycott group may decide to act like a judge in a criminal court proceeding and "sentence" the boycott target to a specific period of punishment, often a year, for its offensive behavior. This was the action taken in 1990 by the Los Angeles chapter of the National Organization for Women (NOW) when it decided to boycott Alfred Knopf, Inc. for a year for publishing a book (*American Psycho*) that the boycotting group considered to be highly offensive to women. Moreover, the American Family Association (AFA) once announced plans to initiate a one-year boycott of the corporation that sponsored the most offensive television programs (highest sex and violence content, as determined by the AFA).

Boycott Completeness

Boycotts also differ in how much they ask of consumer participants. Some boycotts, called *commodity boycotts*, ask consumers to refrain from buying all brands and models in a product or service category (e.g., all brands of granulated sugar), while others limit their attention to one brand (a *brand-name boycott*) or one manufacturer or retailer (*a single-firm boycott*). Commodity boycotts are often difficult to execute successfully, especially if the target product is one for which many consumers have established strong allegiances, such as coffee or meat.

Other areas in which boycotts may be less than complete concern the price of the boycotted items and the degree of abstinence requested of consumers. To illustrate the latter circumstance, the initiators of a coffee boycott in the 1970s, fully realizing that many consumers would not be able to make do without this beverage, called for a 50 percent drop in daily purchases and consumption. To illustrate the partial price circumstance, consumer leaders in the early days of the postwar era reacted to rapid increases in meat prices after government price controls were lifted by calling for a boycott of all meat selling for more than 59 cents a pound. In each of these instances we have a case of a *partial boycott*, rather than a *complete boycott*.

Yet another example of a partial boycott is one restricted to certain days of the week, such as the 1973 meat boycott called for

Tuesdays and Thursdays. Partial boycotts allow reluctant participants to buy and consume a boycotted product or service by following what often appear to be rather undemanding rules.

Boycott Sponsors

Boycotts have been launched by a wide variety of sponsoring
organizations. Among the most common are consumer groups,
labor unions, organizations representing ethnic and racial
minorities, religious groups, women's rights groups, and environmental groups. Still others include gay rights groups, antiwar
groups, health groups, pro-life and pro-choice groups, animal
welfare groups, anti-pornography groups, and groups combining
two or more interests.

Boycott Actions

An examination of news accounts of boycott actions reveals that
many of them follow a path of escalating militancy, a path that
begins with an announcement that a boycott action is under consideration. Some boycotts do not go beyond this point, and we
refer to them as *action-considered boycotts*. However, those that
do go further usually take the same next step, namely, to
announce that a boycott is being called and that participation in
the action is requested. Many boycotts go no further; these are
called *action-requested boycotts*. Those that go beyond this stage
often issue an announcement indicating that the boycott is being
organized and noting what preparations are under way. We refer
to boycotts that stop at this juncture as *action-organized boycotts*. Finally, the boycotts that go beyond organization and
preparation to take such concrete actions as initiating demonstrations and/or picket lines to publicize and stimulate the boycott activity are referred to as *action-taken boycotts*.

Many protest groups apparently do nothing more than engage
in an action-considered or action-requested boycott (Friedman,
1985); since some of these efforts seem more concerned with publicity in the news media than with action in the marketplace, we
refer to them as *media-oriented boycotts*. The focus on the news
media often reflects the fact that the organizations calling for the

boycotts lack the necessary resources or appropriate circumstances to implement a full-scale marketplace boycott. So they decide instead to attack the image of the target by (1) generating press releases that depict the target in an unfavorable light and (2) endeavoring to have these releases carried by the various news media. Sometimes, as we have noted, media-oriented boycotts escalate into action-organized boycotts and action-taken boycotts, and if these initiatives focus primarily on boycott activities in the marketplace (e.g., frequent picketing or demonstrations at retail stores), we refer to them as *marketplace-oriented boycotts*. It should be clear, however, that these boycotts, like virtually all organized protest actions, are media-oriented as well. But their use of the news media to attack the image of the target is secondary to their use of the boycott in the marketplace to damage the target economically by depriving it of sales.

It is important to note too that some media-oriented boycotts that escalate into action-organized boycotts and action-taken boycotts remain primarily media-oriented. Thus a boycott group may decide to organize and stage a series of dramatic demonstrations to capture the attention of television news cameras or newspaper reporters. These demonstrations may occur far away from the retail marketplace—at, for example, the headquarters building of the target being boycotted.

Yet another distinction between boycott actions is that between what was once referred to as a *"positive" boycott* and a *"negative" boycott*. The positive boycotts take the form of a "black list" of items to avoid buying. In this sense it is synonymous with the consumer boycott as we have earlier defined it. The negative boycott is a positive boycott with a twist: The focus is on what to buy rather than what not to buy. For this reason it often takes the form of a "white list" of items to purchase and is sometimes referred to as a *buycott*. Other names sometimes used to refer to it are "girlcott" (girl being the opposite of boy), "procott" (pro being the opposite of anti), and "anti-boycott." Perhaps the most common example of the buycott is the effort on the part of organized labor to encourage consumers to buy products with a union label. More recently, several organizations have launched campaigns to encourage consumers to "buy American."

As our last distinctive type of boycott action we refer to the *obstructionist boycott.* Boycotts of this type place obstacles in the way of consumers who are attempting to purchase a boycotted product or service. Perhaps the best-known variety of an obstructionist boycott is the *sit-in*, a technique used by African Americans at segregated lunch counters in Southern communities in the 1950s and 1960s. By "sitting in," the protesters occupied lunch counter seats for hours at a time, thus preventing other customers from being served. Other varieties include a *stand-in*, used by protesters in the 1880s to occupy an auction hall they were boycotting. By crowding themselves into the hall, protesters left no room for real customers to place their bids. Still other varieties are the *call-in* and the *mail-in*. The former has been used to clog 800-number purchase order lines with everything but purchase orders (usually complaints), and the latter has been used to send in postage-paid credit-card application forms at the boycotted organization's expense. In the latter case thousands of such forms were mailed in at American Express's expense in the early 1990s calling for the company to yield to the boycotters' demands.

Yet another variety is the *clog-in*, a practice employed in 1997 by Canadian activists who were upset with media magnate Conrad Black due to his monopoly ownership of Canada's daily newspapers. (Black was said to own 59 of the nation's 105 dailies.) The activists urged Canadians to clog the coin slots for the newspaper boxes selling Black's dailies with such jamming material as bent coins and sticky paper.

Obstructionist boycotts are not common, perhaps because most acts of purchase are difficult if not impossible to block by placing physical obstacles in the way.

Boycott Functions

Boycott actions vary with regard to function. While many have practical ends in mind (*instrumental boycotts*), others are more concerned with venting the frustrations of the protesting group (*expressive boycotts*). The latter are often characterized by short campaigns (usually a day or a week, but one electrical utility boycott was called for one hour) and by vague statements of goals, such as lowering prices, without specifics (in this instance, exactly how much lower). An especially apt example of an expressive boycott is the "Don't Buy Anything Day" nationwide boycott of all retail stores that was called in 1973 to demonstrate to American business that it is dependent on the consumer.

As we saw earlier in this chapter, still another functional type of boycott, one that some may see as an "instrumental-expressive" hybrid, is the *punitive boycott*. Unlike the purely instrumental boycott, which attempts to persuade a target to take "corrective" action, the punitive boycott is often an expressive response to a seemingly irreversible *fait accompli*. For example, once a company has developed and marketed a new product at substantial cost in time and money, the company may be reluctant to drop it simply because it is offensive to a boycott group. Under the circumstances the boycott group may decide to "punish" the firm by calling for a boycott for a fixed period of time, say, a year. By taking this initiative the boycott group both expresses its frustration with the target's actions and signals the target (and potential targets) that a future action of an offensive nature may well be punished by a boycott campaign. In this sense a punitive boycott may be expressive in the short term and instrumental in the long term.

Yet another functional type of boycott (although one that is rarely practiced) is the *catalytic boycott*. This is a calculated political ploy that might be considered by a public interest research organization (PIRO) that is attempting to secure government action on newly made recommendations contained, say, in a study report the PIRO has just issued. A call for a boycott might well be initiated if the study report found, for example, that a particular corporate initiative considered offensive by the PIRO could be weakened or overturned by appropriate government action.

By calling for a boycott, the PIRO hopes to attract more news media attention to its report than would ordinarily be the case, in the hope that news coverage would stimulate government officials to take corrective action.

It was this approach that was apparently taken by the Environmental Defense Fund and the Environmental Action Foundation when they jointly called for a boycott of companies using the term "biodegradable" in their consumer communications to wrongly refer to a characteristic of their plastic garbage bags. The organizations needed a catalyst to get the attention of the Federal Trade Commission and the offices of the state attorneys general, and the boycott call served this function very effectively. What is especially interesting about this tactic is that the call for a catalytic boycott may be taken by an organization with no intention of managing a boycott campaign. The call is simply used to secure news media attention, which, it is hoped, will trigger government action.

Boycott Targets

A distinction should be made between the parties serving as the targets of a boycott and the parties whose actions are offensive to the boycotters. Sometimes they are one and the same, as in the case of a boycott called against a retailer who is alleged to charge excessively high prices. In other instances, however, the offending party may not be directly accessible to the boycotters, so they choose another party as their target, one they believe can be forced to bring pressure to bear on the offending party. An illustration of this kind of indirect action is the case of a group that finds itself dissatisfied with the government policies of a city, state, or foreign nation and acts upon its feelings by boycotting the businesses operating in the affected geographic area. Thus we find that boycotts may be viewed as direct or indirect with regard to the actions taken against offending parties. Since indirect boycotts have a "stand-in" quality to their targets, we have referred to them elsewhere as *surrogate boycotts*, and to complete the analogy, we have referred to direct boycotts as *nonsurrogate boycotts* (Friedman, 1985). It may also be useful to think of surrogate actions as *transformational boycotts* in that their objective is to transform issues concerned with objectionable practices external to the marketplace (such as a foreign government's oppressive policies) into consumer-accessible marketplace issues. Put somewhat differently, transformational boycotts attempt to change political issues into economic ones so that they can be acted upon by consumer "voting behavior" consisting of dollar expenditures (or more appropriately, in the case of boycotts, the cessation of dollar expenditures) in the retail marketplace.

Surrogate boycotts have typically taken two forms. The first and by far the more common form consists of *travel boycotts* to a geographic area whose governing body or electorate has offended the boycotting group. To illustrate, when Nelson Mandela was shunned by the Cuban American government leaders of Miami, Florida, during his visit there in 1990, local African American leaders retaliated by organizing a travel boycott of the city, with the emphasis on persuading national associations not to hold their annual meetings in Miami. Similar actions of a retaliatory nature have been taken by other protesters who, at one time or another, have called for travel boycotts of such states as Alaska, Arizona, California, Colorado, Florida, Idaho, Illinois, Iowa, Louisiana, Missouri, Pennsylvania, North Dakota, Utah, and Wisconsin.

The second type of surrogate boycott consists of *headquarters boycotts*. This is an extension of the travel or tourism boycott to include a call for boycotting businesses that have their headquarters in the boycotted geographical area. A recent example concerns the highly publicized "baby Jessica" case, in which the courts ruled in 1993 that a Michigan couple's adopted baby had to be returned to its biological parents in Iowa because of irregularities in the adoption procedure followed several years earlier. National surveys of the American public revealed that this was an extremely unpopular decision and a call for an Iowa state boycott resulted. The action called for was a travel boycott as well as a headquarters boycott; major Iowa companies (such as Maytag) were targeted in the boycott announcement simply because their headquarters were located in the state.

In addition to surrogate and nonsurrogate boycotts, one may speak of primary and secondary boycotts. The *primary boycott* is similar to the nonsurrogate boycott in that in both cases the offending party is an economic entity directly accessible to the boycotters through the marketplace. The secondary boycott, however, is quite different from the surrogate boycott. The *secondary boycott* focuses on an economic entity, usually a retailer, who buys the wares of the primary boycott target for the purpose of reselling them to consumers. Needless to say, the planners of a secondary boycott would like to see *all* the retailer's wares boycotted either as a punishment for dealing with the boycotted products of the primary target or as an incentive for discontinuing this practice. This could mean boycotting a supermarket (a secondary boycott) that carries the milk and eggs produced by an offending local dairy that is already being boycotted (a primary boycott). An alternative to this practice that has sometimes been deemed legally permissible is for boycotters to inform the customers of the secondary boycott target that it is selling certain goods that are the focus of a consumer boycott because they are made by a firm whose actions are considered offensive by the boycotters. The boycotters are thus allowed to focus on the subset of offending goods in an informational campaign but not on the totality of goods being sold by the secondary boycott target. Usually a major goal of such campaigns is to persuade the retailer to discontinue carrying the products provided by the primary boycott target.[4]

Yet another boycott target distinction is between for-profit and not-for-profit organizations. The latter type, by far the more uncommon of the two, typically consists of charitable organizations, such as the United Way, that either contribute to causes that are offensive to boycotters or refrain from contributing to causes favored by the boycotters.[5]

Offending Actions

No taxonomy of boycotts would be complete without attention to the nature of the target and offender actions that trigger boycotts. As we shall see presently, most of these are perceived violations of rights, such as consumer rights, animal rights, worker rights, women's rights, and environmental rights. Indeed, the focus here is often on perceived victims and, in particular, on the characteristics of the various entities that boycotters believe to be harmed by the actions of offending parties. Perhaps not unexpectedly, a close parallel often exists between these characteristics and the characteristics of the boycott sponsors. Borrowing from the terminology of McCarthy and Zald (1973), we refer to a boycott effort in which the sponsors and perceived victims are members of the same constituency, such as an organized labor action, as a *beneficiary boycott*. A boycott effort in which the sponsor and perceived victims represent different constituencies, such as an animal rights campaign, is considered a *conscience boycott*.

Some observers view the beneficiary and conscience boycott categories as a euphemistic distinction between selfish and selfless actions; in practice, however, this simple distinction is often difficult to maintain.

Determining Boycott Success: The Criterion Problem

Before identifying factors believed to affect boycott success, it is necessary to consider what is referred to in many applied fields (e.g., psychotherapy) as "the criterion problem." Criteria for the success of consumer boycotts are often not easy to identify because boycott leaders are reluctant to pin themselves down. Consumer boycotts are, after all, political actions, and few political leaders are willing to issue statements listing their objectives with sufficient specificity to permit empirical tests of success or failure. (Some believe that an important exception to this generalization was the ERA surrogate boycott of the 1970s; leaders of women's rights organizations identified the passage of the proposed Equal Rights Amendment to the U.S. Constitution as the objective of their travel boycott to states whose legislatures had not passed the amendment.)

A second criterion problem considers the need to draw a distinction between the *short-term* and *long-term effects* of boycotts. While the dividing line between the two is often not clear, short-term success has been claimed by many boycotts, but long-term success has apparently proved more elusive. (See Appendix A for an illustration of this mixed type of outcome.)

Related to the second criterion problem is a third which focuses on the distinction between two levels of success for a boycott. The first is called a *micro-success* and the second, a *macro-success*; the difference between them is akin to achieving a tactical victory versus a strategic victory. In some instances, of course, the distinction does not hold in that the campaign objectives revolve around a single skirmish, and if the boycotters win it they achieve a tactical victory as well as a strategic victory. For example, the campaigns carried on by animal rights groups to eliminate the use of animals in the testing and development of cosmetics are not characterized by this distinction. If a cosmetic company agrees to discontinue animal testing, the animal rights groups can conclude that it has attained a strategic victory as well as a tactical victory because a net decrease in the amount of pain and suffering inflicted upon animals had been realized—one of the primary goals of the animal rights movement.

In contradistinction, if an antiwar campaign is launched against a major manufacturer of consumer goods that also produces military weapons, it is possible to achieve a tactical victory with little or no effect on the larger strategic goals of the antiwar movement. This was the case with two independent boycott campaigns in the late 1980s and early 1990s, one against AT&T and the other against General Electric (GE). After the boycotts were under way both companies severed their connections with the offending military activities; however, in both instances the weapons activities continued under other corporate auspices, and, interestingly, the new owners were companies immune to boycott threats because they neither manufactured nor sold consumer goods. Nonetheless the acts of dissociation with the weapons activities by AT&T and GE were heralded as victories by the boycott groups. By the criteria noted here, each would be a micro-success but not a macro-success since the boycotts did not result in the discontinuance of the military activity.

A fourth criterion problem concerns the distinction between *execution criteria* and *consequence criteria*. The former asks whether the boycott was implemented as planned or, in other words, whether the consumer commodities to be boycotted were indeed not purchased. The latter asks whether the larger organizational objectives of the boycott activity were realized (e.g., lower prices, union recognition, or corporate divestiture from South Africa). For a given boycott activity, it should be clear that performance on one type of criterion is not necessarily related to performance on the other. For example, even a hint or suggestion of a boycott by a powerful group may be enough to achieve its goals (the consequence criterion) without having to actually engage in a boycott (the execution criterion). Conversely, a boycott group may be successful in persuading consumers not to buy a specified commodity only to find that the target refuses to yield to the group's demands. While the consequence criterion is clearly important to boycott groups and their targets, the execution criterion is also important to the targets because boycott success here means a loss of retail sales.

Even if agreement could be reached on criteria for judging the success of a boycott, analysts would still encounter problems in applying them. As already indicated, the consequence criteria are often vaguely stated and, indeed, may change over the course of a boycott. Furthermore, reliable hard data on the execution criterion may be difficult to secure because both sides have a vested interest in presenting evidence favorable to their positions. And finally, even if a reliable change in criterion data can be identified, it may be unclear whether the change is due to the boycott action. (Time-series analysis can be helpful here; this was the statistical approach taken by Pruitt and Friedman [1986] in a study of the impact of boycott announcements on stock market prices for target companies.)

The last-mentioned point is particularly relevant to boycotts called to further consumer economic goals or labor goals. In the case of consumer economic boycotts, lower prices are often the goal, frequently for products that have recently risen sharply in price. When fewer consumers buy the products after a boycott has been called it is sometimes not clear how much the decrease in demand is due to the boycott and how much is due to the products' rapid rise in price (i.e., the products may have become prohibitively expensive for many consumers). Moreover, if the price rise is anticipated by consumers, matters become more complicated, and cause-and-effect analysis more uncertain. As Jones (1977) has indicated in a discussion of the rather abrupt increase in retail prices that triggered the 1977 nationwide coffee boycott, much of the decreased demand apparently derived from the fact that shoppers, upon realizing that prices were about to rise rapidly, had stocked up.

In the case of boycotts directed at labor issues, cause-and-effect connections are also often difficult to discern, but not usually for the reasons noted for consumer economic boycotts. In dealing with labor issues, such as union recognition or, more typically, contract renewal, multiple approaches are frequently taken by the labor organization, including, of course, work slowdowns or strikes or the threats of such actions (Rogers, 1981). In these cases the boycott is only one weapon in an arsenal, and it is virtually impossible to tease out its effects independently of others employed by the labor organization.

Finally, with regard to the execution and consequence criteria for boycotts, a distinction should be made between degrees of success and failure. To the extent that the criteria are realized, one may speak of a boycott, from the boycotters' perspective, as being *productive*. To the extent that the criteria are not realized one may consider a boycott to be *unproductive*. In some rare instances boycotts have been neither productive nor unproductive, falling instead into a *counterproductive* category, often as a result of consumer opposition to the boycott action. In such instances, with regard to boycott execution, sales of a boycotted product have actually increased, or with regard to boycott consequences, the boycotters' demands have not only not been met, but the circumstances prompting these demands have gone from bad to worse.

Such a boomerang effect apparently occurred in Savannah, Georgia, in 1977 in response to the campaign of an anti-ERA group to boycott the sale of Girl Scout cookies, an action taken to protest the endorsement of the proposed ERA by the national board of directors of the Girl Scouts of America (GSA). Representatives of the GSA have cited evidence to support the claim that the boycott, which was opposed by the Savannah chapter of the League of Women Voters, backfired and actually increased sales (Friedman, 1985).

Having noted the diverse types and dimensions of consumer boycotts, we move next to consider various factors that may influence boycott success. Perhaps no topic relating to consumer boycotts has elicited more interest than this one. Social theorists have for years seen this arena as a testing ground for their conceptual formulations. And practitioners on both sides of the boycott fence have a pragmatic interest in the topic. Boycott campaigners want to know how they can make their efforts more successful, and corporate targets of boycott campaigns seek empirically based guidelines to help direct their responses. Knowledge of which factors influence boycott success could help both sides plan their actions more effectively.

◆2◆

FACTORS AFFECTING BOYCOTT SUCCESS

Although researchers (e.g., Rea, 1974; Garrett, 1987) have suggested numerous factors that may influence the success of consumer boycotts, the scholarly literature has been largely limited to economic variables and only a few boycott types. Less available in the literature are analytical works that recognize the full variety of boycott types and, perhaps more importantly, acknowledge the need for a behavioral science approach for examining the actions of boycott sponsors and participants as well as those of their targets.

In this chapter we draw upon the perspective of instrumentality theory (Vroom, 1964) from organizational psychology in an effort to identify variables believed to predict boycott success. Instrumentality theory, sometimes called valence, instrumentality, and expectancy (VIE) theory, makes a sharp distinction between the work effort required to successfully complete a task (our execution criterion), the likely outcomes of task completion (our consequence criterion), and the positive or negative values associated with these outcomes. While space limitations do not allow for full explication, the reader should note that Vroom's basic instrumentality model has been expanded by others, including Graen (1969), Lawler (1971, 1973), Naylor, Pritchard, and Ilgen (1980), Pinder (1991), and Porter and Lawler (1968).

What the theory seems to say to consumer groups is that before initiating a boycott they should ask themselves if (1) consumers care about the boycott issues and objectives, (2) the boycott task is likely to be successfully executed, and (3) its execution is likely to lead to the desired consequences specified by the boycott objectives. These three questions are especially appropriate for groups considering instrumental boycotts (as compared to expressive boycotts) in light of the means-end pragmatic framework of VIE theory.

Table 2.1 presents boycott strategies for instrumental actions differing with respect to two dichotomies: media-oriented boycotts vs. marketplace-oriented boycotts and surrogate boycotts vs. nonsurrogate boycotts. Perhaps the first point to be made about this table is that the type of boycott that has received the most attention in the economic literature (e.g., Hirschman, 1970; Rea, 1974), namely, the marketplace-oriented, nonsurrogate boycott, may be the least common of the four types presented. Indeed, it could be persuasively argued that media-oriented boycotts (both surrogate and nonsurrogate) are now the most commonly occurring type, and for an obvious reason: Most parties calling for consumer boycotts commit few if any resources to their execution in the marketplace. This may be because the resources are not available or because the boycott organizers choose not to expend them for this purpose. Whether conducted

Table 2.1   Strategies Envisioned by Boycott Leaders for Various Types of Instrumental Boycotts

Orientation	Surrogate Status	
	Nonsurrogate boycott	Surrogate boycott
Media-oriented boycott	Adverse effects on target's image lead to desired change in target's behavior	Adverse effects on target's image lead target to apply pressure on offending party leading to desired change in behavior of offending party
Marketplace-oriented boycott	Adverse effects on target's image and sales lead to desired change in target's behavior	Adverse effects on target's image and sales lead target to apply pressure on offending party leading to desired change in behavior of offending party

at the local, regional, national, or international level, a market-place boycott requires substantial organizational and economic supports for such activities as picketing, demonstrations, and leafleting over the course of the boycott campaign.

In the three sections that follow, we look first at the factors believed likely to affect the success of media-oriented boycotts (both surrogate and nonsurrogate). Next, we examine factors affecting the success of these boycotts. The third and final section looks at the extra step in the boycott sequence of actions found for surrogate boycotts and suggests factors that influence their success.

Factors Affecting the Success of Media-Oriented Boycotts

What the foregoing suggests is that press statements are often issued indicating that a consumer boycott is under consideration or is being called when the individuals or organizations making the announcements lack the wherewithal to follow through with a marketplace boycott. It is well to ask if these statements should "count" as consumer boycotts. By the definition given earlier in this book, they would qualify because they technically are attempts, albeit weak ones, to get consumers to refrain from making certain purchases. Their primary purpose, however, is to secure prominent coverage in the news media so as to damage the image of the targets of the boycott. The logic here is straightforward. Given the power of the news media, no company in the business of offering goods or services to consumers can afford to risk having its image tarnished by news accounts suggesting that it may be acting improperly.

Instrumentality theory would suggest that leaders of a media-oriented boycott bear in mind certain execution and consequence considerations. Central to both considerations is the valence question, that is, how consumers are likely to value the boycott issues and their outcome.

Execution Considerations

To increase its likelihood for success, a media-oriented boycott should issue its public announcements in a manner that maximizes its potential for coverage, especially prominent coverage, by the news media. Execution factors believed to be important here are as follows:

1. *The announcements should be made by well-known organizations and/or individuals.* Two examples from the 1970s and 1980s are Jesse Jackson's announcements of boycotts being considered by PUSH (People United to Serve Humanity) and Cesar Chavez's announcements of boycotts called by the United Farm Workers. Both organizations and both leaders were well-known to the American public at the time of the announcements.

2. *The announcements should identify one or more well-known firms as the boycott targets.* A boycott called in the late 1970s by migrant workers hired to pick tomatoes in northern Ohio was directed not at the tomato growers but at the Campbell Soup Company, the growers' most widely recognized corporate customer. According to the boycott's leader, it was Campbell's national reputation that led to its selection as the boycott target. Similarly, while social and religious groups cited many firms in the 1970s for their questionable practices relating to the distribution of infant formula in developing countries, Nestle's prominence was largely responsible for its selection as *the* infant formula boycott target.

3. *The complaints against the targeted firm noted in the announcements should appear to be legitimate and relatively uncomplicated.* Looking first at the need for legitimacy, here is a case where announcements of conscience boycotts, such as environmental actions, may be more attractive to the news media than announcements of beneficiary boycotts, such as labor union actions, since the latter may well be dismissed as the not-unexpected self-interest proclamations of major organizations with little appeal to news media audiences. And given the very real news media limitations of time and space, the less complicated the complaint, the more likely it will receive attention.

4. *Wherever possible, drama should be employed in the boycott announcements to the news media.* Sound bites and photo opportunities have become the media parlance of the day, and

boycott leaders need to have the media savvy to make successful use of such devices. To illustrate, in 1988 Cesar Chavez captured media attention for a grape boycott over a period of weeks with a hunger strike, and national celebrities helped the effort along by engaging in one-day sympathy fasts. Similarly, the Campbell boycott organizers presented the news media with many photo opportunities in 1983 during their dramatic monthlong march from Toledo, Ohio, to Campbell's headquarters in Camden, New Jersey.

Consequence Considerations

If these are some of the factors believed likely to predict news media coverage of boycott announcements, what others, the reader may ask, are likely to predict whether or not the targeted firm will react to the news media coverage in the manner desired by the boycott leaders? Many candidates could be identified here, but we will focus on the ones believed to be most likely to have an effect.

1. *The more widespread and prominent the news media coverage, the more likely the target will yield to the demands of the boycotters.* As we have seen earlier, while success on the execution criterion does not logically imply success on the consequence criterion, practically speaking, it would seem that the one often leads to the other.
2. *The more image-conscious the target, the more likely it will yield to the demands of the boycotters.* Image management is an increasing concern of many companies and especially those with prominent positions in retail markets (Garrett, 1987).
3. *The higher the likelihood that the target perceives the news coverage of the media-oriented boycott as leading to a marketplace-oriented boycott, the greater the chances that it will yield to the boycotters' demands.* Damage to image is one thing; damage to sales is quite another. And just as a tiny spark can quickly ignite a forest fire, so can a single news media account fan the flames of consumer dissatisfaction. An illustration of this kind of explosive action occurred in 1966 when a consumer boycott of supermarkets in Denver spread

in a few weeks to about a hundred communities across the nation (Friedman, 1971).

4. *The more inflexible and non-adaptive the target's policies regarding reactions to outside organizational pressures, the more likely it will refuse to yield to the demands of the boycotters.* In each of two labor-oriented consumer protests of the 1970s (the Farah boycott and the Coors boycott), the resistance of the firm's leader to what were apparently seen as threats to his autonomy resulted in years of "stonewalling" before remedial actions were taken.

5. *The more realistic the boycotters' demands, the more likely they will be met.* It may not be realistic, from the perspective of cosmetics companies (and perhaps from the perspective of the American public), for an animal welfare group to demand that they no longer conduct a particular laboratory test found to be painful to animal subjects when (1) the test is used to ensure that new cosmetics and cleansers are safe for human use, and (2) alternative tests are not available to perform the same function. However, a demand that the companies allocate funds for research to develop a viable alternative test may well be seen as realistic. Indeed, this is what led the cosmetics industry in 1981 to fund, at a cost through 1989 of $4 million, the establishment of the Center for Alternatives to Animal Testing at Johns Hopkins University (Feder, 1989).

6. *The more capable the target is of launching a successful counteraction to the boycott, the less likely it will yield to the boycotters' demands.* In 1988 a boycott was called against Peugeot, the French automobile manufacturer, based on the allegedly poor crash-worthiness of its car. Peugeot responded by questioning the crash-worthiness measures used by the boycotters and by showing how other measures yielded a more favorable crash-worthiness rating.

Factors Affecting the Success of Marketplace-Oriented Boycotts

Since news media coverage is usually a critical concern for marketplace-oriented boycotts, the four hypothesized factors noted under execution considerations for media-oriented boycotts would appear to apply here as well. Similarly, since damage to a target firm's image (as well as its sales) is a concern of a marketplace-oriented boycott, most of the six hypothesized factors noted under consequence considerations for media-oriented boycotts would also seem to be relevant here. Additional factors are identified in this section related to execution, consequences, and consumer attitudes for a boycott that escalates beyond the release of news media announcements to include the cessation of purchases in the marketplace.

Execution Considerations

To encourage consumer participation in a marketplace boycott, the desired changes in purchase behavior should be easy to perform and without adverse consequences, either economically or psychologically. This reasoning suggests that boycott leaders consider the following factors:

1. *The products or services targeted by boycotts should be easy for consumers to identify.* Fresh produce has sometimes posed a problem in this regard for boycotts called by the United Farm Workers. In particular, lettuce harvested by union workers has not always been easy for shoppers to differentiate from boycott-targeted lettuce harvested by their nonunion counterparts.

2. *Boycotts should target as few brand names as possible with one being the ideal.* It is a cognitively simple task for consumers to keep one brand name in mind in their efforts to cooperate with a marketplace boycott, but as the number increases so does the difficulty of the task. To illustrate, the infant formula boycott was reactivated in 1988 with two firms, Nestle and American Home Products, as the targets. A consumer wishing at that time to participate in the boycott would have had to be cognizant of literally dozens of brand names produced by these two firms, including Advil, Anacin, Beech-Nut, Chef Boyardee, Easy Off, Hills Brothers, Libby's, Nescafe, Preparation H, Quik, Stouffer's, Taster's Choice, and Woolite.

3. *Boycotts should be planned at a time when there are few, if*

any, competing boycotts on related issues. This is a corollary to the multiple brand-name recommendation in that the more related marketplace boycotts that are under way, the more brand names shoppers have to remember and act upon in their trips to the market. To illustrate the problem, peace movement sympathizers wishing to participate in boycotts against weapons contractors as well as boycotts against war toy manufacturers may find that they are overwhelmed cognitively by the large number and variety of targeted brands.

4. *Boycott targets should be selected to ensure that acceptable substitutes are readily available for the boycotted products or services.* There are at least three elements involved here: accessibility, price, and taste. For some products, such as gasoline, all three are unlikely to pose a problem, in that in most communities one can find a brand other than the one being boycotted, and of comparable quality and at approximately the same price. If, however, a convenient neighborhood shopping mall or downtown shopping area is being boycotted, many consumers may not be willing to shop at stores farther away. Taste factors may also loom large, especially for commodity boycotts. To illustrate, many coffee drinkers find it difficult to switch to other beverages, and committed carnivores are likely to have trouble supporting a meat boycott.[1]

5. *Boycott targets should be selected to ensure that consumer violations of the boycott are publicly visible.* This suggestion focuses not on the ease of complying with a boycott but rather on the social stigma that may be associated with not complying with it. The stigma is, of course, likely to be particularly strong for highly publicized and polarized local actions against retail stores, such as the case in the mid-1980s of a boycott called by the NAACP and Detroit black ministers who targeted retail stores in the neighboring, predominantly white city of Dearborn in retaliation for Dearborn's decision to prohibit non-Dearborn residents from using its public parks. This recommendation suggests that boycotts of non-publicly purchased goods (e.g., through mail order catalogs) may not have a high likelihood of success.

Consequence Considerations

Once a marketplace-oriented boycott has been implemented the next questions to ask concern the response by the target. As indicated earlier, a marketplace-oriented boycott is media-oriented of necessity; thus the earlier discussion of consequence considerations for media-oriented boycotts would also pertain here. However, additional factors would seem salient relating to the impact of the boycott on sales.

1. *The more successful the boycott is in the marketplace, the more likely the target will yield to the demands of the boycotters.* "Successful" can, of course, be defined in various ways, including decreases in total purchasers, in total units purchased, in sales volume, and in estimated profits. But in any case, a boycott that has a major deleterious economic effect can be expected to make a target give serious thought to meeting the boycotters' demands.

2. *The larger the adverse impact on the target of the drop in sales due to the boycott, the more likely the target will yield to the demands of the boycotters.* Large companies with many product lines and subsidiaries may be in a position to weather the boycott. Small producers, on the other hand, especially those with few product lines, are often more vulnerable to a sales downturn and thus may be more likely to yield to boycott pressures.

3. *The more distant the perceived time horizons for a boycott, the more likely the target will yield to the demands of the boycotters.* Time horizons are easier to project for seasonal businesses. To illustrate, a successful marketplace boycott of a professional sports team is likely to be especially worrisome to management if it occurs at the beginning of the season rather than near the end. Over the course of the off-season months passions may well cool, causing fan interest in the boycott to wane.

Factors Affecting the Success of Surrogate Boycotts

While nonsurrogate boycotts, whether media-oriented or marketplace-oriented, are characterized by execution and consequence phases relating to the boycott targets, surrogate boycotts have an additional phase that concerns the consequences of the actions of the target (the surrogate) on the offender. Usually, this entails one or more businesses as targets and a governmental entity as offender. In each instance an effort is sometimes made to have the targeted businesses act as lobbyists for the boycotters relative to the offending government entity. What factors are likely to determine whether these efforts succeed? Let us look at some candidates.

Consequence Considerations

Several obvious prospects consider the political power and inclinations of the boycott targets and the nature of the boycotters' demands.

1. *The more political influence the target companies have, the more likely the government will yield to the demands of the boycotters.* In some cases the political influence of the target may be considerable. For example, the merchants of a small town are likely to have substantial influence with the local police department, and, indeed, local "police brutality" boycotts called by African Americans against a town's merchants in the South have been successful (Tulsky, 1978). On the other hand, state or national government entities are likely to be subjected to a wide variety of powerful political forces, thus diluting the influence of the target.
2. *The more forceful the lobbying efforts of the target, the more likely the government entity will yield to the demands of the boycotters.* While this point may seem self-evident, it is important to distinguish between its public and private manifestations. To placate the boycotters the targeted company may publicly urge a legislator to vote a certain way on an issue, but privately assure him or her that the company does not care which way the legislator votes.
3. *The more politically feasible the demands of the boycotters, the more likely the government entity will yield to them.* A demand that a left-wing policy be adopted by a right-wing or even moderate government entity is unlikely to be met; however, a request may well be honored if it is for something

more politically realistic, such as an apology from a government leader for comments he or she made that were insensitive to a minority group.

Factors Affecting Boycott Success: A Research Agenda

We began this chapter by drawing upon instrumentality theory to provide a conceptual framework for our discussion of types of boycotts and stages within each type. While instrumentality theory is not without its problems both conceptually and empirically (Bandura, 1987; Schwab et al., 1979; Stahl and Harrell, 1981), the notions of execution and consequence stages and the value component associated with them appear to be useful ones for analyzing consumer boycotts and for generating research hypotheses concerning factors that contribute to their success. While most of the hypothesized relationships noted herein do not go far beyond applications of basic principles in the behavioral and social sciences, they nonetheless constitute a first systematic attempt to establish a research agenda for boycotts that speaks to the concerns of social activists. Follow-up efforts should, of course, examine the hypotheses empirically, although, as we said in Chapter 1, reliable data with which to do this may not be easy to come by.

One way out of this dilemma may be to look for creative alternatives to standard survey research methods for studying boycotts. As we have seen, boycott leaders, targets, and offenders are all, to some degree, political actors performing on a public stage. This being the case, one has to wonder if they answer questions more candidly when posed by survey interviewers than by news media interviewers. To the extent that they do not, the scientific validity of their responses may be questioned. How to resolve the problem? What may be needed is more reliance on qualitative research methods, such as participant-observer techniques and case studies, to supplement the survey research methods already in use.

Having offered a definition of consumer boycotts as well as a taxonomy and theoretical framework that suggest the rich variety of dimensions and dynamics assumed by boycotts, we are now ready to examine some of the major boycott types in more detail. Each of the next seven chapters is devoted to a single type, with the first focusing on labor boycotts. Before beginning these chapters the reader should note that for the sake of economy of expression we have often omitted the term "consumer" from the title of each type under examination. Thus instead of "consumer-labor boycott" we simply say "labor boycott." However, it should be understood that the boycotts discussed under the abbreviated titles are all consumer boycotts as defined in Chapter 1.

◆3◆
LABOR BOYCOTTS

As indicated in Chapter 1, labor boycotts have posed serious evaluation problems for analysts seeking to determine their effectiveness because boycotts are usually employed not alone but in conjunction with other tactics. And these problems have been exacerbated lately with the use of a multipronged corporate campaign strategy by unions seeking to advance or protect the interests of their members.

Before examining this strategy and other recent efforts of organized labor, we look at some of the early labor boycotts in American history. The overview nature of our treatment should not be taken to mean that these early efforts were insignificant. Indeed, a good case could be made that the boycott initiatives of labor groups just before the turn of the century were the most numerous and successful in American history. To aid this review we are fortunate to have as primary guides two impressive doctoral dissertations written by young economists in the second decade of this century. *Boycotts and the Labor Struggle* was the 1913 contribution of Harry W. Laidler while completing his studies at Columbia University, and *The Boycott in American Trade Unions*, published just a year later, was Leo Wolman's dissertation at Johns Hopkins University. Laidler's scholarly study of boycotts continued for many years; indeed, he contributed the entry on the topic in the 1930 edition of the *Encyclopedia of the Social Sciences* (Laidler, 1930, pp. 662–666).

The Turn-of-the-Century Labor Boycotts

In theory, labor has a two-sided relationship with management. On the producer side, labor provides to management the workers necessary to generate goods and services. On the consumer side, it provides a ready market for the goods and services produced.

For many years organized labor focused on the producer side rather than the consumer side in its efforts to influence management. In particular, if its powers of persuasion in a labor-management dispute proved to be unconvincing, labor resorted to a withdrawal of its services or threatened such a withdrawal. Was this strike tactic an effective one? The answer, according to Laidler, was a very qualified yes.

> If labor is thoroughly organized, if every man in a certain trade or industry stands staunchly with his fellow in a labor struggle; if the army of the unemployed refused to "scab," and if, finally, the worker's economic power to resist proves as great as that of the employer, the mere cessation of work, if continued long enough, will probably be sufficient to bring the employing class to terms. (1913, p. 56)

Unfortunately for the American labor interests at the turn of the century, however, these textbook conditions rarely existed in practice. Labor market conditions of the time made securing new workers relatively easy for employers; indeed, many of the positions were unskilled, and an influx of new immigrants was available to fill them. Moreover, the "worker's economic power to resist" was usually modest at best.

Thus the unionists of the time had to look elsewhere for an effective weapon. The boycott, which can be viewed as the counterpart of the strike on the consumer side of the labor-management relationship, was suggested as the alternative. The reasoning, according to Laidler, was as follows:

If we can tell the unfair employer that he may fill our places with other workmen, but that he will be unable to sell the goods his new employees produce; if we can assure him that, unless he concedes our demands, labor and its friends will leave his goods unsought, and that it will take many a day to regain his former patrons, our argument will gain double weight. Should we not then unite to cease all dealings with "unfair" firms, and thus cut off, as far as possible, not only their labor force but their market as well? (1913, p. 57)

So this was the logic behind the early union efforts to embrace the boycott as a substitute for, or complement to, the strike. These efforts came at the time the word "boycott" was coined and used effectively in Ireland to ostracize the English landlord class. They also came at a time of widespread labor battles in America fought by a leading union, the Knights of Labor.

The Knights of Labor

The power and extensiveness of boycotts in the 1880s and 1890s, especially when used by the Knights, have been repeatedly documented.

Almost without warning the boycott suddenly emerged in 1880 to become for the next ten or fifteen years the most effective weapon of unionism. There was no object so mean and no person so exalted as to escape its power. Side by side, with equal prominence, the Knights of Labor boycotted clothing manufacturers and their draymen, insignificant country grocers and presidential candidates, insipid periodicals and the currency of our nation, our national banknotes. . . . There can be little doubt that in actual practice the Knights of Labor were primarily a boycotting organization. (Wolman, 1914, pp. 24–25)

As Fusfeld (1980) has noted, the Knights had an intriguing history. Due to employer opposition, it started as a secret organization in 1869 and assumed a significant role among industrial unions following the depression of 1873. After a nationwide strike by unskilled workers in 1877—a seemingly spontaneous action that spread to the major industrial centers of the nation and led to the use of military force to restore order—the Knights decided to drop its secrecy status as it endeavored to become a national egalitarian organization open to unskilled as well as skilled workers in all occupations and industrial settings.

The philosophy of the Knights of Labor was not radical in the modern sense of the term. The organization believed that workers, as a group or class, deserved a larger share of the benefits generated by their work and that the way to attain this objective was for all workers to devote themselves to the task by joining and becoming active in the Knights. As Fusfeld (1980) has observed, since many of the Knights were uneducated and unskilled or semiskilled workers, such as brickmakers or freight handlers, they had little understanding or appreciation of what a labor union was all about. According to Fusfeld, "turnover among workers was high, strikers were easy to replace by strikebreakers, and most workers had little previous experience with organization and strikes" (1980, p. 16). Not surprisingly, under the circumstances, the Knights launched many strikes that proved to be unsuccessful.

In light of this background, it seemed only natural for the Knights to turn to the boycott as a tactic to supplement the unsuccessful strike. Wolman has expressed this point dramatically:

> Appearing, therefore, in 1879 and 1880 as a compact labor organization, composed in the main of workmen ignorant of the difficulties and necessities of organization; not oversupplied with funds; finding it necessary to employ spectacular and effective, but cheap, methods of aggression; controlling, however, a not insignificant purchasing power, the Knights of Labor immediately seized in 1880 upon the boycott as a unique and logical source of strength. (1914, p. 26)[1]

An important feature of the boycotts called by the Knights is that their targets were often not restricted to a primary offender. Retail units that were customers of offending companies were also targeted and thus the Knights engaged in secondary boycotts as well as primary boycotts. If a county labor federation called a boycott against a dairy violating union work rules, the boycotters would visit stores that carried the milk and cheese products of the dairy and ask the store owners to stop carrying these products or risk a boycott of their wares. In boycotting a printer, the union would make known to all of the printer's business customers, such as hotels, restaurants, and saloons, that to continue patronizing the printer would mean being placed on the county labor federation's "black list." Needless to say, the secondary boycotts were not received warmly by the business community or the courts, particularly when these protest actions extended far beyond the labor-management principals in the dispute to include many tangentially related companies and consumers.

Adding to the frustration of the business community and the courts with the labor boycotts were their large numbers and impressive record of effectiveness. Supporting data come from *Broadstreet's*, a business publication of the time that conducted a national survey in 1885 of boycotts of "unfair" shops and goods in American cities. The survey results revealed a total of 196 boycotts since 1883, with the state of New York alone reporting 59 in 1885.[2] Moreover, 82 of these 196 efforts had reached a conclusion, and it was estimated that 72 percent of the 82 were successful with regard to the consequence criterion noted in Chapter 1, in that they attained the goals of the boycotters in part or whole.

Of special interest are the tactics used by the Knights to realize their boycott objectives. According to Laidler (1913), the following approaches were commonly employed: "public addresses, personal conversation, the distribution of circulars and letters, the sending of delegates, the publication of 'unfair' lists and articles in trade union papers" (p. 67).

The circulars were distributed to all of the unions in a position to lend aid. And if the product being boycotted was distributed and sold nationally, the circulars would likewise receive nationwide distribution. Circulars were also distributed to the public if the boycott target sold its wares to the laboring classes. The circulars usually noted the reasons for the boycott and called upon "the friends of labor" to refrain from dealing with the targeted company.

Trade unionists were also asked to contribute funds in support of boycotts and to send delegates to visit retail dealers of the boycotted goods for the purpose of persuading these merchants to stop carrying these goods in their stores. Boycott delegates would often travel around the nation stopping in communities along the way to visit dealers and to meet with local trade unionists who were urged to aid the boycott effort. They sought support from all their various members in a community, including carpenters, cigar makers, bricklayers, blacksmiths, plasterers, and shoemakers. Since the Knights alone could draw upon local laborers from such a wide array of occupations, their boycotts were of particular concern to the business community.

Also contributing to the success of these labor boycotts was an astute choice of goods and services to be boycotted. As Laidler (1913) has noted, the Knights and other unions soon found that "boycotts may be waged most frequently and effectively in connection with common necessities and inexpensive luxuries purchased regularly by the mass of workers, such, for instance, as newspapers, cigars, hats and certain other articles of clothing, food and furniture" (p. 81).[3]

Although the Knights achieved a boycott success record that was truly impressive, it was not to last. During the late 1880s the unions found that increasingly their boycott efforts were being opposed by legal injunctions. This development, along with a sharp decrease in its membership, led to far fewer boycotts being called by the Knights during the 1890s and beyond.

The American Federation of Labor

The drop in membership for the Knights of Labor occurred at the time a new union, composed mainly of skilled workers, was appearing on the labor scene. Whereas the Knights began in 1869, the American Federation of Labor (AFL) emerged in the early 1880s. While both organizations held to the Knights' reform goals and their belief in legislation and the ballot as the way to end the "tyranny of the capitalists," the two organizations differed considerably in style. According to Wolman:

> The Knights of Labor were emotional, high-strung, spectacular; within hardly more than a half decade the Order attained by the indiscriminate boycotting of its enemies a hitherto

unheard of position of industrial and political power. The American Federation of Labor, while exhibiting on some occasions similar qualities, is, on the whole, characterized in its management by a more measured calmness and a greater deliberation. (1914, pp. 98–99)

By the end of the 1890s, the Knights were defunct, and the AFL, under the leadership of Samuel Gompers, was America's leading labor organization.

For some 20 years stretching from the mid-1890s to 1908, the AFL published a "We Don't Patronize" list in its official magazine featuring dozens of names of "unfair" companies. The AFL also assisted national and international unions with their labor boycott campaigns. These efforts were so successful that they prompted a counteraction in the form of a business trade association to help companies that were the targets of boycotts. The aptly named American Anti-Boycott Association (later renamed the League for Industrial Rights) was founded by two nonunion hat manufacturers, Dietrich Loewe and Charles Merritt, in Danbury, Connecticut, in 1902 when Loewe refused to recognize the hatters' union (the United Hatters). Loewe's rejection of the union led to a strike, which he easily circumvented by hiring nonunion replacements. This action prompted the hatters' union to initiate a boycott, and the AFL aided the effort by placing Loewe's company on its "We Don't Patronize" list.

The United Hatters' boycott plan was carefully conceived and executed with the focus being the distribution system for Loewe's hats. Wherever the hats were sold the union sent a full-time agent or a rank-and-file activist to urge local retailers to cease their dealings with Loewe. In one Virginia city two agents devoted several weeks to persuading the local labor council to place the name of a retailer of Loewe's hats on the "We Don't Patronize" list.

Loewe claimed his company was hurt by the boycott; his estimate of losses was $88,000. He filed a suit in the courts that led to the Supreme Court's first Danbury Hatters' decision in 1908. In *Loewe vs. Lawlor* the court held that it was illegal for the hatters to urge consumers "through the common newspapers and union prints" to boycott goods and services that had crossed state lines. Seven years later, in its second Danbury Hatters' decision, the court concurred with a lower court decision allowing Loewe to collect treble damages from the hatters' union.

The Danbury Hatters' case, according to Laidler (1930), started a new chapter in the legal history of the labor boycott. Prior to this decision the main weapon for combating the boycott had been the injunction. Indeed, in 1908 Samuel Gompers and two of his AFL colleagues had been sentenced to terms in prison and fined in a contempt action that stemmed from such an injunction. The boycott at issue here was called by the International Molders' Union to protest the 10-hour workday demanded by Buck's Stove and Range Company of St. Louis. The boycott was enthusiastically supported by the AFL in part because the head of the company was president of the antiunion National Association of Manufacturers. In 1913 the *Buck's Stove* case was dismissed on appeal due to a legal technicality.

According to Forbath (1991), open union defiance of antiboycott regulations and decrees largely stopped after the Supreme Court's actions in *Loewe vs. Lawlor* and *Buck's Stove*. Forbath notes that "'unfair' lists gradually disappeared from union journals, and boycotting lost its prominent place in the labor movement's arsenal and common culture" (1991, p. 94).

Nineteenth-Century Tactics: Boycotts vs. Strikes

That very large numbers of labor boycotts were initiated in the last two decades of the nineteenth century is hardly surprising. Given the poor economic conditions of the time (e.g., a national depression occurred in 1873) and the labor militancy that came shortly thereafter (i.e., a nationwide strike was undertaken by unskilled workers in 1877), conditions were right for an organization like the Knights of Labor to champion direct action successfully as a group strategy. And given the weakness of the strike as a labor tactic (i.e., workers would often not cooperate when asked to withhold their services, and even if they did cooperate, businesses usually had no problem replacing them), the boycott was a natural weapon to add to the union's arsenal.[4]

Moreover, the boycott, according to Wolman, offered some distinct advantages over the strike. First, it was far less costly to implement. As Wolman observed, "unlike the strike, it does not postulate the unemployment of a large number of workingmen, many of whom must be paid strike benefits" (1914, p. 123). At most, according to Wolman, the costs are limited to such minor items as postage, stationery, circulars, and the salaries and travel expenses of one or more national agents.

Second, the boycott offered unions a strategy that was, in theory at least, far more potentially effective than the strike. According to Wolman:

> A strike is, broadly speaking, a contest between a union and an employer during which the employer seeks to replace the strikers with strike-breakers, while the union attempts to dissuade strike-breakers from taking the places of its members. Under normal circumstances, if no violence is used, the contestants are on equal terms. The strike-breaker makes his decision at the seat of the disturbance subject to the influence of both the employer and the union. The ordinary boycott is different. Here the battle is waged by thousands of consumers who are not even remotely connected with the original dispute; they enter the struggle, not because they themselves have any grievance, but because wise foresight tells them that in the future they may make a similar use of the purchasing power of the union that now asks their support. (1914, p. 143)

Wolman concludes his argument by highlighting a basic distinction between the boycott and the strike in potential effectiveness:

> In a strike the employer may obtain a fair hearing and may take measures to protect his business; in a boycott the union acts as judge, declares the employer guilty, invokes to its aid a vast power foreign to the dispute—the membership of affiliated unions—and, if the boycotted commodity is sold for the most past to working men, it succeeds in destroying the employer's business. Strike-breakers often help employers to win strikes; consumers hostile to trade unions can, however, only under the most unusual circumstances be so organized as to render effective aid to a boycotted employer. (1914, pp. 144–145)[5]

A third claimed advantage of the boycott as a labor weapon over the strike is its longer-lasting effects. As Wolman astutely notes, when a strike is called off, the workers usually return to their jobs right away. But for the boycott,

> The publicity given the boycott ... and the deep feelings of hostility engendered by its prosecution produce more lasting effects. A commodity once advertised as unfair retains the stigma for a long time after the boycott is raised. (Wolman, 1914, p. 144)

This effect can, of course, take place at two levels. Retail dealers who have stopped doing business with a boycotted supplier may continue to deny business to the supplier after the boycott is called off because they fear the reestablishment of the boycott. Moreover, consumers who patronize other retail stores during the period of the boycott may, simply through inertia, find themselves staying with these stores after the boycott has ended.

Labor Boycotts Then and Now

The advantages claimed by Wolman of the boycott over the strike in labor struggles suggest some of the monumental changes to affect the boycott weapon over the next hundred years by organized labor. The first notable change is the marked departure from the boycott-friendly legal environment of the 1880s and early 1890s—the time when so many of these labor boycotts occurred.

The Changing Legal Environment

As Forbath (1991) has noted, the labor boycott was a relatively new legal concept in the 1880s, one not yet integrated into federal or state statutes or in judicial decisions of the time to nearly the same extent it is now; thus boycott targets had to resort to court-imposed injunctions on a case-by-case basis to combat the union campaigns.[6] The Supreme Court decisions of the early twentieth century changed the government position dramatically, and the more hostile period for boycotts that followed sharply limited union use of the tactic. The most dramatic changes here were with regard to secondary boycotts. As we have seen, these actions were extremely common in the 1880s and early 1890s, and they often succeeded by their implicit (or explicit) threats to innocent third parties (the retail dealers of boycotted goods) to stop selling the targeted goods or risk being punished economically by the working-class people of a community. And once activated, a secondary boycott was often difficult to stop, even by an injunction, since the organizers could continue their efforts covertly.

Since the Supreme Court decisions of the early twentieth century there has been a host of legislative and judicial actions at federal and state levels affecting labor boycotts. Much of the attention has been directed at secondary boycotts. For example, the Taft-Hartley Act of 1947 barred secondary boycotts, viewing them as unfair labor practices. The prohibitions were continued by the Landrum-Griffin Act of 1959, which outlawed secondary boycotts considered to be "coercive," in that the adverse effects are felt by businesses other than the one from which the union is seeking concessions. But what exactly constitutes "coercive" is not clear. As Hager has noted, "Federal secondary boycott law is notoriously dense and confusing" (1991, p. 793).

Some clarification has come with the Supreme Court's 1988 *DeBartolo* decision, which ruled that the distribution of handbills to consumers at a secondary boycott site is permissible while picketing aimed at consumers may or may not be. The idea here is that leafleting is generally less coercive than picketing and thus deserves to be a protected union practice.

Some picketing is protected as well, as a result of the Supreme Court's 1964 *Tree Fruits* decision and related cases. According to Hager,

> Picketing is not protected, however, if it requests a general boycott of an enterprise carrying a struck product or if it requests boycott of a struck product that constitutes so large a proportion of a secondary enterprise's business as to turn the struck product boycott into an enterprise boycott. (1991, p. 793)

But complicating matters are the specific legalities of each case. According to Stencel (1991), it is probably legal for a union in a labor conflict with a manufacturer to hand out leaflets in front of a retail store that sells the manufacturer's products, asking shoppers not to purchase them. It is also probably legal for the union to ask the store not to carry the manufacturer's products. However, Stencel believes that if the union engaged in both activities it might well find itself on somewhat shaky legal ground. Legal scholars expect to see no simple resolution of the legal status of the secondary boycott in the foreseeable future; more litigation and legal debate seem to be in the offing.

While the legal environment has certainly affected labor boycott use and effectiveness over the years, it is only one of four factors that have been important to a union finding itself at an impasse in a labor conflict. The second factor is the availability of the strike, especially if it is likely to be effective in attaining union goals. If a strike is expected to work, a union might well decide to call one (or at least threaten to do so). The third factor is the nature of the labor issue and the extent to which a strong case can be made in its favor to the consuming public. To illustrate, a 10-cents-an-hour wage dispute in the 1990s is unlikely to generate consumer support for a boycott. The fourth factor considers the nature of the good being manufactured or sold by the prospective boycott target. If, to use an extreme example, the prospective boycott target manufactures industrial equipment exclusively, there appears to be no obvious way a consumer boycott can be used to influence the company's policies.

Examination of the four factors discussed here reveals that the first (the legal environment) and fourth (the goods produced or sold by the target company) are limiting factors or constraints in that a boycott cannot usually be successfully pursued if it is illegal or if it is not implementable because there are no consumer goods to boycott. The middle two factors offer the potential, however, to influence the decision to initiate a boycott as well as its outcome.

The Nature of the Labor Boycott Issue

Perhaps the more important of the middle two factors is the nature of the boycott issue. In Chapter 1 we distinguished between two types of boycotts, *beneficiary* and *conscience*, and noted that the two differ with regard to the relationship between the boycott sponsors and the perceived victims of the target's actions. If the two entities represent the same constituency we have a beneficiary boycott; if they represent different constituencies we have a conscience boycott. With the growth of organized labor to a position of national power in the years following the Great Depression, union calls for boycotts became increasingly viewed by the consuming public not as appeals to conscience to help poor victimized workers, but as power-play pleas to take sides in contract disputes between two large organizational forces in the economic arena. It became a question of which one of the two powerful interests deserved an increase in its share of the consumer's dollar, and this question was of little interest to many (if not most) consumers. With this realization in mind, some labor groups tried to find ways to position their issues not only as beneficiary concerns but also as conscience concerns. Thus the United Farm Workers in the 1980s and 1990s cited evidence to support a broader statement of boycott objectives—one that went beyond better working conditions for themselves to include a pesticide-free crop, which would mean healthier food for American consumers.

The Boycott as the Labor Weapon of Last Resort

The other factor that has affected boycott use and effectiveness is the availability of the strike as a union weapon and its likelihood of success in a conflict situation. Needless to say, workers usually have to be already unionized for a strike call to have a reasonable chance of succeeding since not only do nonunionized workers normally have no strike fund to support their unemployed status, but they are typically much easier to replace than their unionized counterparts.

For unionized workers a strike is usually called in a labor struggle prior to a boycott, with the boycott held in reserve to be activated if and only if the strike is not succeeding. This point has been made by Laidler (1913) and by more contemporary analysts. For example, Kushner (1975) has stated, "Usually the boycott in the labor movement is resorted to when the picket lines have ceased to be effective. It has . . . been viewed as a last-ditch effort to salvage a losing strike" (p. 176). This observation has been recently echoed by Merilyn Toro of the AFL-CIO, who notes, "Generally speaking, labor boycotts are called only as a last resort" (1992, p. 1).

Why a last resort? This policy recognizes the obvious. Many action initiatives of unions engaged in modern-day labor struggles are beneficiary campaigns carried out to advance the welfare of affected groups of blue-collar or white-collar workers, rather than the welfare of the community at large (or the welfare of a more economically deprived segment of the community), and the consuming public is unlikely to lend its support to these boycotts. Needless to say, without this support these boycotts are unlikely to succeed.

Labor unions are well aware of these facts of life, but they call for boycotts anyway. And they do so for two reasons. First, by listing the boycott target and particulars in their newsletters, they are hoping beyond hope that luck will be on their side in that the boycott will be embraced by consumers. Second, even if the boycott call should fail, they are fulfilling their obligation to the labor movement by expressing solidarity with their members and with other unions. The AFL-CIO has been a leader here, and it still claims that the boycott is one of the most powerful tools that labor has other than the strike. This comment may say less about the power of the boycott and more about the growing weakness of the weapons in the arsenal of labor unions in the current era.

The Labor Boycott as a Union Organizing Tactic

If public sympathy has been conspicuously absent for labor boycotts called by established unions such as the AFL-CIO in support of their members' battles with corporate management, the same cannot be said for labor boycotts called to establish unions to represent nonunionized workers. In the last 40 years these efforts have focused on the plight of the poor and disenfranchised members of society, such as migrant farm workers, many of whom immigrated to the United States from Mexico. Still other examples are new immigrants from Mexico and Central America employed for low wages and few benefits in the textile mills of the South.

The stories about these workers and the often deplorable conditions under which they labor have pricked the conscience of many Americans, who have demonstrated their support of boycotts called to secure union rights for these workers. Major corporations that have been the targets of union-sponsored campaigns over the last 30 years includes Farah, J.P. Stevens, and Campbell Soup. Each of these three corporate campaigns has been a success, due in no small part to the effectiveness of the consumer boycotts called against the firms.

By far the most successful of the union-organizing efforts was that of the United Farm Workers Organizing Committee (UFWOC) in California, which started in the 1960s under the charismatic leadership of the late Cesar Chavez. The UFWOC campaign was launched as a new and promising chapter in a long history of unsuccessful initiatives to organize and improve the lot of migrant farm workers, a group that was denied the right to organize by the National Labor Relations Act. (All agricultural workers were excluded from the union-organizing provisions of the act, a development that led to low wages and high profits for California agriculture.)

As might be expected, strikes had not worked well in organizing farm workers largely because of the ease of hiring strike breakers, the mobility of the workers, and the absence of a substantial strike fund to support the strikers and their families. Fortunately for the farm workers, table grapes were available as a boycott product in that this product offered the advantages of being a discretionary purchase sold in relatively few market locations; indeed, about half of all U.S. sales of table grapes occurred in supermarkets in 10 major cities.

Chavez knew that the UFWOC was no match for the California growers in economic power. His strategy was to use the consumer boycott, a powerful moral weapon that drew upon the Gandhian model of nonviolence. His campaign, which was openly admired by Martin Luther King and Robert Kennedy, was a source of frustration to the growers, who were used to overpowering the farm worker opposition with their money and influence. But the nonviolent approach also frustrated many of the workers, who had already spent a lifetime turning the other cheek.

Supporters of the UFWOC in organized labor expressed surprise at the use of the boycott strategy. One unnamed AFL-CIO official, recognizing that the boycott had become a formality rather than a force in union strategy, reacted to Chavez's call for a boycott by exclaiming, "I thought they were crazy." But as Kushner has noted (1975), "Suddenly the boycott became the farm-workers' most important weapon to the amazement of old-timers in the labor movement" (p. 176). Kushner also claims that the weapon was extraordinarily effective in pressuring the growers. Indeed, he notes, perhaps with a bit of hyperbole, "There never was a boycott as successful as the one initiated by the farm union" (p. 176).

Chavez, of course, was a critically important factor in the success of the UFWOC boycott. Unlike the leaders before him, he had the ability to work effectively with the Mexican American farm workers whom he represented as well as the diverse populations of liberal Americans who supported the boycott. Included here were the trade unionists in the AFL-CIO and United Auto Workers, student leaders, and activists in the various church movements of the time. The cooperation of these various groups was crucial to the success of the boycott, and in city after city they worked in support of the UFWOC effort.

How this worked in practice was detailed by Dolores Huerta, a UFWOC leader who led the union boycott campaign in New York:

> In each of the five boroughs, we organized neighborhood coalitions of church, labor, liberal and student groups. Then we began picketing the A&P, the biggest chain in the city. For several months we had picket lines on about 25 to 30 stores and turned thousands of dollars away. A lot of the managers had come up through the unions and were sympathetic to us. In response to consumer pressure, the store managers began to complain to their division heads, and soon they took the grapes out of all of their stores, 430 of them. (Smith, 1990, p. 252)

The success of these efforts was impressive. In just six months, New York, the largest urban market for grapes in the United States, had seen a drop in grape shipments of 30 percent. Indeed, all of New York's major supermarket chains stopped selling table grapes.

And what happened in New York was repeated on a lesser scale in each of 35 other major urban markets for table grapes. From 1966 to 1969, the UFWOC claimed that its 100 organizers had been responsible for an almost one-third drop in table grape sales in these major markets. Moreover, the boycott was not limited to the United States. In Toronto, Canada, UFWOC organizers worked with trade unionists and activists in the church movement to make the city off-limits to table grapes.

The response of the growers to this North American onslaught was a multimillion-dollar publicity campaign devised by the San Francisco firm of Whittaker and Baxter. The firm established a consumers' rights committee to discredit the fledgling union and its boycott. The campaign claimed that the boycotters were making nonnegotiable demands and engaging in threats, intimidation, and violent acts of vandalism such as the fire-bombing of supermarkets. These various initiatives of the growers proved to be too little and too late, as did their attempts to secure legislative and judicial action to stop the boycott.

The dramatic successful ending of the UFWOC boycott came on July 19, 1970, at the UFWOC dining hall just outside of Delano, California. On this landmark day, according to Kushner,

> Cesar Chavez's army of farm workers, supported by much of the labor movement and others, had toiled for almost five long years, and the fruits of their labors, having fallen slowly over the span of several years, were now beginning to come down in bunches. (1975, p. 171)

Crowded around the head tables in the dining hall were the union's leaders along with 26 grower-employers of more than 7,000 farm workers, and together the union leader and the growers signed the historic table grape agreement.

Following this agreement there were many twists and turns in the evolution of the UFW; many more boycotts were called, but none was nearly as successful as the table grape boycott that established the UFW. With the death of Cesar Chavez in 1993 the gradual slide in membership and influence that occurred for the union in the 1980s and 1990s has continued.

The Labor Boycott in the Context of the Corporate Campaign

In the last 30 years unions have begun to look beyond the traditional tactics of strikes and boycotts in their confrontations with management. A more systematic approach was championed by Ray Rogers, a labor organizer and consultant who referred to it as the "corporate campaign." According to Rogers (1971), the corporate campaign is a "confrontation strategy" that

> considers all avenues of pressure and would include the possibility of a strike, a boycott, and other traditional tactics. However, these would be timed and coordinated as part of an overall conceptualized strategy to maximize their effectiveness. A corporate campaign attacks a corporate adversary from every conceivable angle. It takes on the power behind a company. It shows clearly how to cut off the lifeblood of an institution. Its proponents recognize that powerful institutions are both economic and political animals and must be challenged in both the economic and political spheres. It moves workers' and poor peoples' struggles away from their own doorsteps to the doorsteps of the corporate power brokers. (p. 60)

Unlike traditional union strategies, the corporate campaign puts pressure on management in a manner that is external to the workplace. As Mishel (1985) has noted, strikes, sit-ins, and slowdowns are internal workplace tactics that undermine management's production capabilities. A corporate campaign combines these internal tactics with external nonworkplace tactics such as boycotts and shareholder resolutions.

The theory underlying the corporate campaign strategy is straightforward. According to Mishel (1985),

> A corporation is an organization which exists to make money, the more the better. Each corporation relies on its own resources and those of other organizations and individuals. A corporate campaign strategy is based on an assessment of an employer's links to other organizations (banks, interlocking corporations, government, corporate customers) and individuals (customers, shareholders, neighbors, citizens). A corporate

campaign systematically uses the resources available to the union—its membership, its ties to other unions, church and community groups, its political clout—to put pressure on the vulnerable links. The basic elements of a corporate campaign are research, the mobilization of the union's resources, coalition building and public outreach. The basic thrust is to broaden the conflict from one which is solely between a limited group of workers and their employer to one which is between a corporation and all levels of government, community groups, its customers, the entire labor movement. (p. 70)

As Mishel notes, a variety of external corporate links can be used as pressure points by a skillful corporate campaigner.

1. *Financing*. A corporation may secure financing from a bank that has one or more officers represented on the corporation's board of directors. A union can put pressure on the bank in many ways, such as threatening to withdraw union funds unless the bank dissociates itself publicly from the corporation's antilabor policies by having its officers resign from the board of directors.

2. *Shareholders*. Many public corporations have a small number of shareholders who own very substantial blocks of stock. These large shareholders may be mutual funds, investment bankers, pension funds, or wealthy individuals. Since their holdings are so large, these owners may be in a position to influence corporate policy, and thus they qualify as prospective pressure points for corporate campaigners. Possible mechanisms of influence include shareholder resolutions and face-to-face meetings.

3. *Customers*. Many corporations produce or market consumer goods and these firms are, of course, prospective candidates for consumer boycotts. In other instances corporations such as banks or insurance companies may have unions for customers and thus they may be able to apply pressure by threatening to withdraw their business from these firms.

4. *Corporate Governance and Community*. Corporations are often interlinked through representation on their boards of directors. Corporations are also linked to the community by

corporate foundations and by the participation of corporate officials in community organizations and charitable activities. Each of these corporate extensions presents a potential pressure point for corporate campaigners to exert influence.

5. *Public Image*. With huge sums of money being spent yearly on corporate advertising, most firms are very sensitive to any effort to undermine their public image. An effective corporate campaigner will look for embarrassing or questionable corporate practices to expose to public scrutiny, such as safety and health violations, plant closings, excessively high executive compensation, and environmental abuses.

6. *Government*. The many links of corporations to government provide even more potential pressure points for activation by corporate campaigners. Included here are various government regulations that corporations may be violating related to the environment (e.g., air and water pollution) and the workplace (e.g., employment discrimination as well as health and safety practices). Also, the government may be a customer of corporations (e.g., the defense and aerospace industries), and such misdeeds as cost overruns or inflated pricing may be used to pressure government to cease or curtail its dealings with the corporate offenders.

7. *International Links*. Many companies have links to foreign countries, which provide pressure points to be targeted by corporate campaigners. Boycotts have been a commonly used tactic here; perhaps the best-known instance was the Shell boycott, which was prompted by the company's ties to South Africa during apartheid.

Generally, unions have used corporate campaign strategy sparingly, with the typical offense, according to Mishel (1985), consisting of such extreme practices as corporate lawlessness or takeaway demands. Beneficiaries of the strategy have frequently been unorganized workers who are attempting to unionize or to have their newly established unions recognized by management. Corporate targets of such campaigns in the last few decades include Equitable Life Insurance, Beverly Enterprises, Litton Industries, and J.P. Stevens.

Mishel (1985) notes that another use for corporate campaigns is to make matters difficult for companies that have destroyed a union or have defied industry practices by refusing to honor well-established labor-management agreements. Two examples he cites are actions taken against Phelps Dodge and Louisiana Pacific. Still another extreme action that may prompt a corporate campaign is a plant shutdown, either threatened or actually carried out. Corporate campaigners attempted to use this strategy in conjunction with a threatened consumer boycott of General Motors cars in the Los Angeles area in the 1980s in an effort to persuade General Motors not to close its plant in neighboring Van Nuys. This campaign, which was documented by organizer Eric Mann (1986), was temporarily successful; however, the plant did close in 1992.

The Stevens Campaign

Do corporate campaigns, and especially those employing boycotts, offer a successful strategy for labor unions? The question is difficult, if not impossible, to answer because of the many problems associated with the evaluation of any intervention strategy in a natural context—the same sorts of problems we found in Chapter 1 when we looked at how one determines if boycotts are successful. One case, however, has generally been viewed as a success, and that is the maiden voyage of the corporate campaign under the direction of Ray Rogers.

This case, which has been described in some detail by Rogers (1981), concerns a boycott initiated by the Amalgamated Clothing and Textile Workers Union in conjunction with a corporate campaign in the late 1970s. The target was the J.P. Stevens Company, and the union pressed to get textiles workers represented by it to secure their first contract with Stevens. As Rogers (1981) noted, through his efforts as a union aide, the focus of the campaign became the corporate headquarters of Stevens along with those institutions and organizations linked to Stevens through large stock holdings and loans and through interlocking boards of directors. The corporate campaign was successful in forcing two chief officials of Stevens off the board of directors of Manufacturers Hanover Trust Company, which at the time was the fourth-largest bank in the country. The bank's action was taken in response to pressure from large numbers of religious, community, and political organizations as a result of a campaign spearheaded by organized labor. Further pressures to isolate Stevens from the business community led to the resignation of the CEO of Avon Products Company from the Stevens board and to the resignation of the Stevens board chairman from the board of the New York Life Insurance Company.

Did the corporate campaign strategy work? Rogers claims that it did because union recognition soon followed for the Stevens workers, and in the labor contract that was subsequently signed, Stevens insisted that the following paragraph be included:

> Subsequently to the date of the Agreement the Union will not engage in any "corporate campaign" against the Company. Accordingly the Union will not in any manner attempt to effectuate the resignation of members of the Board of Directors of Stevens, or to effectuate the resignation or removal of Stevens executives from the board of directors of other companies, or to restrict the availability of financial or credit accommodations to Stevens, or by deliberate conduct to affect materially and adversely the relationship between Stevens and any other business organization. (Rogers, 1981, p. 62)

The Hormel Campaign

In contradistinction to the dramatic union victory for the corporate campaign strategy over Stevens was its frustrating failure in combating George A. Hormel & Company, a major meat packer headquartered in Austin, Minnesota. Unlike the other labor-management confrontations we have examined that used the corporate campaign strategy, this one was precipitated not by union recognition considerations but by a contract renewal impasse. The story is a complicated one, and a summary account is needed to understand the role of the corporate campaign strategy as well as the boycott that was called as part of this strategy.

Problems started when Hormel announced in late 1983 that it planned to cut the wages and benefits of the unionized workers in its Austin plant. The Austin union, Local P-9 of the United Food and Commercial Workers International Union (UFCW), adamantly refused to accept the cuts. The union position was not difficult to understand since it was being asked to accept $8.25

an hour for jobs then paying $10.69 an hour, and the company had just reported annual profits of nearly $30 million. Nonetheless Hormel claimed that the cuts were needed in order for Hormel to remain competitive, especially when compared to other meat-packing companies paying substantially lower wages.

Two union activists played important roles in determining what happened next: Jim Guyette and Ray Rogers. Their personalities and actions have been dramatically showcased in *American Dream*, Barbara Kopple's Academy Award-winning documentary film about the Hormel labor conflict. As Terrance Rafferty (1992) has noted in reviewing the film:

> The president of the local, a deceptively soft-spoken and unassuming man named Jim Guyette, was a militant, a leader who inspired his constituency by his unyielding adherence to principle. Guyette's blunt personality was not ideally suited to the intricate art of collective bargaining, and Hormel's negotiators obviously felt that the company's position was so strong that they didn't have to compromise much. Against the advice of the international union, P-9 hired a free-lance New York consultant named Ray Rogers, whose organization, Corporate Campaign, espoused an unorthodox approach to labor disputes. Rogers' strategy consisted mainly of generating negative publicity about the company and its major corporate stockholders, and maintaining that sort of corporate pressure until the harassed employer would be compelled to settle on the union's terms.
>
> [His] arrival [in Austin] kicks off a period of euphoric solidarity for the rank and file of P-9. He's a fantastic cheerleader: when he speaks at a union meeting, it turns into something like a high-school pep rally before the big game. (p. 88)

Viewers of the film describe its early moments as something akin to the heyday of the American labor movement in the 1930s. Rogers awakened extraordinary feelings of hope and optimism in the Hormel workers—emotions marking a sharp contrast to the inertia and frustration that seemed omnipresent in American union members in the 1980s. Indeed many observers of the 1980s believed the labor movement had simply stopped moving, and others judged that its movement had been backward rather than forward.[8] The large unions appeared to have more in common with their more institutionalized corporate counterparts than with the unions of old; increasingly, their actions seemed bureaucratic and arbitrary, rather than principled and democratic. Moreover, membership rolls for unions were decreasing, and they were being defeated in their battles with an anti-union Reagan Administration. And even more importantly, when faced with threats of layoffs and plant closings and the kinds of concessionary contracts offered by Hormel, unions seemed incapable of effectively confronting corporate management.

A tragedy of sorts unfolded in the documentary film and the story it tells so effectively. When attention turns to the international union we find that Rogers did not enjoy the confidence of some UFCW officials. As one UFCW executive put it, "Ray acts as if he is a Messiah, and that worries me." Still another, who was the chief negotiator in the union's international meat-packing division, told the P-9 members that Rogers' strategy was "doomed," knowing as he did that the local union lacked the power to defeat Hormel.

What happened next was that a split developed over strategy between the local and international unions; P-9 found that it was fighting two battles instead of one. In the end a strike was called, which proved to be catastrophic in its effects on the local and the community. Hormel replaced some of the striking workers while others opted to cross the picket line and return to work. And then the old P-9 was ousted and a new local formed as part of the international union. So the remaining members of the abandoned local found themselves adrift, both jobless and disconnected from their international union. Before reaching this nadir the striking workers, now known as the United Support Group, called for a nationwide consumer boycott of Hormel products; later the major fast-food customers of Hormel (Burger King and Pizza Hut) were added to the boycott list. The corporate campaign also attempted to get union members and their sympathizers to stop doing business with a Minnesota-based bank that was a close corporate ally of Hormel.

Although the United Support Group appeared determined to continue the boycott "until all 850 meat packers still out of work were rehired," it is difficult to imagine how the group thought this objective could be attained. A new contract had been signed and a new local established with new officers elected to represent it. And all these changes occurred more than ten years before making their undoing a virtual impossibility.

It would seem, however, that the boycott may have served an expressive, rather than an instrumental, function for the United Support Group and its sympathizers. As Green (1990) has noted in his account of the labor conflict, the Austin local and its supporters fought a fierce battle during the bone-chilling winter of 1986, and, in so doing, it took on some formidable forces: a large multiplant corporation, strike breakers recruited from economically depressed local farming communities, the leadership of the UFCW parent union, and National Guard troops who were called in by the Minnesota governor. After fighting and losing such an extraordinary battle, it would seem that the frustrations experienced by these wounded warriors must have approached the unbearable. By continuing to boycott Hormel, the United Support Group, while severely limited in numbers and resources, appeared to have found a way to go on—by expressing its frustrations against the corporate entity responsible for its defeat in the workplace.

Assessing the Effectiveness of Labor Boycotts

Has organized labor found the boycott to be an effective means to attain its ends? The question is far easier to pose than to answer. Indeed, few labor boycotts have been rigorously assessed with regard to effectiveness.[9] In this section we share some observations stimulated by the foregoing historical accounts and analysis. Taken together they may help the reader gain some insights into the boycott effectiveness question.

1. *Boycotts and strikes may often be two sides of the same sword.*

    As we have already seen, in many labor conflicts an unsuccessful strike is followed by a call for a boycott, and the boycott often fails as well. What we have neglected to note, however, is that a strike action may also, in effect, be a boycott action. Workers picketing a supermarket while on strike present a clear boycott signal to customers who are contemplating shopping there. They may well be jeered upon entry and exit, and if they are regular customers, they may find themselves too embarrassed to cross a picket line staffed by the store clerks who have been waiting on them for years. Moreover, the picket signs carried by the strikers may include boycott messages. A good example is the pre-Thanksgiving strike called by flight attendants for American Airlines in 1993. Some of the picket signs called for a boycott indirectly ("Let's clear the air") while others were very direct ("Don't fly American"). And yet, at no time during this labor dispute did the flight attendants' union officially call for and publicize a boycott of American Airlines.

The lesson here seems to be that you need more than a scorecard to identify the players. You have to observe each one in action to know who is a boycotter and who is a striker and who is occupying both roles. And if indeed workers are occupying both roles, it is not possible to distinguish the effects of the boycott from those of the strike.

2. *Even when a boycott and a strike are initiated as separate and distinct actions, it may not be possible to arrive at an independent assessment of the boycott.*

As we have repeatedly seen in this chapter, boycotts seldom happen in isolation from other labor protest initiatives. The Ray Rogers-type corporate campaign, for example, draws upon as many tactics as practicable in an effort to conduct a successful campaign, and this emphasis on multiple approaches makes it difficult, if not impossible, to isolate the effects of a consumer boycott.

3. *What we have conveniently called consumer boycotts to satisfy labor goals may actually be merchant or retailer boycotts.*

A good example is the J.P. Stevens boycott. This action was undertaken to provide support for the union-organizing effort directed at the manufacturer. Much of the union effort followed the pattern we earlier observed in the Danbury Hatters' boycott at the turn of the century. In particular, the focus was on retail stores, including such giants as Macy's in New York. Union-supplied informational pickets at these retail outlets were so effective in discouraging shoppers from entering that the stores decided to discontinue carrying J.P. Stevens goods. And, of course, once that action was taken there was no way many of these shoppers could conveniently buy J.P. Stevens products. Thus a so-called consumer boycott was, in a real sense, a merchant or retailer boycott.

4. *Labor boycotts are more likely to be effective if they use conscience campaigns rather than beneficiary campaigns.*

As has been suggested in this chapter, perhaps the worst case scenario for a labor boycott is a beneficiary campaign to aid well-paid employees (e.g., an airline pilots' union) seeking public support during negotiations with corporate management for a new contract. Many consumers, faced with dozens, if not hundreds, of other protest actions crying out for public support, are likely to look the other way.

Conscience campaigns, on the other hand, have made headway, as we have seen, with the boycott efforts of migrant farm laborers in California and Ohio. Other efforts to organize the disenfranchised are likely to have a chance at drawing consumer support especially if the boycott campaigns are well-planned and implemented, and if the issues at hand focus on major inequities and/or labor abuses.

5. *The current era may not be particularly conducive to strident action by labor unions, be they strikes or boycotts.*

Many observers believe that President Reagan dampened union enthusiasm for strikes in 1981 when he shocked the nation and the labor movement by permanently replacing striking air-traffic controllers. As one AFL-CIO official put it, "We believe it was a signal that it was OK to fire strikers . . . something that hadn't been done before." Although federal law bans employers from firing striking workers, they may be "replaced permanently" so that business can continue. In the words of former UAW President Doug Fraser, "They have the right to strike. They gave that to you in one hand, but in the other they threaten to replace you if you do."

As a result, labor unions are pushing their demands on management but not on the picket lines through strikes and boycotts. Instead the two sides are opting for the relative quiet of the corporate conference room where union and management leaders are increasingly trying to resolve issues through mediation and sometimes even through arbitration. Indeed, many labor and management leaders have enrolled in joint training classes to learn how to negotiate peacefully and effectively, so that each side gets its points heard and understood.

The clearest example of the downturn in labor activism is the change that occurred in the UAW contract negotiations with the major automobile manufacturers in 1993 as compared to 1990. The 1990 negotiations sparked two years of sporadic strikes, while in 1993 the talks began early and contracts were extended with no serious consideration of a strike.

Should the trend continue, some labor analysts believe strikes and other militant union actions may become obsolete—a development that reflects the dramatic decline in the power of organized labor in the 1980s and 1990s.

Concluding Comments

Labor boycotts have assumed a significant role in American affairs for more than 100 years, starting with the myriad campaigns of the Knights of Labor in the 1880s and extending to the present-day "Don't Patronize" lists of the AFL-CIO. During its heyday the very mention of the word "boycott" evoked fear and hatred on the part of its targets, and legal as well as organizational remedies were pursued to counteract the various boycott initiatives.

In more recent years the boycott has been used in two principal ways. The first is as a last-resort solution to a labor-management conflict, usually one resulting from unsuccessful negotiations to renew a contract. Boycotts called under such conditions often have a last-ditch quality of desperation to them in that they are activated after all other reasonable approaches have been pursued unsuccessfully, including, in many cases, a work stoppage or strike. Moreover, when the boycott is finally called, it is often unclear whether it is being seriously pursued or, as sometimes seems more likely, it is simply added to a "Don't Patronize" list. Under the circumstances it is hardly surprising to learn that boycotts used in this first way are rarely successful.

The second principal way that boycotts have been used is as a tactic in support of a union-organizing campaign for a group of unrepresented workers. As we have seen, in the 1880s it was the poor, often uneducated immigrant who was aided by the boycott campaigns to gain union recognition undertaken by the Knights of Labor. A century later it was, once again, the poor, often uneducated immigrant who was likewise helped by union-organizing boycott campaigns, only this time they were launched by new leaders of the unrepresented, such as the United Farm Workers. The nineteenth-century immigrants who were the beneficiaries of the boycott campaigns came from northern and eastern Europe to pursue a new life in America's cities, while many of their twentieth-century counterparts hailed from Central America and sought to establish themselves in America's farmlands.

Both groups were poor and powerless. They also worked under extremely difficult conditions, both physically and mentally, for wages that most observers considered exploitative. It is no wonder that these boycott campaigns were so often successful in touching the conscience of Americans. It is no wonder too that many Americans expressed their support by refusing to purchase the goods produced and sold by the offending firms. The UFW grape and lettuce boycotts are two campaigns that elicited these kinds of responses.

However, as we have indicated, the labor boycott situation is beset by many seemingly intractable complexities. Some labor boycotts of the union-organizing variety were more oriented toward the media than the marketplace, and success here was less a matter of conscience than a matter of embarrassing a corporation with a national reputation, such as Campbell Soup. Moreover, it can be argued that some consumer boycotts were not really consumer boycotts at all but retailer or merchant boycotts. And some labor strikes may have been consumer boycotts as well as strikes in that the message they communicated to the public was not to buy. Finally, in light of the devastating decline in power for labor unions in the last few years, such militant actions as strikes and boycotts appear to be rapidly disappearing from the repertoire of union tactics for dealing with management. Only time will tell if this new and discouraging state of affairs for labor union militancy is a temporary phenomenon or a permanent change in labor's approach to advancing the welfare of workers.

Social scientists are fond of saying that there are two sides of the economic coin: production and consumption. In this chapter we have examined the ways in which the boycott tactic has been used by employees to confront perceived inequities and worker dissatisfaction on the production side of the economy. In the next chapter we move from the workplace to the marketplace and look at the role of the boycott in coping with various kinds of consumer dissatisfaction.

◆4◆

CONSUMER ECONOMIC BOYCOTTS

As we saw in Chapter 3, for more than 100 years, American workers have seen the value of establishing unions to serve as a countervailing power to that of their employers. And while the labor movement has weakened considerably in the last two decades, no one seriously questions the greater power of workers when they speak and act as an organized unit rather than as isolated individuals.

One would think that this labor lesson in empowerment would have been learned over the years by consumers. After all, they also have an economic choice, and that is to cope as solitary individuals with the increasingly large corporations with whom they deal in the marketplace or to cope with them through organized consumer action. And consumers, both individually and jointly, often find much that is disturbing in their marketplace interactions with corporations. Indeed, consumer complaints and dissatisfactions are common, with many directed at high prices, unsafe products, exaggerated advertising claims, and poor quality of goods and services.

Curiously, one of the great enigmas of economic behavior is the reluctance of Americans to form organizations for advancing their interests as consumers. For years, observers of the consumer movement (e.g., Chase and Schlink, 1927) have called attention to the problem. As one economist put it more than 60 years ago:

> We organize on the basis of almost every other conceivable interest—political, social, economic, religious. Clubs for this and that exist everywhere. We are very assiduous in organizing on the basis of our interests as producers. Groups of business men organize into trade associations; laborers into unions; lawyers, teachers, doctors into their professional associations. (Coles, 1938, p. 33)

Many students of the consumer movement would agree that the Coles statement holds true to (or almost to) the same extent today as it did in 1938. As a result the consumer right to be heard and represented through dedicated organizations remains weak, and especially when compared to other actors in the private sector who are represented by powerful organizations such as the U.S. Chamber of Commerce or the National Association of Manufacturers.

The foregoing should not be interpreted to mean that there are no national organizations to represent consumers. Indeed, for more than a half-century, the nonprofit Consumers Union, publisher of the monthly magazine *Consumer Reports*, has been recognized as the nation's leading consumer organization. And for several decades, the Washington-based Consumer Federation of America, an umbrella organization consisting of 240 groups with 50 million members, has been an effective advocate for the consumer interest. Interestingly, however, these two not-for-profit national organizations, as well as a host of others at the state level, have rarely initiated or supported consumer economic boycotts. More typically, they conduct research on consumer issues, disseminate and publicize research findings, and lobby legislators and administration officials on behalf of the consumer interest. Their mode of operation is thus more moderate or conservative than that of their labor union counterparts, and a boycott action would appear to be stylistically uncharacteristic of these organizations.

In light of this background the reader may wonder what role, if any, consumer economic boycotts have had in advancing the consumer interest. The answer appears to be a modest one, with few significant boycott actions having been launched in the last few decades. And, as indicated, when these actions have been initiated, the responsible groups have often not been the establishment organizations in the consumer movement such as Consumers Union or the Consumer Federation of America. Instead it has been *ad hoc* consumer groups usually led by women that have typically launched consumer economic boycotts. As we shall see, many have come and gone in what a historian would see as a twinkling of the eye—time periods ranging from a few weeks to a few years.

It should come as no surprise that women in general and homemakers in particular have been at the forefront of direct grassroots actions such as boycotts to further the consumer interest. For centuries the traditional division of labor meant that it was homemakers who did the shopping, and thus they were the ones who most directly felt the impact of adverse changes in price or availability of consumer goods. Especially critical were sharp price rises and acute shortages for food, particularly for such staples as milk or meat. The result was often women-led protests and revolts. As English historian E. P. Thompson has noted in describing food riots of the eighteenth century, it was women who were "most involved in face-to-face marketing [and hence] most sensitive to price significancies." He adds, "it is probable that ... women most frequently precipitated the spontaneous actions" (1971, p. 116). Moreover, while the reasons for such actions are not clear, historian Herbert Gutman (1973) suggests a sensibility, with roots in preindustrial times, focusing upon the illegitimacy of charging unfair prices for necessities like foodstuffs. And it was due to this perceived illegitimacy that some historians saw the rioters' purpose as meting out justice and punishment (Baxandall et al., 1976).

What often distinguishes these boycotts from other types is their concern with consumers receiving value for the money they spend in the marketplace. Thus anything that served to decrease the value received from such consumer transactions was a potential source of concern to the *ad hoc* consumer groups. And businesses believed by the groups to be responsible for the value decrement have been seen as fair game for boycotts.

What are the value threats that typically concerned the *ad hoc* groups that resorted to consumer economic boycotts? To answer this question one has to realize that consumer educators (e.g., Garman, 1993) tend to view the concept of "value" as a dual function of the quality or worth of a commodity purchased in the marketplace and the price paid by the consumer. Thus consumer advocates are likely to become concerned if for a given product or service a marked increase in price or decrease in quality should occur, and for no apparent reason or for a reason that does not seem to be justifiable. Consumer advocates may also show concern if they have reason to believe that an existing price is set at an artifically high level (due, for example, to oligopolistic practices) or if quality has been held to a level lower than need be. And while there are many dimensions to quality, health and safety are generally viewed as key ones, in that a consumer product is usually not considered to be of high quality if its use endangers the health or safety of consumers.

What this brief overview suggests is that price and quality are the two elements that have triggered consumer economic boycotts in the United States in the last few decades. And of the two, price has dominated quality as a boycott inducer, perhaps because changes here are usually clearly signaled, while changes in quality often are not.

Another characteristic of consumer economic boycotts is that they tend to be commodity-oriented rather than oriented to a particular product brand. The reasons for deemphasizing individual product brands are not hard to discern. If a particular producer, say Domino, should blatantly move in an untoward consumer direction with regard to the price or quality of its packaged sugar, individual consumers would presumably note the untoward change, with many switching to another brand. Moreover, if many consumers acted in this manner, they would send Domino a message equivalent to an organized marketplace boycott of the firm; and it seems likely that the message (a dramatic drop in sales) would have an effect similar to the one communicated by an organized marketplace boycott of the branded product.

The point is that consumers appear not to gain very much by resorting to an organized consumer economic boycott of a particular branded product, especially if a competitive brand of equal or near-equal attractiveness is available to them. (Nonetheless, consumer economic boycotts of individual branded products sometimes do occur, and to illustrate their dynamics one such boycott is discussed in a postscript to this chapter.)

Consumer economic boycotts have frequently been activated, however, when two conditions have been met: The stimulus is a seemingly large and unfair price increase, and the product in question is not a single brand or model, but a whole commodity class. This circumstance occurred fairly often in the 1970s when boycotts were called in response to large and seemingly unjustified price increases for milk, sugar, coffee, and meat. And it is important to note that these commodities are all staple items that many consumers view as essential to the diets of their families.

The careful reader will note what appears to be a contradiction between some of these items (i.e., coffee and meat) and the guidelines relating to the execution of marketplace boycotts delineated in Chapter 2. There we followed conventional wisdom (as well as psychological theory) by suggesting that protest leaders *not* boycott items for which there are no effective substitutes in the marketplace—effective with regard to price, consumer acceptance, and accessibility. We gave as an example the "committed carnivore" who may have difficulty complying with a meat boycott. But what the guideline really says is that ideally one should not select all coffee brands or all meat products as boycott targets. Sometimes the real and the ideal differ, however. If the price increase for a food commodity is great enough or the rationale behind it suspect, consumers may initiate a boycott anyway. Frequently, however, boycott leaders faced with the "committed carnivore" or the "coffee addict" have dealt with the no-effective-substitute problem by calling for a reduction rather than an elimination of product purchases or consumption. In Chapter 1 this practice was referred to as a partial boycott.

To sum up the foregoing, consumer economic boycotts tend to be actions taken by *ad hoc* consumer groups rather than established consumer organizations. The actions often result from an abrupt and seemingly unjustified untoward change in economic value—a decrease in product or service quality or, more typically, an increase in price. Moreover, most consumer economic boycotts focus not on a single brand of product or service but on a whole class of commodities, and these items tend to be food staples.

In the remainder of this chapter we examine some of the more significant consumer economic boycotts that have occurred in the United States since the turn of the century. The first of these, the 1902 meat boycott, is a very early example of consumer activism in that it predates the three stages of consumer activism identified some years ago by Herrmann (1970) and Kotler (1972).

The 1902 Meat Boycott

President William McKinley's successful campaign for reelection in 1900 used a slogan promising American workers "a full dinner pail." The worst of the depression of the 1890s had passed, and there appeared to be good reason for optimism. But after the cost-of-living index had fallen 9 percent for the 1891–1897 period, it began to climb and by 1902 had increased 9 percent above the 1898 level. During this same four-year period food prices jumped 8.3 percent. And for some foods the increases reached truly startling levels. For example, the cheapest cuts of beef increased in one year from 5 cents to 12½ cents a pound.

As historian Steven Piott (1981) has indicated in a fascinating account of the circumstances that generated these price increases, consumers of the time were upset about the dramatic declines in their purchasing power and resorted to boycotts as a means of protest. Piott notes that consumers strongly suspected that the loss in purchasing power was caused by corporate consolidation, a phenomenon referred to at the time as the formation of "trusts." In 1899, more than 100 trusts were incorporated, and this number was more than twice the total for *all* years prior to 1899. As Thorelli (1955) has documented, the number increased to more than 300 by 1903. Piott sums up the situation wryly: "Prosperity had not come to rural and urban America but to corporate America" (1981, p. 32).

The story of the consumer economic boycotts of meat starts with the establishment of the Beef Trust:

> By the turn of the century the Beef Trust possessed economic power over an industry exceeded only in extent by the Stan-

dard Oil Trust. Gustavas Swift had combined refrigerated railroad cars and refrigerated warehouses to create the first national meat packing company in the late 1880s. Other packinghouses quickly followed his example and soon formed a system based on a mutuality of interest. About 1885 these major meat packers, especially the Armour, Swift and Morris concerns, combined their efforts. They formed a pool to dominate a large portion of the food industry by controlling and regulating shipments of dressed meats to the markets. . . . To complete the arrangement, the pool adopted a uniform method of figuring the cost of fresh meat so that profit margins would remain identical. This pooling agreement continued in undisturbed form until the spring of 1902. (Piott, 1981, pp. 33–34)

Interestingly, it was producers rather than consumers who first protested the actions of the Beef Trust. In response to complaints from butchers and Western cattlemen a special committee of U.S. senators held hearings in 1888 to investigate the meat-packing industry. After two years of study the committee found that the Beef Trust did indeed exist, and it also found evidence of collusion in the "price fixing of beef, the division of territory and business, . . . and the compulsion of retailers to purchase from the major packers" (Piott, 1981, p. 34). These findings helped secure passage of the Sherman Antitrust Act in 1890.

The consumer boycotts that followed the producer protests were led by the worker organizations of the time:

In Bloomington, Illinois, 2,000 employees of the Chicago and Alton Railroad shops agreed that none of their members would eat meat for a thirty-day period. The workers hoped to encourage others to follow their example and force the Beef Trust to reduce the prices of meat. Dayton, Ohio, protestants started an endless chain letter crusade against the Beef Trust. Thousands of letters broadcasted the high price of meat and encouraged abstinence for one week. Four hundred workers in Bellefontaine, Ohio, signed an agreement refusing to eat any meat for thirty days. The Central Labor Union of Amsterdam, New York, composed of twenty-five subordinate unions and 5,000 members, began a thirty-day boycott to abstain from using any meat handled by the so-called "meat trust." (Piott, 1981, pp. 44–45)

Sometime later the state of Missouri held hearings on the Beef Trust. Testimony not only confirmed that the trust was responsible for artificial increases in meat prices but also that it had provided diseased meat to St. Louis consumers. The Missouri investigation generated more newspaper coverage and this, together with the continuing high beef prices, led to more boycott actions.[1]

> At Lynn, Massachusetts, nearly 1,700 employees of the General Electric Company, representing at least 4,000 consumers, formed an antibeefeating league. Members pledged to abstain from beef consumption for thirty days, and promoters expected 5,000 company employees to join before the boycott ended. In Middletown, New York, 300 members of the Laborers' Union voted unanimously to abstain from western beef for one month. The Central Labor Union in Portland, Maine, unanimously adopted a resolution protesting the advance in meat prices and organized a similar thirty-day boycott. In Topeka, Kansas, 2,500 Sante Fe Railroad shop employees began a thirty-day beef boycott and caused an immediate 50 percent drop in meat sales in the workingclass neighborhoods. The continued high beef prices in St. Joseph, Missouri, and Omaha, Nebraska, caused consumers to switch to a fish diet. And in New York City 500 Jewish men and women met and formed the Ladies Anti-Beef Trust Association, threatening to start their own cooperative stores if the price of meat did not come down. (Piott, 1981, p. 48)

As noted, many of these consumer responses were successful. At prohibitively high price levels, meat purchases dropped with many shoppers opting for cereal foods instead. One dramatic result of this change in consumption behavior was that literally thousands of small butcher shops were forced to close their doors.

Piott sees much of value resulting from the organized consumer actions:

Their actions forced the judicial system to respond. Investigations at the state level, such as the one in Missouri, exposed corporate arrogance which, in turn, deepened consumer indignation. These investigations . . . showed the popular reaction to economic consolidation. This consumer-oriented response to the Beef Trust served as a model for state antitrust activity and for progressivism. (Piott, 1981, pp. 51–52)

The New York Kosher Meat Boycott of 1902

While Piott's study of the Beef Trust and the consumer reactions to it present a "big picture" account, historian Paula Hyman's research provides us with a microaccount of a local consumer boycott stimulated by the Beef Trust actions (Hyman, 1980). This is an in-depth description of a consumer economic boycott undertaken in 1902 by Jewish immigrant women in New York City. The targets of the boycott were kosher meat markets on the Lower East Side and in upper Manhattan, as well as the Bronx and Brooklyn.

The origins of the boycott have been documented in detail by Hyman; we quote her at length to give the reader a feel for the social and cultural context surrounding the boycott.

In early May, 1902, the retail price of kosher meat had soared from twelve cents to eighteen cents a pound. Small retail butchers, concerned that their customers would not be able to afford their product, refused to sell meat for a week to pressure the wholesalers (commonly referred to as the Meat Trust) to lower their prices. When their May 14th settlement with the wholesalers brought no reduction in the retail price of meat, Lower East Side homemakers, milling in the street, began to call for a strike against the butchers. As one activist, Mrs. Levy, the wife of a cloakmaker, shouted, "This is their strike? Look at the good it has brought! Now, if we women make a strike, then it will be a strike." Gathering support on the block—Monroe Street and Pike Street—Mrs. Levy and Sarah Edelson, owner of a small restaurant, called a mass meeting to spread the word of the planned boycott.

The next day, after a neighborhood canvass staged by the

organizing committee, thousands of women streamed through the streets of the Lower East Side, breaking into butcher shops, flinging meat into the streets, and declaring a boycott. "Women were the ringleaders at all hours," noted the *New York Herald*. Customers who tried to carry their purchased meat from the butcher shops were forced to drop it. One woman emerging from a butcher store with meat for her sick husband was vociferously chided by an elderly woman wearing the traditional sheitel that "a sick man can eat tref meat."[2] Within half an hour, the *Forward* reported, the strike had spread from one block through the entire area. Twenty thousand people were reported to have massed in front of the New Irving Hall. "Women were pushed and hustled about [by the police], thrown to the pavement . . . and trampled upon," wrote the *Herald*. One policeman, trying to rescue those buying meat, had "an unpleasant moist piece of liver slapped in his face." Patrol wagons filled the streets, hauling women, some bleeding from their encounters with the police, into court. About seventy women and fifteen men were arrested on charges of disorderly conduct.

After the first day of street rioting, a mass meeting to rally support and map strategy was held at the initiative of the women activists, who had formed a committee. . . . The next day, May 16, Lower East Side women again went from house to house to strengthen the boycott. Individuals were urged not to enter butcher shops or purchase meat. Pickets were appointed to stand in front of each butcher shop. On each block funds were collected to pay the fines of those arrested and to reimburse those customers whose meat had been confiscated in the first day of rioting. The *Tribune* reported that "an excitable and aroused crowd roamed the streets. . . . As was the case on the previous day, the main disturbance was caused by the women. Armed with sticks, vocabularies and well sharpened nails, they made life miserable for the policemen." On the second day of rioting another hundred people were arrested. The boycott also spread, under local leadership, to the Bronx and to Harlem, where a mass meeting was held at Central Hall.

On Saturday, May 17th, the women leaders of the boycott

continued their efforts, going from synagogue to synagogue to agitate on behalf of the boycott. Using the traditional communal tactic of interrupting the Torah reading when a matter of justice was at stake, they called on the men in each congregation to encourage their wives not to buy meat and sought rabbinic endorsement of their efforts.

By Sunday, May 18th, most butcher shops on the Lower East Side bowed to reality and closed their doors. And the boycott had spread to Brooklyn, where the store windows of open butcher shops had been broken and meat burned. That night, the women held another meeting, attended by more than five hundred persons, to consolidate their organization, now named the Ladies' Anti-Beef Trust Association. Under the presidency of Mrs. Caroline Schatzburg, it proposed to continue house-to-house patrols, keep watch over butcher stores, and begin agitating for similar action among Christian women. Circulars bearing a skull and crossbones and the slogan "Eat no meat while the Trust is taking meat from the bones of your women and children" were distributed throughout the Jewish quarters of the city. The Association established six similar committees to consolidate the boycott in Brownsville, East New York, and the Bronx. Other committees were set up to visit the labor and benevolent societies, labor union meetings, and lodges and to plan the establishment of cooperative stores. The Association also sent a delegation to the mayor's office to seek permission for an open air rally. Local groups of women continued to enforce the boycott in their neighborhoods. In Brooklyn four hundred women signed up to patrol neighborhood butcher stores. Buyers of meat continued to be assaulted and butcher shop windows smashed. In Harlem two women were arrested when they lay down on elevated tracks to prevent a local butcher from heading downtown with meat for sale. Throughout the city's Jewish neighborhoods restaurants had ceased serving meat. (Hyman, 1980, pp. 94–95)

In just a few weeks the boycott brought results. On May 22 the Retail Butchers Association yielded to the boycotters and affiliated with them against the Meat Trust. A few days later Orthodox Jewish leaders also decided to join the boycott. By June 5 the boycott was over. The wholesale price of meat was reduced to 9 cents a pound and the retail price to 14 cents a pound. And though meat prices began to rise after the conclusion of the boycott, Hyman still considers it to have been a "qualified success."

Hyman's account of the New York meat boycott does not ignore the social aspects of the protest activity. In her view the boycott's source of strength was its neighborhood orientation. As we have seen, the boycotters went house to house seeking support for their actions. They assumed that as neighbors they all shared a set of collective goals and that they were willing to experience sacrifices to attain them. Boycott participants picketed local butchers and refused to speak to "scabs" who violated the boycott. The ongoing presence of the boycott leaders in the neighborhood made it difficult for local residents to avoid surveillance. In short, the neighborhood provided a sense of community and solidarity for the boycott participants.

Also of interest is Hyman's observation concerning the economic role played by the boycotting women, a role that complemented on the consumption side the parallel economic role played by many of their husbands on the production side. As one of the leaders put it: "Our husbands work hard. They try their best to bring a few cents into the house. We must manage to spend as little as possible. We will not give away our last few cents to the butcher and let our children go barefoot" (Hyman, 1980, p. 99).

Finally, mention should be made of the violent nature of the boycotters' actions and the police officer's reactions. While such activities were not uncommon in urban America at the turn of the century as it experienced the inevitable adjustment problems associated with absorbing masses of new immigrants (a circumstance we have already seen in Chapter 3 in conjunction with labor conflicts of the time), the violent actions of the boycotters were roundly condemned by the press. In an editorial, the *New York Times* of May 24, 1902, observed, "It will not do to have a swarm of ignorant and infuriated women going about any part of this city with petroleum destroying goods and trying to set fire to the shops of those against whom they are angry."

Post-World War II Consumer Economic Boycotts

Price-oriented consumer economic boycotts continued in the 1940s, 1960s, and 1970s. After World War II, price controls were lifted in stages. By the spring of 1946 the process was complete, and the result was an enormous jump in meat prices. In a personal account of what happened by a boycott leader in Washington, D.C., Anne Stein (1975) recalls that hamburger doubled in price, from 35 cents to 70 cents a pound, after price controls were discontinued. Stein by then was a veteran in the trade union movement; she had started working in protests in the 1930s.

To combat these high prices a local *ad hoc* group was formed called the Washington Committee for Consumer Protection. The *ad hoc* group drew upon trade union groups, including the women's trade union league, the Rochdale co-ops (a middle-class cooperative movement led by Sara Newman), as well as women shoppers and women voters.

The first action taken by the newly formed consumer protection group was to organize a meat boycott. But instead of simply saying "Don't buy meat" or "Don't buy meat on certain days or weeks," the group came up with a price-oriented boycott criterion. In Stein's words,

> Our slogan was "Don't buy meat over 60 cents a pound." We had a button which said "Don't buy high." It was a good slogan, don't buy high, because that gave you an alternative. It also gave you a lever. If the butcher could not sell anything that was over 60 cents a pound, then he began stocking things that were selling and that did not have a push-back process, because you can't have low cuts without also cutting your high-priced cuts. So they were either wasted or they were reduced. (1975, p. 158)

Stein and the other boycott organizers worked hard to get consumers to express their support.

> The form that our first action took was a pledge. We asked every consumer to pledge . . . not to buy any meat over 60 cents a pound. And in two weeks we got 40,000 signatures, in Wash-

ington, which was not a very large city at that time. We covered every single supermarket in the city. All day long. We had shifts at every supermarket; every organization contributed petitioners [and] signature gatherers. And everybody signed. (1975, p. 158)

According to Stein, the meat boycott apparently worked, at least in the short term. In the six-week period immediately after the boycotters' pledge drive,

it was impossible to sell any piece of meat over 60 cents in Washington. And within a week all these stores began distributing leaflets, "sale on steak for 59 cents a pound." Everything was selling for 59 cents a pound! It was really fantastic. (1959, p. 159)

And interestingly, just as the meat boycotters of 1902 blamed the meat trusts for the high prices, so did their 1946 counterparts lay the responsibility with the meat packers (rather than the retailers or the farmers). The boycotters claimed that they were fighting the "monopoly packers."

Stein notes that the lifting of price controls on milk at the end of World War II stimulated higher prices, which in turn prompted two milk boycotts to be called by an *ad hoc* coalition of middle-class and working-class women. The boycotters targeted fresh milk and urged consumers to buy such substitutes as powdered milk, condensed milk, or evaporated milk. Without citing evidence to support her conclusion, Stein surmises that the coalition was successful in bringing milk prices down.

The 1966 Nationwide Boycott of Supermarkets

The next major consumer economic boycott for which we have full documentation occurred in the fall of 1966 when a wave of consumer protests started in Denver, Colorado, and spread to communities across the nation in response to a sudden rise in supermarket prices. Unlike many of the nationwide protests that we have examined here, this one was the subject of a survey research study shortly after it ended (Friedman, 1971).

The 1966 consumer protest represented the first time since

1902 that consumers from many sections of the nation exhibited their disturbance with higher prices through boycotts, demonstrations, and other direct actions. The protest received widespread coverage by the news media although, as is often the case with such reporting, only a fragmentary picture emerged of the participants, their actions, and the consequences of these actions.

A mail survey conducted in August 1967 focused on the local leaders of the consumer protest. A complete account of the survey is presented in Appendix A; suffice it to say here that many sources were explored in an attempt to secure a large and representative sample of protest leaders. Although the actual sample realized fell short of this ideal, it did provide a national cross-section of local leaders for 64 of the consumer protests.

What did this survey study find? First, consistent with the pattern of price protests reviewed so far in this chapter, all of the 64 leaders were women. As a group they could be described as young, well-educated, middle-class homemakers. Since these characteristics, along with their tendency to affiliate with the Democratic Party, have all been empirically associated with perceived legitimacy of social protest actions, it is not surprising that such direct action tactics as boycotts and demonstrations were employed by a majority of the local groups. Moreover, direct action tactics in general, and boycotts in particular, were seen by the 64 respondents as the most effective of their protest actions. The study findings indicate that these and other actions were directed primarily at the elimination of trading stamps and games and the reduction of advertising expenditures.

Did the nationwide protest have the desired effect of reducing prices? The answer seems consistent with the pattern found earlier: Most of the local leader respondents reported success in lowering prices at the time of the protest but not beyond, and this assessment appears to concur with economic analyses of price changes during and after the consumer protest period. Perhaps as a result of the frustrations experienced from having "won the battle but lost the war," 49 of the 64 local leaders reported that their groups had disbanded within a year of the consumer protest. And only a minority (29 percent) of these leaders thought it highly likely that their groups would reassemble in the event of another rapid rise in food prices. As one boycott veteran put it,

"Some homemakers may be fighters, but it's hard to get enough of the fighting kind to fight over the same thing at the same time."

The Food Commodity Boycotts of the 1970s

Consumer economic boycotts in reaction to rapidly rising food prices continued in the 1970s with a nationwide meat boycott called in 1973, followed by sugar and milk boycotts in 1974 and a coffee boycott in 1976–1977. These boycotts along with others for the 1970s have been examined as part of a decade-long focus on consumer boycotts (Friedman, 1985).

The Meat Boycott

In the first week of April 1973, consumers reacted to meat price increases of 8 percent from February 20 to March 20 by organizing a nationwide meat boycott. The boycott, which received extensive coverage in the news media, including daily stories on its progress, appeared to be an *ad hoc* grassroots reaction to the pocketbook pressures felt by many homemakers across the land. As columnist Joseph Kraft of the *Washington Post* noted on the boycott's third day,

> The most striking feature of the boycott is its spontaneous character. One set of stories by careful reporters traces the origins of the boycott to a housewife in the suburbs of Hartford, Conn. Another set of stories by careful reporters claims the resistance was set in motion by an actress in Southern California.
>
> The truth is nobody knows how the boycott was started. What is known is that it suddenly became the thing to do all over the place. (1973, p. A19)

What is also known is that protesting women from Los Angeles to New York took to the streets with picket signs during the first week of April, leafleting supermarkets with meatless menus and urging shoppers to join the boycott. In Washington, D.C., consumer groups rallied at the White House where they delivered a "precious commodity"—a steak, which was brought to the rally in an armored truck.

What was the impact of the 1973 meat boycott? The familiar

pattern noted earlier for price-rise boycotts appeared to follow here as well. Consumers did buy less beef during the boycott period, although it is not clear why this occurred. It could have been a continued reaction to rising prices or an effect of "stocking up" by consumers in the weeks before the boycott. (Some butchers claimed that their customers stocked up beforehand so they could support the boycott painlessly.) And, of course, it could have been a real effect of the boycott. More likely than not, all of these factors contributed to a reduction in meat purchases. The reduction did not have the effect desired by the boycotters, however.

Though some prices fell, they did not remain at lower levels long beyond the boycott. And this despite the attempts of the boycott leaders to continue the boycott on a part-time basis (Tuesdays and Thursdays only). Though the boycott failed to meet its instrumental goals, it did have other compensating effects, according to the boycott leaders. As spokesperson Lynn Jordan noted in the May 1973 newsletter of the Virginia Citizens Consumer Council,

> It was as a consciousness-raising experience that the boycott was perhaps most effective. Consumers now know they can move mountains. And government and industry now know that they know. (1973, p. 1)

The Milk and Sugar Boycotts

The *ad hoc* groups that formed to lead the meat boycott focused their efforts on milk and sugar in 1974. Mother's Day was picked as an appropriate start date for a statewide boycott of milk called by two California groups to protest high prices and a recent state-approved increase of 5 cents per half gallon. Fight Inflation Together (FIT) and the California Citizens Action group urged consumers to switch from liquid milk to powdered milk for one week. The groups blamed the high prices on "excessive profits" at processing and retail levels. The California call for a boycott followed one several months earlier in Concord, New Hampshire, where the owner of a small chain of corner-store groceries called for a milk boycott to combat what he referred to as "ridiculous" price increases. He claimed that he had been forced to increase his store prices from 95 cents to $1.25 per gallon during the previous five months. While the impact of the milk boycott calls is not known, the lack of news media attention to protest actions and their consequences suggests that the effects were minimal.

American Consumers Together, another *ad hoc* group formed during the nationwide meat boycott of 1973, urged consumers in November to participate in a partial sugar boycott (Tuesdays and Thursdays) for the next few months. The boycott call was in response to prices that rose from 79 cents the previous year to $2.20 in early November for a 5-pound bag of sugar. Immediate indications of government support came from various sources including the Boston City Council, which voted to make the week of November 25 Boycott Sugar Week in the city. A more nationally visible endorsement came from President Ford's newly established Citizens Action Committee to Fight Inflation. Economic columnist Sylvia Porter, who headed the committee, asked American consumers to reduce their use of sugar "immediately and drastically." Additional support came from New York City's Consumer Affairs Department, which urged consumers in December to continue the boycott promoted by the Ford Administration and by Elinor Guggenheimer, the New York City commissioner of consumer affairs.

Actual boycott group actions appeared to be few and far between, although in Hartford, Connecticut, members of the Connecticut Committee to Boycott Sugar and two other groups joined to stage their own version of the Boston Tea Party. Wearing colonial costumes, they dumped "sugar"—actually white sand—from a prominent bridge into the river below in an effort to promote the boycott. A similar action occurred in Concord, New Hampshire, where symbolic sugar in the form of sawdust was dumped into the Merrimack River in a protest against high sugar prices organized by a local community action program "to help get poor people back into the eating business."

Retailers in the United States joined government officials and consumer organizations in advising shoppers not to buy sugar (e.g., Giant Food in Washington, D.C.), and perhaps it was their combined efforts that led to consumer cutbacks. But once again, stocking up beforehand and rapidly increasing prices (more than $4 for a 5-pound bag at its zenith) are plausible rival hypotheses.

In any case, by mid-December prices began to fall, and by February 1975, 30 percent decreases were common. How much of the change was due to decreased domestic demand is difficult to say because the sugar price increases apparently had resulted from a variety of international developments, including the failure of the European sugar beet crop in 1974, a lack of cheap labor to harvest sugar cane, and the Soviet Union's entry into the international sugar market.

The Coffee Boycott
Even though coffee prices rose dramatically in the mid-1970s (from $1.29 a pound in mid-1975 to more than $3.19 a pound in early 1977), national consumer groups seemed reluctant to promote a coffee boycott, according to Mouat (1977), for two reasons. First, there was the feeling that the price increases had a legitimate basis—short supplies caused by a killer cold front that destroyed half the buds on Brazil's coffee trees. And second, national consumer leaders had genuine doubts about the feasibility and potential effectiveness of boycotts as an economic tactic—largely because of the questionable success of the earlier commodity boycotts in the 1970s. Although not noted by Mouat, another factor may have been coffee's special status as a product with addictive-like qualities. It is one thing to give up fresh milk or meat or granulated sugar; substitutes are readily available and at comparable prices. But coffee drinkers cannot easily get a caffeine stimulant from other consumer beverages, with the possible exception of carbonated sodas.

Despite these prospective problems, Guggenheimer and her Consumer Affairs Department decided to take the lead by calling in late 1976 for a 50 percent drop in per capita consumption and issuing 400 notices and appeals to individuals and groups around the world. Her efforts received support from unexpected sources. A grocery chain in Chicago urged customers not to consume any coffee on Wednesdays; a chain in New York offered 20-cents-off coupons in its stores that could be applied toward the purchase of such coffee competitors as tea, cocoa, or hot chocolate; a Dayton, Ohio, chain distributed 300,000 flyers to shoppers calling on them to switch to tea, cocoa, natural juices, or "anything but coffee"; and anticoffee in-store displays began appearing in chains in Washington, D.C., Baltimore, Kansas City, and cities in several New England states. Moreover, New York City restaurants began offering major discounts on tea, with one, the posh 21 Club, providing it free. Soon Guggenheimer's efforts were also supported by consumer groups such as American Consumers Together, the Consumer Federation of America, the Community Nutrition Institute, and the state consumer organizations for Maryland and Virginia.

By mid-June of 1977, significant drops in price had occurred at both the wholesale and retail levels, prompting some observers to hail the success of the boycott. Indeed, Guggenheimer publicly announced that the campaign was "in sight of victory." But she prudently added, "I'm not saying that our asking people to drink less was the only factor, because price certainly was the major influence, but I think we helped." The "stocking-up factor" should also be noted: A *New York Times* survey found that many consumers did just that when they sensed that prices were about to move upward (Jones, 1977, p. D1).

We end this review of price-increase boycotts by noting several generalizations about their behavior from the turn of the century to the recent past:

1. Price-increase boycotts have usually been initiated by *ad hoc* groups rather than established national consumer organizations.
2. Their organizers have often been homemakers, as have been many of their supporters.
3. They have targeted foods, especially staple items such as meat, sugar, and milk.
4. Their approach has been media-oriented, as well as marketplace-oriented, with volunteers helping with initiation and implementation of the boycott effort.
5. The boycotters have often blamed various middlemen for the rise in prices—meat packers, wholesalers, and distributors—rather than farmers or retailers. Indeed, sometimes retailers and farmers have expressed support for the boycott.
6. The boycotts have often been followed by decreases in sales for the targeted items, but the drops were rarely sustained,

and it is not clear that they were causally connected to the boycott activity.

7. Prices have often dropped as well during the boycott period, but typically they have returned to preboycott levels after the boycott has ended.

The price-increase boycotts appear to be a vanishing breed, with the last one having occurred almost a generation ago in 1977. While the reasons for their disappearance are not altogether clear, several candidates seem plausible: the decreasing number of available homemakers with many more women now being in the workplace on a part-time or full-time basis; the increasing stabilization of food prices; the decreasing role of food staples in the American family diet, with made-from-scratch meals being replaced by convenience foods and eating out; and the increasing appeal of other, more dramatic issues to prospective boycott activists. With regard to the last-mentioned point, many activists apparently feel that price-increase issues are boring and unengaging, especially when compared to the currently popular animal rights and environmental issues. And the switch away from price issues may also relate to the financial rewards derived from working outside the home. For many women this money has contributed substantially to their household incomes, and thus even a fairly large increase for a favorite food item may have become a matter of no great urgency (Friedman, 1991).

What these various circumstances make clear is the fragility of consumer organizations that are almost completely dependent on the contributions of volunteers, a point made by both Forbes (1985) and Herrmann (1991). This point is underscored by two tenets of resource mobilization theory, a popular sociological approach to understanding social movements. The theory goes beyond earlier formulations focused on group grievances to make clear that grievances are necessary but hardly sufficient to account for the dynamics of social movements (McCarthy & Zald, 1973, 1977; Tilly, 1978). One must go beyond grievances to ask what resources are available to the aggrieved groups and what organizational entry points exist for using these resources effectively. As we have seen repeatedly in this review of consumer economic boycotts, the boycott groups typically suffered on both accounts, with few resources other than volunteers and even fewer connections to powerful organizations that could help the boycotters attain their goals.

To sum up, what is made clear from this look at the historical record is that over the course of the twentieth century in the United States, women in general, and homemakers in particular, have sometimes looked to the boycott as a vehicle for influencing consumer policy relating to the prices of essential goods consumed by themselves and their families. Through such direct action techniques as demonstrations, picketing, and leafleting, they have made their voices heard in the marketplace and in the halls of government. By engaging in these grassroots activities, these women have complemented on the consumption side of the economic coin their husbands' activities on the production side. Indeed, the consumer boycott is the economic mirror image of the labor strike.

One of the ironies associated with the consumer economic boycott period is that the marketplace assertiveness it required in its women leaders at the grassroots level emerged during a traditional period in American social life, one that stressed the benefits of nuclear families, with husbands as wage earners and wives as homemakers. Starting in the late 1970s, that period began to pass, perhaps in part because the marketplace assertiveness was passing as well. The "new woman," now busily engaged in both home and workplace pursuits, had neither time nor energy to volunteer to a consumer economic boycott, and a larger income helped them absorb price increases that a boycott might earlier have contested.

While it is tempting to romanticize the past and to yearn for the "good old days" of consumer assertiveness at the grassroots level, one should not forget that the boycotts rarely succeeded in lowering prices beyond the short term. They typically consumed many hours of largely volunteer time and energy in a losing cause. Nonetheless, the boycotts did serve an important expressive function; indeed, their very existence sent a message for all to hear—consumers have a right to expect a fair price and they insist that this right be recognized in the marketplace.

POSTSCRIPT

A Consumer Economic Boycott of Another Kind: The Case of Peugeot

As we noted in the beginning of this chapter, most consumer economic boycotts have been initiated in response to price increases and especially for food commodities. But a few consumer economic boycotts have dealt with the question of the value received by consumers for the dollars they spend in the marketplace.[3] The quality issue was of central concern to Rosemary Dunlap and the consumer group Motor Voters, which she started in California in 1979 and moved to the Washington, D.C., area in 1985. According to Dunlap, Motor Voters is "an independent, nonprofit consumer organization incorporated in 1982 and dedicated to promoting auto safety, reducing traffic deaths and injuries and improving automotive business practices." It has several hundred members and an all-volunteer staff consisting primarily of Dunlap, who is president of the organization. Dunlap and her group led a movement based in San Diego in the early 1980s to reform California laws protecting car buyers; a major result was the passage of what has been referred to as the "California lemon law."

On August 22, 1988, Dunlap held a press conference at the National Press Club in Washington to announce that Motor Voters was initiating a boycott against Peugeot, a French manufacturer that was selling 2 million cars a year in Europe at the time. One reason for targeting Peugeot was that its existing model, the Peugeot 505, had performed poorly in some U.S. government crash tests. According to Dunlap,

> We looked at their whole record since 1979. Out of eight crash test scores, they had seven that were disasters and, unlike other auto makers who work to improve their performance, they didn't seem to care. (Hinds, 1989, p. 52)

In response to the charges, Peugeot said the crash tests had little importance in that the government agency that conducted them had not claimed the Peugeot was unsafe or that it would perform any worse than its competitors in actual accidents. In fact, according to Hinds (1989), insurance industry data on accidents, which reflect driver temperament and skill as well as actual road conditions, indicated that Peugeot drivers were not injured more often than drivers of most other cars. But according to Peugeot, the company, unlike most others, had not tried to improve its performance in the crash tests, and its reputation was damaged as a result (Hinds, 1989).

Another reason for selecting Peugeot as a boycott target was tactical in nature. Even though it is a large European automaker, its U.S. sales were small, and thus the company was seen as an appropriate match for a likewise small Motor Voters. Also, it was about to introduce in American showrooms a car that had received accolades from European automobile writers (the Peugeot 405 was voted the best European car of 1988), and yet, most disturbingly from Motor Voters' perspective, the new model had not provided its passengers with air bags.

Motor Voters had one simple demand of Peugeot in launching its boycott—that the company offer air bags in their U.S. models. The boycotters were supported in their campaign by various consumer and health organizations including the Center for Auto Safety, the U.S. Public Interest Research Group, Physicians for Auto Safety, and both the Virginia and the Massachusetts Head Injury Associations. According to Dunlap, the boycott was primarily media-oriented rather than marketplace-oriented, and the group was successful in securing coverage for its efforts in such major news media outlets as the *New York Times*, the *Los Angeles Times*, and *USA Today*. This is not to say that there was no picketing at dealerships; on weekends Dunlap and her colleagues displayed signs saying "Say no to Peugeot" at dealerships in the Washington, D.C., area, but she saw this effort as very modest.

Was the boycott effective? Personal interviews with Dunlap and the Peugeot official in charge of public relations during the time of the boycott yielded conflicting responses, but two developments were indisputable. Sales for the new 405 model were substantially below expectations, and in August 1991, Peugeot announced that it would no longer build cars for export to the United States. Why was Peugeot pulling out of the American market? Dunlap claimed that the boycott was partly responsible for the low sales and Peugeot's decision to leave, but the company disputed these claims. The Peugeot official interviewed cited several possible reasons for the sales drop that led to the pullout:

1. Peugeot's major advertising campaign to launch the 405 may have created unrealistically high consumer expectations.
2. There were limited inventories of the 405 in U.S. showrooms and this did not help sales.
3. Competition was intense, with many consumers preferring comparable-size Hondas or Toyotas.
4. Peugeot thought it could rely on a base of brand-loyal Peugeot owners in the United States, but many of these owners perceived the 405 as smaller than its predecessor even though the internal dimensions were actually larger.

The Peugeot official interviewed claimed that the boycott had a negligible effect on the sales and image of the 405 model.

Before closing this section on the Peugeot boycott by Motor Voters, it should be noted once again that this was a most unusual consumer economic boycott. It focused not on price but on quality, and not on a whole commodity class, such as meat, but on a particular brand and model of product. Usually one would expect a variety of commercial and noncommercial forces in the marketplace to identify and weed out an inferior brand or model through independent product test reports, comparative advertisements, or word-of-mouth communications, but this process can be very slow and inefficient. Motor Voters apparently saw itself as a mechanism for speeding up the communication process so that more consumers would know and know soon about the lack of air bags in the new Peugeots. Whether their effort made a difference in the Peugeot decision to pull out of the American market is likely to remain a mystery.

◆ 5 ◆

MINORITY GROUP INITIATIVES

African American Boycotts

While many, if not all, of the boycotts we have examined so far touch upon universal themes affecting "everyman" or "everywoman," others are of chief concern to certain subgroups of the American population. These subgroups, or minorities, often claim that the issues they are confronting relate to problems peculiar to their circumstances as a minority group. Thus Jewish Americans may claim that a foreign policy issue involving the status of Israel is of special concern to them since Israel has become the Jewish homeland. And African Americans may claim that racial discrimination in the workplace or the marketplace has historically affected them more than other minorities and that these issues are thus a major concern to them. Similarly, women, while not technically a minority, are usually perceived as having less economic and political power than men, and, this being the case, they are likely to feel especially vulnerable when confronted with issues of discrimination in the workplace or the marketplace.

All this is not to say that minority group boycott issues are not of concern to the American majority. Indeed, individuals from the majority population have often stood side by side with minorities to shoulder the burdens of their problems and to mobilize resources in support of the minority response. However, the majority member response to such problems has usually been limited to a supportive one, and for this reason (and others) it makes sense to view the underlying issues as minority issues and the boycotts that they engender as minority boycotts.

Among the minority groups affected by issues that have led to consumer boycotts are African Americans, Jewish Americans, Native Americans, Italian Americans, women, and gays. Interestingly, since the turn of the century, African Americans have been responsible for more consumer boycotts than all the other groups combined. Most of these boycotts have concerned consumer economic and labor issues, broadly speaking, while others have dealt with civil rights issues. We look first at consumer economic boycotts called by African Americans and then move on to other types affecting this group. Indeed, this whole chapter is devoted to African American boycotts. In the following chapter we look at boycotts and boycott issues involving other minorities and especially Jewish Americans, women, and gays.

To start this chapter on African American boycotts, we note that the post-World War II era witnessed a turbulence in its social order that has profoundly affected the nature of human relationships. We refer of course to the civil rights movement, which for 20 years prior to 1954 took the form of a legal struggle by the National Association for the Advancement of Colored People (NAACP), culminating finally in the historic *Brown vs. Board of Education* Supreme Court decision.

In the more active phase of the movement that followed this landmark decision, we see the manifestations of long-harbored dissatisfactions relating to civil rights issues and related consumer and labor issues. To confront these various issues African Americans have over the years turned to the consumer boycott as a primary tactic.

Why the consumer boycott? According to E. Randel T. Osburn of the Southern Christian Leadership Conference,

> The boycott is the most potent economic empowerment weapon that blacks have. . . . That's what the oil embargo was about in the '70s. Everyone uses economic pressure. . . . The minute we silence that cash register, they can hear everything we say. (Anonymous, 1991)

Consumer Economic Boycotts
Initiated by African Americans

Among the consumer dissatisfactions of African Americans engendered by civil rights deprivations were inadequacies in public transportation and in access to retail markets and decent housing. In all these instances we see how segregated practices flagrantly violated the consumer's right to choose—the third of the four declared rights that President Kennedy put forth in his widely acclaimed first consumer message to Congress in 1962. Many African American consumers and their white supporters reacted to these violations with direct action. Boycotts, sit-ins, and protest marches soon became familiar weapons of these groups in their clashes with the business elements of their communities. Indeed, much of the history of the civil rights movement can be viewed as a series of direct confrontations beween a minority group and an inequitable marketplace.

Under the circumstances, one might have expected to find American consumer leaders at the forefront of this struggle. While it is true that the consumer problems of African Americans were largely peculiar to this minority group and that only a relatively small fraction of the American population was affected, nevertheless this small fraction represented millions of people, and their problems as consumers were unquestionably in greater need of urgent attention than those of any other single group. But the postwar efforts of consumer advocates largely failed to embrace this struggle for equal consumer rights as a legitimate concern for consumers at large (Friedman, 1968).

In this chapter we see how African Americans looked largely to their own resources to respond to deprivations of their consumer rights. We start with the boycotts of streetcars at the turn of the century.

The Streetcar Boycotts in the South in the Early 1900s

More than 25 Southern cities experienced consumer economic boycotts by blacks from 1900 to 1906. The boycotts have received little scholarly attention, and a debt of gratitude is owed to August Meier and Elliott Rudwick (1968–1969) for their pioneering work in the area. The boycotts occurred at a time of increasing hostility on the part of Southern whites and indifference on the part of Northern whites, a dual circumstance that may have encouraged acceptance of and accommodation to subservience as the prevailing attitude of southern blacks.

The boycotts were initiated in response to Jim Crow streetcar laws enacted as part of the wave of segregation legislation passed in Southern states at the turn of the century.[1] According to Meier and Rudwick (1968–1969), Georgia passed the first such law in 1891, and municipal ordinances were passed in 1900 in Atlanta, Rome, Augusta, and Montgomery, followed by Jacksonville in 1901, Mobile in 1902, and Columbia, Houston, and San Antonio in 1903. Moreover, state segregation laws were passed in Louisiana and Virginia in 1902, in Arkansas and Tennessee in 1903, in Florida in 1905, and in Texas, Oklahoma, and North Carolina in 1907.

Meier and Rudwick (1968–1969) note that the streetcar companies generally opposed the Jim Crow laws. The companies were concerned about the expense and difficulty of enforcing the laws, and they feared a loss of black customers, who often constituted a majority of the local riders.

Although technically the new segregation laws represented an abridgment of the consumer right to choose in that blacks were required to sit in the back of the streetcar, symbolically they represented much more—unjust acts whose effect was "to humiliate, to degrade, and to stigmatize the negro." As one of the stigmatized angrily put it, "Do not trample on our pride by being 'jim crowed,' Walk!"

And walk they did. Boycotts were called in many southern cities, including Atlanta, Houston, Jacksonville, Little Rock, Memphis, Mobile, Montgomery, Nashville, New Orleans, Newport News, Norfolk, and Savannah. Indeed, all the states of the old Confederacy were affected and the clear connection between the segregation laws and the boycotts was observed in the Mobile *Daily Register* of May 17, 1905: "In every city where it has been advisable to separate the races in the street cars the experience has been the same, the negroes ... have invariably declared a boycott" (Meier and Rudwick, 1968–1969, p. 760).

In their early stages the boycotts attracted much black cooperation, fueled as they were by humiliation and frustration, but informal social pressures were employed as well.

> In San Antonio, a few days after the movement began, six Negroes were arrested for pulling a youth off a trolley car. In Columbia, the few who rode "were 'guyed' when the cars passed groups of negroes on the streets." In Savannah, those who opposed the boycotts were publicly denounced at mass meetings as "demagogues and hypocrites." The city's police quickly took to arresting Negroes who stood on downtown street corners, heckled riders as they got off, and urged those ready to board the trolleys to take a hack instead. (Meier and Rudwick, 1968–1969, p. 764)

The boycotters needed alternatives to the streetcar to get where they were going, and often walking was the medium chosen. In addition, private carriages, hacks, and drays were called into service. The latter two vehicles were especially important, for, as Meier and Rudwick (1968–1969) have observed, "It is doubtful that the boycotts could have occurred at all except for the Negro hackmen and draymen, who in that period still dominated these two occupations in a number of southern cities" (p. 764). To help the boycotters, the hackmen reduced their fares in such cities as Houston, Jacksonville, and Savannah.

For a variety of reasons Meier and Rudwick (1968–1969) view the boycotts as a conservative form of protest. First, their leaders were an elite group of respectable citizens consisting primarily of businessmen and professionals. Second, the boycotts were attempting to preserve the desegregated status quo, rather than make radical changes to society. And third, their methods were nonconfrontational in that the protesters did not insist on sitting in the white section of the trolleys.

Although some of the boycotts lasted for just a few weeks, others extended for far longer periods, with the longest being the trolley boycott in Augusta, Georgia, which continued for three years. But every one of the boycotts failed to reverse the legal tide of segregation in the South. As the only protest mechanism realistically available to African Americans, however, the boycott tactic continued to be embraced even though failure was inevitable.

In the view of Meier and Rudwick (1968–1969), "The remark-able thing is not that the boycotts failed, but that they happened in so many places and lasted as long as they often did" (p. 775).

The Bus Boycotts of the 1950s

Some 50 years later African Americans in the South once again vented their frustrations relating to the problems they experienced with urban public transportation, only this time buses rather than streetcars were the focus. The bus boycotts that followed were of historic importance. As historian Aldon Morris, a close student of the bus boycotts, has noted,

> The modern civil rights movement and the modern direct action organizations grew directly out of bus boycotts. Boycotts brought wide-spread economic and social disruption to three capital cities, Baton Rouge, Montgomery, and Tallahassee. Buses became the first target of the movement because members of the black community had begun to see bus discrimination not as a private misery but as a public issue and a common enemy. It had become a widespread social grievance shared throughout the community. (Morris, 1984, pp. 48–49)

We look next at the three urban bus boycotts referred to by Morris.

The Baton Rouge Bus Boycott

The replacement of Jim Crow streetcars with Jim Crow buses in the South resulted in a continuation of many of the painfully humiliating experiences for African American passengers. Under the Jim Crow system every bus had a "colored section" in the rear and a "white section" in the front. A portable sign labeled "colored" separated the two sections. Once the white section filled, "coloreds" had to move to the rear, taking the sign with them. When they filled their section, "coloreds" were forced to stand even if there were vacant seats in the white section. If, as often happened, the colored sections filled first, blacks had to stand over empty seats set aside for white passengers.

In March 1953, black leaders in Baton Rouge were successful

in securing City Council passage of an ordinance allowing blacks to be seated from back to front on a first-come, first-served basis. The ordinance raised problems immediately since it permitted blacks to fill the bus completely, if they all boarded before whites; this meant that blacks could sit in the front seats formerly reserved for whites. The bus drivers balked at this behavior and ordered blacks not to fill the front seats. When the City Council overruled the drivers they went on a four-day strike. During the strike the Louisiana attorney general ruled in favor of the drivers by declaring the ordinance illegal since it violated the state's segregation laws. So when the strike ended, the drivers once again ordered black passengers to take seats in the back of the bus.

Three months later, in June 1953, Baton Rouge's black community initiated a boycott against the Jim Crow bus system. The boycott was led by the Reverend T. J. Jemison, pastor of one of Baton Rouge's largest black churches. According to Morris (1984), Jemison had several valuable assets that helped him lead the boycott to a successful conclusion. Among these assets was the high respect with which he was held in the black community. In addition to being a church leader, he was an educated man with two college degrees. He was also well-connected in the black community, having served as president of the Baton Rouge chapter of the NAACP. Moreover, he was a newcomer to the community, and as a result had made few enemies to obstruct his leadership of the bus boycott.

As a church leader Jemison had close local ties to the black masses and to the network of black clergymen, and it was these two linkages that gave the boycott its strength. Indeed, a church-related organization, the United Defense League (UDL), was established to lead the boycott. While church-related, the UDL also included other important organized groups in the Baton Rouge black community.

To finance the boycott, money was raised at nightly mass meetings in the churches. The money was used to pay for a "free car lift" and an internal "police force." The free car lift consisted of private cars that transported the boycotting workforce just as the buses had done prior to the boycott. To make matters simple the cars followed the same routes as the buses, picking up and dropping off passengers on the way. The internal police department was used to patrol the black community and to provide body-guards for the boycott leaders.

Was the boycott successful in its execution? According to Jemison it was completely effective. He claimed that no one was riding the buses by the afternoon of the boycott's first day. He further claimed that "For ten days not a Negro rode the bus" (Morris, 1984, p. 18). Although his claim may be slightly exaggerated (a *New York Times* story at the time found 90 percent compliance), it seems clear that the vast majority of the black passengers, who accounted for at least two thirds of the total riders, was participating in the boycott. It was estimated that as a result the bus company suffered losses of $1,600 a day during the boycott.

The boycotters had one primary demand—that blacks be permitted to fill seats on a first-come, first-served basis, and that no seats be reserved for whites. Within a few days of the boycott's inception local white officials offered a compromise, which largely accepted the first-come, first-served system for seating but proposed two exceptions: The long rear seat in each bus would be reserved for blacks, and the two side front seats would be reserved for whites.

The executive committee of the UDL voted to recommend that the compromise be accepted. At a mass meeting attended by 8,000 blacks a majority voted in favor of accepting the compromise.

The boycott ended officially on June 25, 1953. It was seen as a major victory against segregated busing. According to Morris, "It was the first evidence that the system of racial segregation could be challenged by mass action" (1984, p. 25). He notes too that the Baton Rouge success influenced other clergy who led bus boycotts in the South. As we shall see shortly, the subsequent bus boycotts in Montgomery and Tallahassee were directly affected by it in that their clergymen leaders consulted closely with Reverend Jemison and modeled their protest action after his. Morris concludes, "It was the Baton Rouge movement, largely without assistance from outside elites, that opened the direct action phase of the modern civil rights movement" (1984, p. 25).

The Montgomery Bus Boycott

A strong case can be made that this protest action is the best-known and most influential consumer boycott in America's history. It marked the beginning of the modern civil rights movement in the United States and introduced to the world the man who would become the movement's leader, the Reverend Martin Luther King, Jr. Not unexpectedly, more has been written about this boycott than any other; this brief summary touches on some of the highlights.[2]

The Montgomery bus boycott was triggered on December 1, 1955, by the refusal of Rosa Parks to give up her seat on a city bus to a white man. Her actions, which were a violation of local segregation laws, came just two and a half years after the successful Baton Rouge bus boycott. Despite the many books and articles written about the Montgomery boycott, many misunderstandings persist. For example, Rosa Parks is sometimes portrayed as a retiring apolitical woman who, owing to fatigue from a long day's work, finally decided she had had enough, and stepped out of character by defying the local authorities. In fact Parks was anything but retiring or apolitical; she had long been involved in local and state black political activities, having served, for example, as secretary for the local NAACP chapter from 1943 to 1955. Moreover, she had refused several times in the 1940s to comply with the bus segregation laws, and once in the early 1940s was ejected by a bus driver for her refusal to comply (coincidentally, by the same driver who called the police to arrest her on December 1, 1955).

A second common misunderstanding concerns the organization of the boycott plan and its initial implementation. The leadership for this mammoth effort is often wrongly ascribed to King; only after the boycott got under way was he asked to take charge. The early planners and initiators were two long time Montgomery residents with a history of leadership in the black community. One was E. D. Nixon, a local leader in union matters and black political pursuits. Known as a local militant, Nixon was the man Montgomery blacks would seek out if they experienced trouble with whites and needed help. The second principal was Jo Ann Robinson, a professor of English at the local black college, Alabama State College. Robinson headed the Women's Political Council, a group of middle-class black Montgomery women considered to be one of the most active and assertive black civic organizations in the city.

The Women's Political Council had already played a leadership role with regard to black problems with local buses. In 1954 the council informed the City Commission of black dissatisfaction with (1) standing over empty seats in the white sections, (2) having to board the buses by the doors in the rear after paying their fares in the front, and (3) having to walk twice as far, on the average, as whites to reach bus stops since there were half as many in the black community (every other corner) as there were in the white community (every corner). The City Commission agreed to act on only the third problem by establishing bus stops at every corner on the bus routes in the black community. The next year a black girl named Claudette Colvin was arrested for refusing to give up her bus seat to a white person. Members of the Women's Political Council were firm in their support of the girl, and her arrest led the council to consider developing plans to boycott the local bus system. However, local leaders such as Nixon were hesitant to make Colvin the focus of a major resistance effort against the white community, especially when they learned that she was expecting a baby out of wedlock (Morris, 1984).

Nonetheless the germ of an idea had been planted to initiate a boycott. And once planted it was hard to suppress, as Robinson noted dramatically in her account of the Montgomery movement:

> "What must we do? What can we do?" I asked, half aloud, half to myself. And the answer seemed to come from everywhere at once: "Boycott! Boycott! Boycott! BOYCOTT!" I did not have the slightest idea how—without involving others who might get hurt—to begin a boycott against the bus company that would put that company out of business. But the Women's Political Council took the idea under advisement. (Garrow, 1987, p. 27)

With the arrest of Parks, Robinson and her colleagues conferred with Nixon about translating the idea into action. Though Nixon had been reluctant to agree to a boycott when other blacks had been arrested for violating the segregated bus rules—in each instance he thought either the time was not right or the individual arrested did not present a strong enough platform to support a massive attack on local segregation practices—this time he thought he had an ideal test case. Parks was a quiet, dignified middle-aged woman active not only in black political and community activities but also in the church. In referring to her several days after her arrest, King said to his congregation:

> Just the other day one of the finest citizens in Montgomery—not one of the finest Negro citizens but one of the finest citizens in Montgomery—was taken from a bus and carried to jail and arrested because she refused to give up her seat to a white person. . . . Mrs. Rosa Parks is a fine person. And since it had to happen, I'm happy it happened to a person like Mrs. Parks, for nobody can doubt the boundless outreach of her integrity. Nobody can doubt the height of her character, nobody can doubt the depth of her Christian commitment. (Kennedy, 1989, pp. 1016–1017)

On the night of the Parks arrest (Thursday, Dec. 1), Jo Ann Robinson, after conferring with other local black leaders, decided to organize a bus boycott for the following Monday (Dec. 5). With two trusted students she worked through the night at her college's duplicating room to produce 50,000 copies of the following message for distribution to the black community:

> Another Negro woman has been arrested and thrown in jail because she refused to get up out of her seat on the bus for a white person to sit down. It is the second time since the Claudette Colvin case that a Negro woman has been arrested for the same thing. This has to be stopped. Negroes have rights, too, for if Negroes did not ride the buses, they could not operate. Three-fourths of the riders are Negroes, yet we are arrested, or have to stand over empty seats. If we do not do something to stop these arrests, they will continue. The next time it may be you, or your daughter, or mother. This woman's case will come up on Monday. We are, therefore, asking every Negro to stay off the buses Monday in protest of the arrest and trial. Don't ride the buses to work, to town, to school, or anywhere on Monday. You can afford to stay out of school for one day if you have no other way to go except by bus. You can also afford to stay out of town for one day. If you work, take a cab,

or walk. But please, children and grown-ups, don't ride the bus at all on Monday. Please stay off of all buses Monday. (Garrow, 1987, pp. 45–46)

The next day the two students and Robinson, together with other members of the Women's Political Council, distributed the announcements throughout Montgomery's black community.

Interestingly, the one-day boycott was planned as a surprise action by Robinson and her colleagues. However, a black domestic worker who considered herself loyal to her white employer took the handbill to her as she went to work on Friday. In moments the local news media knew of the boycott, and coverage appeared in the newspapers and on television on Saturday and Sunday. Ironically, this publicity may have helped the boycott because many blacks who did not receive the handbill heard of the boycott plan through the news media.[3]

Following the Baton Rouge example, nightly church meetings were held to organize the boycott. At the Friday night meeting attended by more than 100 sympathizers a transportation committee was established to help the boycotting blacks get to where they were going on Monday. Cars were volunteered, taxis contacted, and routes mapped out to get workers to their jobs.

The one-day Monday boycott was a dramatic success in that fewer than 10 percent of Montgomery's blacks rode the city buses (Wright, 1991).[4] And since 75 to 80 percent of the passengers who normally rode were black, the boycott resulted in a huge loss in revenues for the bus company. Moreover, Robinson claims that white ridership was down on that day as well, so that many buses were empty for the length of their routes (Garrow, 1987).

By Monday afternoon local black leaders were well aware of the success of the boycott and looked for someone to lead its continuation. Although E. D. Nixon had been asked to assume this role he decided that a black minister would be a better choice. His logic was that "ministers would follow one another and then we wouldn't have to be fighting the churches to get something done." Nixon had been impressed with the young Reverend King, a 26-year-old newcomer to Montgomery with a doctorate from Boston University and an impressive gift for oratory.

At an afternoon meeting of local black leaders on Monday it

was decided that a new local organization would be formed to continue the boycott and that it would be called the Montgomery Improvement Association. King was selected by the group as its leader. That evening his oratorical gifts were made dramatically evident at a mass meeting of 6,000 blacks who came together at the Holt Street Baptist Church to discuss the bus boycott and its future. According to Kennedy,

> He delivered, extemporaneously, a short but impassioned address that sounded many of the major themes upon which he would elaborate during the remainder of his life. He did so with the mix of patriotism and outrage, simplicity and sophistication that make his speeches among the most memorable in American history. (1989, p. 1021)

The speech ended with these inspiring words:

> We are going to work together. Right here in Montgomery, when the history books are written in the future, somebody will have to say, "There lived a race of people who had the moral courage to stand up for their rights. And they injected a new meaning into the veins of history and civilization." And we're going to do that. God grant that we do it before it's too late. (Wright, 1991, p. 85)

The response of the thousands gathered inside and outside the church was one of pandemonium. The audience apparently felt that Montgomery blacks had found not only a way to combat the daily humiliations of segregated buses but also an inspiring young minister to lift their spirits while mobilizing their energies to confront the white power structure of the city. Little did they know how long they would need this leadership to sustain them. The boycott lasted a total of 382 days, from December 5, 1955, to December 21, 1956, a period far longer than any of its leaders could have foreseen.

To the surprise of many observers, the bus boycott was very successfully executed. The more than 90 percent of black riders that stayed off the buses on December 5 continued to stay off throughout the boycott period. That abstinence from city bus services was made possible by the creation of an alternative transportation system by the Montgomery Improvement Association. And the system, which started as a crude voluntary effort, soon evolved into something far more sophisticated and reliable as the Montgomery Improvement Association secured the necessary funds to buy vehicles, hire drivers, and develop routes—in short, to establish a "remarkably effective transportation service" that was independent of the white power structure.

Moreover, the Montgomery Improvement Association took steps to develop a sense of community among its members. It published a newsletter edited by Jo Ann Robinson and held weekly mass meetings that rotated from church to church. The meetings cut across class lines. According to King,

> The vast majority present were working people; yet there was always an appreciable number of professionals in the audience. Physicians, teachers, and lawyers sat or stood beside domestic workers and unskilled laborers. The Ph.D.'s and the no "D's" were bound together in a common venture. The so-called "big Negroes" who owned cars and had never ridden the buses came to know the maids and the laborers who rode the buses every day. Men and women who had been separated from each other by false standards of class were now singing and praying together in a common struggle. (Kennedy, 1989, p. 1023)

The strong sense of community was a major factor in the financing of the Montgomery Improvement Association and especially its extensive and expensive alternative transportation system. Those attending the weekly church meetings gave generously, but unlike earlier black boycotts in the South (e.g., the one in Baton Rouge), this one drew large contributions from the outside, especially from the North (Morris, 1986). Northern blacks donated large sums as NAACP units and black churches across the nation organized a fund-raising campaign. Also, labor unions, such as the United Automobile Workers, provided large amounts, as did peace organizations such as the War Resisters League.

A curious aspect of the boycott campaign concerns the demands made by the boycotters and how these demands changed over its duration. At the outset the Montgomery Improvement Association did not seek to overturn the state's segregation laws, or indeed challenge the legitimacy of *de jure* segregation. Instead it was within the constraints of a segregated system that the boycotters, as fare-paying consumers, sought to have their rights to equitable treatment honored (Garrow, 1987, p. 80). This meant more courtesy from the bus drivers and the right for blacks to sit from the rear to the front on a first-come, first-served basis.[5] This right was not inconsistent with the state's segregation laws; indeed, a seating plan of this type was already in place in other Southern cities (e.g., Mobile, Alabama).

However, instead of considering the boycotters' demands for change to be within the existing segregation laws, the bus company rejected them summarily. The company believed that compromise was unwise because it might fuel more black defiance. Ironically, the bus company's rigid reaction helped to radicalize the Montgomery Improvement Association, its leadership, and its goals. From a position of working within the existing bus segregation laws the boycotters moved to one of fighting to overturn them.

After the first few weeks of boycott success, signs of serious strain began to appear in the city of Montgomery. Late in January 1956, drivers in the Montgomery Improvement Association's carpool reported being harassed by the police. On January 30, King's house was bombed. A month later a grand jury returned indictments for 90 of the leaders and supporters of the association. These individuals were charged with conspiring to carry out an illegal boycott.

The boycotters were defended by the NAACP, which took the case to federal court. When it appeared that the courts would rule against segregated busing, the local bus company attempted to put an end to the practice, only to find that the city of Montgomery threatened company drivers with arrest if they permitted desegregated seating.

Finally the federal court in Montgomery did act with a 2-to-1 ruling on June 5, 1956, that bus segregation was illegal. The ruling was upheld by the U.S. Supreme Court on November 13, 1956, and a month later Montgomery officials were served with copies of the ruling by federal marshals. The following day,

December 21, 1956, the boycott ended and blacks, for the first time in more than a year, returned to the buses.

In light of the landmark federal court decisions and their influence on the boycott's outcome it is well to ask what effect, if any, the yearlong protest had on ending bus segregation in Montgomery. It seems clear that by the execution criterion noted in Chapter 1, the boycott was a huge success in that the vast majority of Montgomery blacks stayed off the buses for more than a year. But by the consequence criterion of Chapter 1, it is more difficult to judge the outcome.

On the one hand, some observers claim successful litigation, not the boycott, desegregated the buses (Kennedy, 1989). Barnes (1983) echoes these sentiments:

> White authorities remained impervious to the adverse publicity the boycott brought them, to the economic losses it caused local business, and to the moral pressures of nonviolent resistance. They yielded only when faced with a final mandate from the Supreme Court. (p. 124)

And according to Powledge (1991), NAACP officials of the time, annoyed that the Montgomery boycott had been undertaken without their direction, did not hesitate to point to their successful role in the federal courts in winning the boycott objectives.

> Thurgood Marshall, the special counsel for the NAACP . . . , was said to have commented that if the demonstrators had just stayed home and saved all that walking and waited for him to get the court's ruling, they could have spared themselves a lot of trouble. And John Morsell, the second in command at the NAACP's national headquarters, was quoted as saying that someday some bright reporter would discover that it wasn't the boycott that desegregated Montgomery's buses, but an NAACP lawsuit. (p. 86)

On the other hand, since federal court decisions do not take place in a social vacuum, the dramatic and heroic actions of Montgomery blacks during the many months of the boycott—actions that received nationwide publicity in the various news media—may have influenced the judges' thinking. But even if this influence was minimal, some people see the consequences of the boycott painted on a far larger canvas, one not dreamed of by its local leaders when their campaign got under way in late 1955. For the boycott, more than any other single action, brought the civil rights movement to the attention of the nation. As Capeci (1980) has observed, the boycott

> provided a leader in King, a philosophy in nonviolence, a tactic in direct action, and, as important, a tangible triumph. Blacks were poised for change, needing, in Lerone Bennett's words, "an act to give them power over their fears." The boycott, of course, did much more, for under King's leadership it achieved legitimacy and prepared both races for a prolonged assault on inequality. (p. 733)

And particularly important to Powledge (1991) is that Montgomery blacks fought their yearlong fight using a tactic that was difficult to sustain.

> The method chosen in Montgomery—the boycott—was one of the toughest to initiate and adhere to because of its built-in inconvenience. It's easy to boycott the gasoline refined by a notorious polluter or the beer brewed by an ultraconservative zealot, for there are plenty of alternatives available at little or no penalty. There was, however, no alternative bus company in Montgomery. The blacks maintained the boycott through the cold winter months and the moist heat of a south Alabama summer. (p. 83)

And as we shall now see, the boycott also sparked similar actions in other Southern cities. We look next at one in Tallahassee.

The Tallahassee Bus Boycott

Five months after the Montgomery boycott began, a bus boycott started in the much smaller city of Tallahassee (total population, according to the 1950 census, was 27,237, of whom 9,373 were nonwhite). The precipitating event occurred on May 27, 1956, when two black female students attending Florida A&M College refused to give up their seats on a bus to whites. This act of defiance, which took place on the "white section" of the bus, resulted in the arrest of the students. Upon hearing of the arrests, fellow students at all-black Florida A&M met and unanimously decided to boycott the city buses until the end of the term, which was just two weeks away.

What would happen after the students left in two weeks was the question posed to the local black community. The answer, as told by Morris (1984) in his study of the Tallahassee boycott, was swift and emphatic. On May 29, a meeting of community leaders was called by two black clergy leaders, the Reverend C. K. Steele, a community leader and president of the Tallahassee NAACP chapter, and Dr. James Hudson, president of a local group of black ministers and former chaplain at Florida A&M. At the meeting a committee was established to approach city officials with a request that the buses be desegregated. Since a negative response was expected, the church leaders called a mass meeting at a church in the black community. At the meeting a bus boycott was called that was to take effect immediately.

Following the Baton Rouge and Montgomery models, a new central organization was formed to coordinate the boycott, and an alternative transportation system was established that proved to be very effective. Indeed, according to Morris (1984), in just a few days no blacks were riding the buses. Funding for the boycott operation was collected by the churches in the black community and brought to the two weekly mass meetings in support of the boycott. As in Montgomery the meetings were rotated among the various churches.

Was the boycott effective? According to Morris the short answer is "very." The longer answer is as follows:

> The mass boycott put the buses out of business in the black community of Tallahassee. Considering that it was concurrent with the boycott in Montgomery, in which the issues were being deliberated by the Supreme Court, the Tallahassee leaders decided to continue the boycott until that ruling was made. When the Supreme Court ruled against bus segregation in Montgomery, blacks in Tallahassee resumed riding buses, with desegregated seating. (Morris, 1984, p. 67)

If the boycott had a larger significance it was to demonstrate that even the smaller cities of the South were not immune from the boycott weapon.

Lessons Learned from the Bus Boycotts of the 1950s
The three boycotts had much in common, according to Morris (1984). In all three cities, new organizations were created to operate the boycotts, and the organizations drew heavily on the black churches and clergy for their leadership and support. Moreover, all three organizations saw an immediate need to establish viable alternative transportation systems to get people to their jobs and to stores. In a larger sense the boycotts represented a break with the legalistic protest tradition of the past, as represented by the NAACP, and the start of an emphasis on "direct action" campaigns to disrupt the established order.

The model for much of what transpired here was, of course, provided by the Reverend T. J. Jemison, the unsung hero whose organizational initiatives in Baton Rouge provided guidance and inspiration to both the Reverend King in Montgomery and the Reverend Steele in Tallahassee. As we have seen, both Jemison and King were newcomers to their communities, and there is reason to believe that this status may have helped them to gain acceptance as boycott leaders.

Finally, a real question arises concerning the consequence criterion for success in evaluating the impact of the bus boycotts. While the Baton Rouge boycott did indeed lead to desegregated busing, the situations in Montgomery and Tallahassee were murky in that it was the actions of the Supreme Court that led to the desegregation of these cities' bus systems, although it is possible that the boycott campaigns influenced the decisions of the individual judges.

Local Boycotts against Korean American Merchants

Like the bus boycotts we have just examined, more recent examples of consumer economic boycotts called by African Americans have followed a behavioral pattern. The typical scenario starts in a large city with an African American neighborhood served by local stores run by new immigrants from Asia. Very often the owners are Korean Americans, and the stores are mom-and-pop operations offering groceries and convenience items. The boycott call usually follows an incident in which an African American customer of the store claims that he or she was mistreated by the store's owner or employees.

Probably the best-known example of this type of boycott occurred in Brooklyn, New York, in 1990. An altercation took place on January 18, 1990, between a Haitian American customer and a Korean American store manager at the Family Red Apple Market (FRAM) grocery store. The altercation soon triggered a year-long boycott of two Korean American-owned groceries, of which FRAM was one.

What happened during the altercation is not clear since the two participants reported completely different stories. The customer charged that she was assaulted by the store manager, while the store manager claimed that he simply asked her to leave when her behavior became disruptive. Apparently some witnesses in the store agreed with the customer's story, while others agreed with the store manager's. The incident ended with the arrival of the police, who arrested the store owner and had the customer taken by ambulance to a nearby hospital for treatment.

Following the incident a crowd of approximately 40 persons gathered in front of the store, according to the police record,

> to protest the assault upon the Haitian woman by the Korean merchants, demanding that the store close permanently. Unidentified spokespersons voiced their opposition to the Korean American treatment of customers in general, indicating that there have been a number of incidents in which customers have been manhandled and there is a lack of respect to all black customers. When [the store] closed at about 2000 hours the demonstrators moved across the street to 1826 Church Ave., another Korean-owned fruit and vegetable market [Church Fruits and Vegetables]. (Commanding Officer, 1990, p. 1)

The second store became a boycott target when it provided refuge to a FRAM employee seeking protection from the angry crowd.

The yearlong boycott become a major media attraction as well as the focus of numerous court battles and flurries of charges and countercharges between offices of local government. For example, the execution success of the boycott was clear from the start, and the devastating effect this had on sales prompted the two store owners in May 1990 to apply for injunctive relief from the courts. Weighing the boycotters' right to protest against the store owners' right to freely engage in trade, the Kings County Supreme Court ordered the boycotters to discontinue their protest activities from a distance of less than 50 feet from the stores' entrances. The court also ordered the New York City Police Department to enforce its order, but the police declined to do so; the department finally proceeded with enforcement after being ordered to do so by the state appellate court. A Mayor's Committee report on the boycott also proved to be contentious, as did the City Council's response to it. Finally, a year after the boycott began, the 50-feet court order was being honored, the city's African American Mayor David Dinkins had shopped in both stores, and there was an easing of the tensions in the Brooklyn neighborhood community that was the site of the boycott (Kandel, 1991).

If the Brooklyn boycott was an isolated incident it would be easy to dismiss as a local phenomenon not worthy of national attention. But similar incidents followed this boycott in other American cities.

- A 110-day boycott by African Americans of a Korean American-owned liquor store in Los Angeles ended in October 1991 through negotiations by representatives of the African American and Korean American communities. The boycott was called as an act of protest after an African American youth was shot and killed by a Korean American store clerk during an alleged robbery attempt.
- Also in October 1991, African Americans in North Philadelphia boycotted a neighborhood store owned by Korean Americans for a total of three months due to an alleged assault of an African American customer by the store owner. The boycott was effective in that it forced the store to close even though its owner was acquitted of the charges made against him.
- In the Englewood community of Chicago, an African American organization announced in April 1992 a boycott against

businesses in the area owned by Korean Americans, claiming that they mistreated local shoppers in the Englewood Shopping Plaza.

- In December 1992 Howard University students in Washington, D.C., began a boycott of a local grocery store owned by Korean Americans because of a racial slur allegedly directed at an African American student who claimed she was short-changed by a store employee.
- In Berkeley, California, an African American organization of students at the University of California called for a boycott of a local convenience store owned by Korean Americans when its owner allegedly sprayed Mace at a female African American student after a dispute broke out between them in February 1993.

Why the problems between Korean Americans and African Americans? According to Sims (1990), many African American shoppers may perceive the Korean American merchants as rude because they infrequently smile and they often place change from a transaction on the counter instead of in the customer's hand. But as Sims notes, these behaviors have a cultural basis. People in Confucian cultures are discouraged from smiling, and women, in particular, are taught not to touch men, so they place change on the counter.

However, some African Americans claim that there is more involved here than cultural misunderstandings. According to Sims (1990), some consumers claim that the Korean American merchants often follow them around their stores as if they suspected them of shoplifting; others claim that the cashiers sometimes do not provide receipts and that often they add a few dollars to a large bill, hoping that the shopper will not notice.

Finally, some shoppers expressed regret that few if any of their local stores were owned by African Americans, and these shoppers accused the banks and the responsible government agencies of providing special loans to the Korean Americans to help them start businesses. As one put it, according to Sims, "This is our community but isn't it odd that none of these markets are owned by blacks. Something is wrong with this picture" (1990, p. A15).

Consumer Labor Boycotts Initiated by African Americans

Just as consumer economic boycotts initiated by African Americans predate World War II, so do African American boycotts relating to labor issues. Perhaps the first significant period of activity coincided with the Great Depression. With unprecedented numbers of urban blacks finding themselves jobless, it was only natural that the boycott tactic would be used in an effort to create jobs in their own neighborhood shopping areas.

The "Don't Buy from Where You Can't Work" Campaigns

As Gary Jerome Hunter (1977) has documented in detail in a fascinating doctoral dissertation on the black urban boycott phenomenon during the Great Depression, tens of thousands of blacks lost their jobs during this period, sometimes to create jobs for unemployed whites. In addition to the huge numbers of industrial positions that blacks lost, large numbers of domestic jobs in white households were eliminated as their occupants tightened their belts by doing their own housework and tending their own children. By the 1932 election, according to Hunter, black unemployment in the urban North exceeded 50 percent.

The middle-class NAACP responded to the problems by launching its New Economic Program, which attempted to create jobs for urban blacks by asking its local representatives to urge white employers in the black community to hire blacks. The response, as Hunter (1977) observes, was disappointing:

> White merchants in black communities replied that economic and family obligations "precluded them from hiring Negroes." A surprising number of employers flatly stated that they would not hire "colored" when so many whites were unemployed, while others stated it was not their policy to employ black workers. Within a year the New Economic Program faded as a feeble attempt to deal with a tremendous problem. (p. 50)

Another effort by the black establishment to cope with the unemployment problem was initiated by the National Negro

Business League, a leading advocate for black economic development. The league had long been impressed by the size of the national black consumer market (estimated at $4.5 billion in 1929) and by the dominance of white businesses in black retail markets (one estimate was that less than 10 percent of the black retail trade was controlled by black entrepreneurs). In fact, except for beauty parlors, barber shops, restaurants, and pressing shops, the retail trade of the black community was almost completely owned by white nonresidents (Moon, 1966). In an attempt to secure a larger segment of these local markets for black business, the National Negro Business League established the Colored Merchants Association (CMA) in 1928.

The CMA endeavored to start local associations that would "collectively purchase wholesale products at discount prices by organizing buyers cooperatives of at least ten black retail stores" (Hunter, 1977, p. 53). The CMA also encouraged the formation of Housewives Leagues at the local level, consisting of black women who agreed to spend their consumer dollars, to the greatest extent possible, in black-operated CMA retail outlets. In effect, then, by establishing the Housewives League the CMA had launched a consumer buycott, with its own units as the direct beneficiaries of the action. Although the CMA effort enjoyed some initial modest successes (20 retail stores organized by mid-1929 and pledges of participation from 9,000 consumers by the Detroit Housewives League), it soon collapsed when thousands of black retailers became victims of the Great Depression. And with the collapse went any prospects of new jobs for blacks within their own neighborhood shopping areas.

In light of these middle-class black failures to deal with the unemployment crisis, the times were right for more militant approaches, and they soon appeared in Southside Chicago, the nation's second largest urban black community. A new generation of black intellectuals, calling themselves the "New Negroes," emerged there in 1919. Its voice became the *Whip*, a weekly newspaper of black business, which declared a buycott in its inaugural issue by stating, "We believe that Negroes should trade with Negroes even at a personal sacrifice in order that the race might have an economic average for which they will not have to compromise" (Hunter, 1977, p. 81).

The *Whip*'s initial attempts at consumer labor actions were only partly successful. Working with a local minister in September 1927, its editors organized a boycott of a Southside department store. After the store experienced a severe loss of sales during the Christmas season its managers yielded to the boycotters by agreeing to hire eight black sales clerks. This long and arduous boycott campaign, while successful, was followed by one that was not. The second boycott, which started in January 1929, targeted the Metropolitan Life Insurance Company. The choice of target was based on the *Whip* editors' claim that blacks bought more insurance policies from Metropolitan than all other insurance companies combined. In light of this claim, they said, "We deserve a fair share of jobs in return for our loyalty" (Hunter, 1977, p. 84). Despite an active campaign, consisting of handbill distributions in the Southside, weekly editorials in the *Whip*, and meetings with local church and civic groups to enlist their support, the boycott failed. A primary reason appears to be that while some loss of new business occurred for Metropolitan (although one has to wonder how many new insurance policies were being bought by urban blacks from any companies during the Great Depression), the company, being national in scope, could absorb them.

In light of the long and frustrating experiences with these two boycotts, Chicago blacks were in need of a quicker and more effortless way to execute consumer labor boycotts effectively. The answer, according to Hunter (1977), appeared in the person of "a street speaker calling himself Bishop Conshankin, chief minister of the Ahamidab Church, one of the dozens of small African-oriented religious movements on the Southside" (p. 85). A colorful and spellbinding soapbox speaker, the charismatic Conshankin, who often appeared in Moslem attire (including a "vivid red turban"), "had few peers in his ability to attract shopping crowds . . . with his 'golden tongue'" (p. 86).

Conshankin in 1928 had used his multifaceted skills to establish a small group of followers consisting of high school students and unemployed workers. He proved to be a highly effective tactician by breaking with the earlier black middle-class efforts at "friendly persuasion" to adopt the picket line, which proved to be a militant breakthrough for urban black leaders of labor boycotts. As Hunter (1977) has noted:

A few dedicated pickets could almost completely stop shopping traffic to any store since few black people were willing to cross a picket line in public display against a race effort. It was more convenient to go to another store. The Bishop's "direct action" pickets also yielded quick results, for few stores could sustain a complete loss of trade even over a short period of time. Within two months Conshankin's movement yielded over three hundred jobs. (p. 86)

The success of Conshankin's campaign attracted hundreds of additional followers. It also attracted imitators, the most notable being "Big Bill Tate," a former prizefighter and well-known street speaker who organized his own boycott campaign aimed at employing blacks as butchers in Southside meat markets. The picketing tactic spread quickly to other black boycott groups, and by the summer of 1929, according to Hunter (1977), thousands of activists were picketing hundreds of stores all around Southside. By the spring of 1930, with the benefit of *Whip* support for the grassroots effort, the newly named "Don't Buy from Where You Can't Work" campaign had created some 2,600 jobs for Chicago blacks. A year later most of the large Southside stores had integrated their workforces, and the boycott movement began to wind down.

The Chicago black boycotts had, however, made their mark. Indeed, news of their successes from 1929 to 1931 swept across black America. While black communities elsewhere seemed incapable of coping with mass black unemployment, the Chicago picketers had made a start, and the result was a most welcome boycott model for others to pursue, a model that had secured an estimated 6,800 jobs for black Chicago workers. Some of the more significant urban boycott campaigns using the Chicago model have been noted by Hunter (1977), as well as others:

• In Baltimore in 1933, a faith healer and mystical adviser calling himself Kiowa Costonie led thousands of black pickets in boycotts of more than a dozen stores, including the A&P, which he claimed had insufficient numbers of black employees. Although the picketing was halted by court injunctions, it left an indelible impression on the black community as the newly integrated stores maintained this employment pattern in subsequent years (Skotnes, 1994).

- In Washington, D.C., in 1933, evangelist Elder Lightfoot Michaux, a minister of the Church of God, worked with young intellectuals who had formed the New Negro Alliance to use the Chicago boycott model to pursue black labor actions in the nation's capital. Such Alliance pioneers as William H. Hastie, John A. Davis, Eugene Davidson, and Albert Demond led boycotts of dozens of stores in black neighborhoods; by early 1936, the alliance claimed that its efforts had created more than 300 jobs for black workers.

- In Richmond, Virginia, a local NAACP chapter, influenced by the New Negro Alliance's successes, initiated a labor boycott in 1934 against local stores including the A&P. The boycott succeeded, and the A&P agreed to hire six black workers.

- In Atlanta, a black labor and consumer boycott of an A&P store led in 1935 by Atlanta University students was aided by the decision of a neighboring competitor (Kroger) to hire a black worker. Ironically, when news of the boycott and the hiring that it triggered spread to other parts of Atlanta, white consumers retaliated against Kroger by boycotting its stores in their neighborhoods. The students eventually called off the boycott after the A&P agreed to treat black customers more courteously; however, the grocery chain did not agree to hire black clerks.

- In New York's Harlem, a number of boycott leaders made their presence felt in labor actions using picketing as a primary tactic. Among these leaders was Chicago's Bishop Conshankin, who had come to New York in 1932 to "set Harlem on fire." As Harlem's newest street speaker, the colorful Conshankin renamed himself Sufi Abdul Hamid. Sufi soon became known as the "Black Hitler" of Harlem because the radical agitator often invoked anti-Semitic rhetoric in his speeches (Moon, 1966; Muraskin, 1972; Weisbord & Stein, 1970). Two of his street speaker competitors, Ira Kemp and Arthur Reed, also led labor boycotts, and a major concern for these leaders was labor discrimination against dark-skinned blacks, who were often rejected by white employers in favor of light-skinned blacks when the employers were forced to

hire black workers to satisfy the demands of black labor boycotters. Sufi, on the one hand, and Kemp and Reed, on the
other, led successful labor boycotts in Harlem in the 1930s.
Following the Harlem riot of 1935, the mantle of black political leadership (which included boycotts) passed to Adam
Clayton Powell, the youthful pastor of one of Harlem's leading religious institutions, the Abyssinian Baptist Church.

• In Cleveland, a shipping clerk named John Holly organized
the Future Outlook League in 1935. One of its primary aims
was to persuade local merchants whose stores were supported by black customers to hire black clerks to serve them.
After an intensive lobbying effort failed to secure a single job
for local blacks, the league decided to use the picketing tactic
in support of a labor boycott. The League's efforts proved to
be successful in that by the end of 1935 it had secured 300
new jobs for blacks in stores that had earlier barred blacks
from working.

As a result of these various urban campaigns an estimated
75,000 new jobs were secured for blacks between 1929 and 1941
(Hunter, 1977). Hunter believes that the most successful campaigns were conducted in Harlem, Chicago, and Ohio (primarily
Cleveland, but other cities in the state as well).

Why had these various "Don't Buy from Where You Can't
Work" campaigns been so effective in securing jobs for blacks?
Several factors were apparently responsible. One, of course, was
the failure of the middle-class establishment approaches of the
NAACP and the Urban League to persuade white merchants in
black commercial areas to hire blacks. Since the civil path of
moderation proved to be ineffective, tens of thousands of jobless
ghetto youths and newly unemployed working-class adults
looked elsewhere for leadership. And what they often found were
charismatic street speakers offering the uncivil, immoderate tactics of picketing and sit-ins—militant actions to be employed in
support of the labor boycott weapon. Face-saving discussions
with white merchants were dropped in favor of in-your-face
assaults on their stores and customers.[6]

These assaults often went beyond the law to include acts of
vandalism directed at the stores and reprisals against their cus-

tomers. As Hunter (1977) has noted in commenting on the early Harlem boycotts, "No language was spared, and often a brick through the window did wonders to uplift the race" (p. 181). Moreover, reprisals often made life difficult (or embarrassing) for blacks who shopped at the targeted stores. In Cleveland the names and addresses of boycott violators were noted and publicized during the implementation of a milk company boycott. In a later boycott of a Cleveland market building, boycotters grabbed the purchases of violators and chased them away. In Harlem photographs of boycott violators were published on the front page of the *New York Age*, a sympathetic local newspaper (Muraskin, 1972).[7]

Obstructionist tactics were also commonly employed, such as threatening to tie up phone lines in New York and Cleveland by having large numbers of boycotters and their sympathizers dial "0" for operator at exactly the same time. The threat was actually carried out in Cleveland when one morning at 9 o'clock, thousands of local boycott supporters overloaded the system with their calls to the operator. Moreover, Adam Clayton Powell in New York organized "bill payers' parades" in which thousands of Harlem blacks paid their gas and electric bills with pennies to express their indignation at the utilities' refusal to hire blacks (Hunter, 1977).[8]

The militancy of the boycotters' actions could not long be ignored by the white merchants, especially since these actions were being performed by masses of consumers, and the results were diminished sales at a time when sales were already far below normal due to the effects of the Great Depression.[9] Many of the merchants yielded within hours of the establishment of picket lines outside their stores. The account of a Cleveland boycott illustrates what often happened:

> The first picket was set up in front of Haicowitz' Grocery store, selected because the merchant had a good first-name relationship with his black customers. Surprised by the appearance of the "shock troops" carrying signs reading "Don't Buy from Where You Can't Work" and the refusal of his patrons to cross the picket line, within an hour Haicowitz agreed to employ Leila Wilson, one of his patrons. The troops then moved on

Florsheim and Clapp Shoe Store, one of the most exclusive stores in the district. After no patrons crossed the picket lines in three hours, the store hired its first black salesman. (Hunter, 1977, pp. 247–248)

While the boycotts secured many jobs for the black community, their impact was not limited to the single area of employment. Indeed, the job crusade can be said to have had an energizing effect on the consciousness of the elite black minority whom W. E. B. DuBois referred to as the "talented tenth." The job crusade generated a grassroots movement that took on a variety of civil rights issues in cities across the nation, often using the militant methods that had been so successfully employed earlier in the labor boycotts. As Hunter (1977) has noted, "the day of the traditional methods of 'conferences and presentations' was quickly coming to a close" (p. 285).

Black Community Boycotts in the Postwar South

Given the success of the urban boycotts during the Great Depression and the success of the Southern civil rights bus boycotts in the 1950s, it is hardly surprising to learn that African Americans in smaller communities in the South adopted the consumer boycott in confrontations with local merchants. The issues that prompted the boycotts covered a wide range of economic and noneconomic issues, including consumer abuse, job discrimination, and police brutality. Sometimes several issues were involved with one the occasion for a boycott and others often added later as old grievances found their way onto local boycotters' agendas.

The names of the affected communities lack the familiar ring of the bus-boycotted Southern state capitals noted earlier in this chapter. They include, for the 1960s, Pine Bluff (1960) and Forrest City (1969), Arkansas; Albany, Georgia (1961); Edwards (1966) and Port Gibson (1969), Mississippi; and Cairo, Illinois (1969). Communities boycotted in the 1970s include Marianna, Arkansas (1971), and Sparta, Georgia (1974); and three Mississippi towns: Byhalia (1975), Tupelo (1978), and Okolena (1979).[10] To illustrate the issues and actions involved in these boycotts, two are examined in some detail, one drawing upon local leadership (Marianna) and the other drawing upon outside leadership (Tupelo).

The Marianna Boycott

At the time the boycott was called in June 1971, blacks made up 60 percent of Lee County and the city of Marianna. Although they represented the majority of the population of this rural eastern Arkansas area, blacks were a largely voiceless majority with little or no direct representation in local government (Brockway, 1975). This lack of representation had contributed to an atmosphere of frustration, tension, and alienation among blacks in Marianna (Terry, 1972). The boycott was triggered when a young black woman was arrested by a black police officer for "talking back" to a white waitress at a local restaurant concerning the purchase of a pizza (Brown, 1978). The following day a boycott was called by black community leaders. These leaders had been active in neighborhood action committees for improving the health care of black residents of Lee County. The leaders worked with local black churches to mobilize the black community around the boycott issue.

The boycott strategy consisted of targeting all the white retail merchants in Marianna. By this approach the boycotters planned to use black purchasing power to secure the attention of the "white establishment," which they believed to be responsible for many acts of discrimination toward black residents (Terry, 1972).

At first the boycotters picketed several of the larger downtown stores. Blacks were stationed on street corners to observe whether the boycott was being adhered to by other black residents. The blacks who did not comply with the boycott were mostly older residents who claimed they were not aware of the boycott. Once these residents became informed about the boycott, most stopped their patronage of the white stores (Brockway, 1975). Many whites within the community became convinced that blacks were using strong-arm tactics of fear and intimidation against other blacks to prevent them from shopping in white stores (Hay & Napier, 1973). Although the boycotters dismissed these charges as "typical white Southern thinking," some isolated strong-arm tactics apparently were used (Brockway, 1975). More widespread, however, were occurrences of racial violence between whites and blacks. In particular, racial violence took a sharp upswing when white crowds began patrolling the downtown area, reportedly to protect blacks who wanted to shop there. Local law enforcement procedures broke down when large groups of whites protested the black boycotts. Fifty state troopers were called in for two weeks, and a curfew was imposed from 4 p.m. to 8 a.m.

In the spring of 1972 the boycotters submitted a list of 41 demands to "the local white establishment." The demands called for the firing of some local officials and the hiring of more blacks in the workplace. Upon request from both blacks and whites a gubernatorial task force came to Marianna to help the community solve its racial problems.

On July 25, 1972, the boycott ended after local black leaders cited several areas in which progress had been made. By the end of the boycott 12 retail stores were either forced out of business or chose to close their doors rather than endure the downturn in sales and profits. As soon as the boycott ended, blacks and whites went back to shopping in the Marianna stores that had remained open.

The Tupelo Boycott

Tupelo is a small rural town in northeastern Mississippi. Blacks accounted for 22 percent of the population at the time of the boycott in 1978. At one point prior to 1978 Tupelo was considered the most progressive community in the state, renown for its racial equality (McNulty, 1978).

The events leading to the Tupelo boycott go back to March 1976 when Eugene Pasto, a black man from Memphis, Tennessee, was picked up by Mississippi highway patrol officers and taken to the Tupelo police station on check forgery charges. Pasto later claimed that two white police officers at the station severely beat him. He followed up his claim by filing a lawsuit and in January a federal judge ruled in his favor. After the court decision additional complaints were made to Tupelo's board of aldermen about the two officers, with demands that they be fired. The Tupelo police chief concluded that the officers had not committed a crime and recommended to the aldermen that they be retained. In February 1978 the aldermen accepted the chief's recommendation with just one dissenting vote, from Tupelo's only black alderman.

The city action outraged the United League of Mississippi, an 11-year-old civil rights organization with 60,000 members. The organization sent its head, Alfred (Skip) Robinson, to organize the black community of Tupelo. As an outsider Robinson incurred some initial resentment from local black community leaders who had planned to deal with the aldermen's action by holding meetings with city officials. But the league won the support of the black community after Robinson successfully argued that Tupelo blacks should not negotiate from a position of weakness (Tulsky, 1978). Robinson then mobilized the black community and organized a boycott.

The boycotters targeted all white downtown merchants and urged them to hire more blacks and to end job discrimination. To support the boycott a series of marches and demonstrations were held protesting the "white control" of the city (Brown, 1978). The boycott stimulated a white militant backlash, including the formation of a Ku Klux Klan chapter in the city.

A major clash between the Klan and the United League members occurred on Tupelo's main street on May 6, 1978, but fortunately for all concerned, no one was injured. However, as the actions of the United League grew more effective (with the assistance of the news media), the Klan perpetrated more acts of intimidation. It burned a cross in Robinson's hometown and pelted a league member's house with tear gas.

Shortly after the events of May 6, the federal district court ruled in favor of the protesters on an important boycott issue. This was a major victory for the black community of Tupelo and the United League. In an emotional statement following the decision, the league's attorney observed: "If it's done nothing else it has brought black people together in a bond of solidarity and pride that is unparalleled in this area. We are no longer afraid" (Brown, 1978, p. 1).

Concluding Comments about Black Community Boycotts

Several observations appear to be in order about these small-town boycotts. First, a sizable black constituency is required to make them work at the execution level, for without a critical mass it will not be possible to have a substantial effect on the sales of the town's merchants. Second, while not absolutely necessary, it is desirable to have available monitors of black consumer behavior on the commercial strips of the boycotted small town in order to spot boycott violators. (It should be noted, however, that while this may help the boycott to be more effective, some may question the ethics of such an approach since the monitors could be viewed by consumers as instruments of intimidation.) A third observation is that for a community boycott to work, one or more neighboring communities must be close by so that the boycotters and their sympathizers can shop there without incurring inordinate costs in time, money, or diminished quality or variety of goods. And finally, community boycotts often have a variety of precipitating issues and types of leaders, and the leaders may be local residents or outsiders who succeed in gaining acceptance for themselves and their boycott initiatives.

National Boycotts in the Modern Era

The Operation PUSH Boycotts

While black boycotts in small Southern towns in the 1970s represent one end of the black protest continuum, the other end for this time period is perhaps most evident in the actions of the Reverend Jesse Jackson and his Operation PUSH—People United to Save Humanity. The Chicago-based Jackson picked Christmas Day of 1971 to announce the arrival of "a rising star in the Midwest," terming PUSH "a religious corporation with an economic mission." The economic mission was to elevate the status of black workers and to increase the profits of black businesses (Cassidy, 1974).

Boycotts or, more typically, the threats of boycotts have been the tactical approach PUSH used to get large corporations to the bargaining table. As Jackson (1973) has noted:

We, in PUSH, have developed the double-edged techniques of organized mass consumer boycotts and negotiations directed at affecting the policy of major corporations. For we are committed to opening up opportunities for those who have been historically left out. (p. 61)

The same tactics had been used earlier by Jackson when he served as director of Operation Breadbasket, the economic arm of the Southern Christian Leadership Conference (SCLC). Perhaps his most dramatic victory at the time was over the A&P food store chain; Jackson led months of demonstrations against Chicago A&P stores, and the chain finally yielded by agreeing to hire more blacks and to provide more shelf space for black-owned product lines.

While PUSH was in many respects a continuation of the Breadbasket operation, organizationally it was independent of its SCLC predecessor, allowing Jackson a free hand to shape his own programs. As Cassidy put it, "Jackson knew he was pouring old wine into new bottles but figured the taste would be sweeter if he could raise his own grapes" (1974, p. 58).

The early efforts of PUSH were highly successful. Its threats of boycotts eventually resulted in the signing of agreements, or covenants, as Jackson called them, with a dollar value of hundreds of millions. And the firms participating in these 1970s agreements included such notables as Avon Products, General Foods, Miller Beer, Joseph Schlitz Brewing Company, and Quaker Oats.

According to the Reverend George Riddick, a PUSH leader in research and negotiations, all of the covenants included agreements in four areas:

1. *Employment*, meaning job development at many levels with the objective of 15 percent representation in entry-level jobs as well as management positions.
2. *Business development*, which means employing black businesses on a contractual basis such as insurance companies, advertising agencies, and banks.
3. *Philanthropic contributions*, especially those in support of the NAACP Legal Defense Fund and the United Negro College Fund.
4. *Policy development*, through representation of blacks and other minorities on corporate boards of directors.

Despite glowing testimonials by black companies reporting increases in business resulting from the covenants, critics claimed that PUSH selected easy targets, companies already moving to involve minorities. Another criticism was that the covenants were simply corporate public relations ploys that might never be implemented—in short, empty promises. And finally, Jackson himself was criticized, according to Cassidy (1974), for allegedly using PUSH as a platform to launch a career in national politics.

Despite these criticisms, PUSH boycotts or threats of boycotts continued into the 1980s with Anheuser-Busch being targeted in 1982 and Revlon in 1986. Both boycotts enlisted the support of activists in cities across the nation to support their campaigns. For example, retail store owners were urged to remove Anheuser-Busch products from their shelves in nine cities including Chicago and Washington. And a Revlon action involving mock funerals held in some 37 cities consisted of the dumping of Revlon products in coffin-shaped boxes. Both boycotts yielded major concessions from their corporate targets including a Revlon agreement to withdraw from the Republic of South Africa in protest of its apartheid government and a pledge of $325 million by Anheuser-Busch to minority programs over a five-year period.

With Jesse Jackson's relocation to Washington, D.C., at the end of the 1980s, leadership of PUSH was passed to the Reverend Tyrone Crider. One of Crider's first major actions was to launch a boycott campaign in 1990 against Nike Corporation, a major manufacturer of athletic footwear. Crider claimed that African Americans accounted for 30 percent of Nike sales and were thus deserving of 30 percent of the corporation's business. He noted that no African Americans held executive positions at Nike and that no Nike ads were placed in African American-owned newspapers, magazines, or radio and television stations.

PUSH not only initiated a boycott but also called for a "blackout," in that it asked wearers of Nike footwear to place black tape over the shoes' Nike emblem. PUSH also organized protests at several stores and at Nike's headquarters in Oregon.

Nike fought back with a defense of its minority policies and with an attack on PUSH itself. Basketball star Michael Jordan, a prominent figure in Nike's advertising campaigns, publicly criticized the boycott as an unfair attack. But while Nike claimed it was an innocent victim of the boycott charges and its sales were not hurt by the boycott, it nonetheless did take steps to meet the

PUSH demands. For example, it appointed an African American to its board of directors and increased minority hiring.

The NAACP Boycotts

Started in 1909, the NAACP has for years been the leading national organization with the goal of securing justice for African Americans. With a 1990 budget of $13.3 million and membership of 400,000, the NAACP has often been viewed as the establishment organization of the civil rights movement due to its aging membership and its traditional reliance on legal approaches, rather than direct-action approaches, to minority problems.

While legal initiatives have indeed been in the forefront (especially during the heyday of the civil rights movement when NAACP director Roy Wilkens often did not see eye to eye with the more militant Martin Luther King), the organization and its members have also espoused confrontational approaches to civil rights problems. Indeed, it was Rosa Parks, Montgomery NAACP secretary and former Alabama state NAACP secretary, whose defiant actions triggered the Montgomery bus boycott in 1955. Two years later it was Daisy Bates, Arkansas state NAACP president, who led the 1957 effort to desegregate Little Rock's Central High School. And it was Medgar Evers, the Mississippi NAACP leader who was later assassinated, who was instrumental in James Meredith's campaign to integrate the University of Mississippi in 1962.

Moreover, it was the NAACP itself that backed several important boycott campaigns, including the 1966 Port Gibson, Mississippi, initiative. This action led to a merchants' suit against the NAACP, which placed it in financial jeopardy for more than a decade until the U.S. Supreme Court ruled in favor of the NAACP in 1982. Other publicized NAACP boycotts include the 1984 campaign against McDonald's and the surrogate campaign later in the same year against the retail merchants of Dearborn, Michigan.

Perhaps the most important contemporary use of the boycott (or the threat of a boycott) has been as a lever to secure corporate signatures on national incentive agreements, similar to

PUSH's covenants, which would expand opportunities for African American employees and businesses. The NAACP, according to Sims (1993), has persuaded some 70 corporations to sign such agreements. Among them are such major companies as Coors, General Motors, McDonald's, Pacific Bell, Safeway, Walt Disney, and United Airlines. A recent signatory was Flagstar Companies, the parent of the Denny's restaurant chain, which agreed to spend $1 billion to increase "black employment, management and equity."

The use of the boycott as a lever to get companies to sign on was most dramatically seen in the case of Coors. This Colorado-based, family-run company had long been a favorite target of liberal boycott groups—including gays, blacks, Hispanics, organized labor, and women. The company's problems can be traced to the conservative style of its owners, which held sway until the mid-1980s. The particulars have been briefly summarized by Prud'homme (1990):

> Trouble started when word of a polygraph test, which reportedly included questions about sexual preference, as well as a misreported story that Coors contributed to Anita Bryant's campaign against homosexual faculty, sparked a nationwide protest by the gay community. Then, in April 1977, Brewer's Workers Local 366 struck the Coors plant over several issues, including the lie-detector tests and rumored searches of employee lockers and automobiles for drugs. (Coors claims it was merely protecting itself against bomb threats.) In solidarity with the striking union, the AFL-CIO called for what became a decade-long national boycott, and was later joined by the National Education Association and various minority groups—Coors reportedly had few blacks, Hispanics, or women on its payroll. Coors bashing took on the proportions of a national sport. (p. 49)

With a new generation of the Coors family assuming the helm in 1984, led by CEO Peter H. Coors, came the realization that the various minorities represented by the boycotting groups were important segments of the growing Coors market (Hicks, 1985). So in 1984 the company agreed to spend an estimated $325 million over a five-year period to recruit more black employees, to increase promotional opportunities for black workers, and to place black executives in positions to formulate corporate policy. The company also agreed to increase the number of black suppliers and vendors, as well as the number of black-owned distributorships across the nation (Fowler, 1984).

The Coors commitment to the black community was established under the threat of an NAACP boycott. Indeed, soon after the commitment was announced, the Los Angeles chapter of the NAACP issued a statement saying that it was canceling its planned boycott of Coors.

The NAACP emphasis on securing corporate agreements that address the needs of the African American community was given a temporary boost with the appointment of the Reverend Benjamin J. Chavis as NAACP executive director in 1992. Long known as a civil rights activist, Chavis was widely seen as a radical departure from the traditional NAACP operational style with its emphasis on legal and judicial approaches to contemporary black problems. Under Chavis's leadership the NAACP was expected to move even more aggressively toward the realization of more so-called fair-share agreements with American corporations. The past rewards had been substantial with an estimated $47 billion in benefits secured by the African American community from fair-share agreements signed between 1986 and 1990 (Sims, 1993). However, with the recent dismissal of Chavis by the NAACP board and the organization's internal movement for new leadership and stability now being pursued under Executive Director Kweisi Mfume (Noble, 1997), it is difficult to say whether the aggressive policy of the NAACP relative to fair-share agreements will continue.

Future Prospects for African American Boycotts

The long history of black boycotts in the United States makes clear what an important role they have played in social protest movements in the last 100 years. From segregated streetcars in the South at the turn of the century to interracial skirmishes in neighborhood grocery stores in the 1990s, boycotts have served as a seemingly ever-ready instrument for African Americans to vent their frustrations with their often impoverished economic circumstances and, at times, to improve these circumstances by winning concessions from producers and retailers of consumer goods.[11] An earlier comment about boycott history in general would appear to apply even more aptly to the history of African American boycotts in particular:

> If there is a generalization to be drawn from these various cases, it is that boycotts . . . have offered an opportunity for the unorganized and the powerless to dramatize their problems and apply pocketbook pressure in an effort to alleviate them. (Friedman, 1985, p. 113)

Are these efforts likely to increase markedly in the future? The answer would appear to be yes for local issues and no for national issues. As just indicated, the national efforts by the NAACP for corporate fair-share agreements may or may not continue, and if they do, they are likely to proceed with infrequent uses of boycotts simply because they are less likely to be needed at this level. The principals in these instances are large, well-informed organizations used to proceeding with negotiations in a businesslike manner. All the cards are on the table, so to speak, and the opponents are skilled professionals who play the game by the rules. Both sides know that a boycott could be called by the protest group if no concessions are made. Both sides know, too, that with some 70 major corporations having already signed fair-share agreements, it is no longer a sign of defeat or weakness for a company to join their ranks. And finally, both sides know that the agreement can have a positive effect on a company's bottom line by broadening the base of minority support for its products and services. Thus, while the threat of a boycott will continue to underlie negotiations for fair-share agreements, it seems unlikely that the threat will trigger a wave of boycott campaigns.

Looking next at local issues and in particular at urban ghetto boycotts of small retailers, we find a far more potentially explosive situation. Instead of an NAACP representative calmly negotiating with his or her corporate counterpart, we have what may well be an angry crowd of the unemployed and the dispossessed shouting at an Asian American store clerk or manager for exhibiting behavior that appears insensitive to them. Under the circumstances it should come as no surprise if the store worker shouts back or attempts to evict the protesters from the premises. Though the two principals differ in language and culture, they share the frustrations of inner-city life—a low-wage existence for the one and a low-wage or no-wage existence for the other—with both ever mindful of the threats of danger seemingly lurking around every corner.

Under such conditions tempers will sometimes flare, and the responses of customers and store clerks may well exacerbate rather than calm a tense situation. Since escape from the often hostile conditions of the inner-city ghetto does not seem likely for most African American consumers and many Asian American business people in the near future, the emotional eruptions of the past appear likely to recur, and the boycott is a natural vehicle for the offended to express their feelings and to seek redress of their grievances. So it seems likely that urban boycotts will continue and maybe even increase in number.

Many of the boycotts that are called, however, may not be executed simply because their initiators lack the wherewithal to do so. Without economic resources or organizational experience, those who call for a boycott may not find a willing audience to join them in mounting a viable campaign.

·6·
BOYCOTT INITIATIVES OF OTHER MINORITY GROUPS

As indicated in Chapter 5, many minority groups have initiated consumer boycotts in the United States. While African Americans have been more active in this regard than other minority groups, the others have stories to tell as well. In this chapter we focus on several of these groups and their boycott efforts.

American Jews

Throughout history Jews have been participants in consumer boycotts both as initiators and targets. As targets in Germany and eastern Europe for more than a century, Jewish merchants and professionals were often subjected to harsh consumer boycotts. More recently, the Arab boycott, while focused on the state of Israel rather than on individual businesses, affected mostly Jewish businesses by depriving them of sales.

As initiators of consumer boycotts American Jews have concentrated primarily on international issues. To illustrate, the political actions of the French and Mexican governments prompted boycotts in the 1970s. These political actions and the boycotts they triggered, however, are minor footnotes to the historical record compared to the almost decade-long anti-Nazi campaign of American Jewry and, indeed, world Jewry, in response to the devastating anti-Jewish actions of Hitler's Nazi Party after its election victory in 1933. The boycott continued as a full-blown campaign under American leadership until the onset of World War II.

The Anti-Nazi Boycott

As Gottlieb (1967, 1968, 1973, 1983) has noted in very thorough accounts of the anti-Nazi protest in the American Jewish community, anti-Jewish outbreaks started in Essen three days after the Nazis were elected on March 5. Ironically, they took the form of highly repressive boycotts (as well as buycotts):

> Several Jewish stores were shut down "voluntarily" after swastika flags had been raised over their doors and windows by specially assigned S.S. squads. This done, the erstwhile brownshirted street fighters proceeded to the second part of their mission, which called for the stationing of S.S. pickets in front of Jewish establishments and shouting to the passerby the "patriotic" cry of "Buy in German shops."
>
> The episode was repeated the following day in Magdeburg, Kassel and Berlin. Bands of uniformed Nazi Storm Troopers, organized into agitating shouting choruses, assembled in front of some of the larger department stores in these cities and coerced the gathering mobs to buy "in German, not Jewish stores." Some of these establishments, which included American chain stores, were able only to admit and let out customers by back doors, while others had to close altogether because stench bombs had been set off in them. (Gottlieb, 1967, pp. 9–10)

As a reaction to the anti-Jewish rhetoric of the new Nazi regime and the occurrence of these boycott actions only days after the election, a spontaneous movement began to arise primarily in the United States and England to boycott German goods.[1] In response to this fledgling movement the Nazis called for an all-day boycott on April 1 of Jewish businesses in all of Germany.[2] On this day, according to a Nazi spokesman, "Not a German man nor a German woman shall enter a Jewish store.

Jewish trade throughout Germany must remain paralyzed" (Gottlieb, 1967, p. 25).

While the anti-Nazi boycott movement was strongest by far in the United States, Jewish communities in many other countries participated as well. Included here were England, France, Romania, Greece, Latvia, Yugoslavia, Egypt, Palestine, Morocco, and several South American nations. Perhaps the leading non-American participant was England, and its active involvement led to the virtual cessation of fur trade between England and Germany (Gottlieb, 1967).

Although far more active than any other country in the anti-Nazi boycott effort, the United States was unable to form a united boycott front either among Americans in general or among American Jews in particular. Many groups took stands but they were unwilling to work together in a single organizational effort under a common leader. Indeed, not only did they not work together effectively, some refused to even support the boycott.

These differing positions, according to Orbach (1982), stemmed from the "vigorous controversy within the American Jewish community as to the mode of response to the Nazi persecutions, with the American Jewish Committee and the B'nai B'rith favoring quiet, diplomatic pressure and the American Jewish Congress favoring open protests" (p. 151).[3]

Boycott Pros and Cons
The boycott proponents and opponents looked to different sources of inspiration and legitimacy to support their positions. The boycott leaders looked to American history with one, William Jay Schieffelin, chairman of the Volunteer Christian Committee to Boycott Nazi Germany, declaring on January 9, 1939, "The [boycott] movement is in the oldest American tradition. Long before the word boycott was used our forefathers made great sacrifices in enforcing a general embargo against trade with Great Britain" (Gottlieb, 1973, p. 221). Still other proponents pointed to the need for Jews to see the boycott as a self-affirming opportunity to express their desire for self-respect by "doing something," even if futile, in the face of adversity rather than watching passively from the sidelines (Orbach, 1982). And

finally, of course, many of the proponents appeared to believe that this "something" they were doing would succeed in improving conditions for German Jews.

The boycott opponents drew upon several major arguments to support their position. Among them was the argument of the traditionalists that the boycott was a "coarse and uncivilized weapon" that is inappropriate for Jews to employ.[4] The point here is that the boycott is "un-Jewish"—a crude, uncultured, unethical sledgehammer of an approach that "is contrary to what Judaism stands for" (Orbach, 1982, p. 154). A second, more pragmatic argument concerned the potentially adverse effects of the boycott on American Jews as well as German Jews. On the domestic side the fear was that if Jews became too visible in an aggressive international campaign their actions might awaken the "sleeping dragon of anti-Semitism" in the United States.[5] On the overseas side there was the greater fear, expressed in an American Jewish Committee position statement, that an anti-Nazi boycott would engender retaliation in the form of intensified persecution of Jews in Germany. As one of the committee's officials, Judge Irving Lehman, said in arguing against support of the boycott, "I implore you in the name of humanity, don't let anger pass a resolution which will kill Jews in Germany" (Gottlieb, 1968, p. 523). Finally, there were those who believed that the boycott would simply not succeed since the Jews were too disorganized and divided to mount an effective campaign (Orbach, 1982).

Boycott Organizations

The first American group to declare a boycott was the Jewish War Veterans in March 1933. They were soon followed in May by the American League for the Defense of Jewish Rights (ALDJR), an organization newly founded by a Yiddish journalist. In a move to broaden the base of boycott support beyond its Jewish base, the ALDJR later changed its name to the Non-Sectarian Anti-Nazi League to Champion Human Rights (ANL). Next came the American Jewish Congress (AJC) in the summer of 1933; it not only declared a boycott but also established the Boycott Committee. And then in October, a major non-Jewish group, the American Federation of Labor (AFL), declared itself in favor of the boycott. Yet another non-Jewish group joined the effort much later when, in 1939, 60 prominent Americans formed the Volunteer Christian Committee.

Still another antiboycott organization formed in 1934 when the Jewish Labor Committee was established claiming to represent some half million Jewish workers. Just two years later the committee's central unit for boycott actions entered into partnership with the AJC's Boycott Committee to form the Joint Boycott Council (JBC). The JBC and the ANL became the leading American boycott organizations; the other boycott groups, such as the Jewish War Veterans, entered into cooperative relationships with these two organizations.[6]

The leaders of the two groups soon became influential on the international scene. For example, JBC chairman Joseph Tenebaum secured passage of a boycott resolution in 1936 at the World Jewish Congress. In the same year ANL leader Abraham Coralnik and his successor, Samuel Untermeyer, organized the World Jewish Economic Conference in Holland to coordinate what had become an international boycott movement and to help identify non-German sources of goods that could serve as substitutes for merchants participating in the boycott.[7]

Boycott Tactics

According to Gottlieb (1967), in the early days of the boycott the JBC and the ANL used a mix of tactics with no single approach differentiating one organization from the other. By 1934, the situation had changed with the more militant JBC having adopted picketing as a distinguishing approach. Used primarily as a retaliatory action against recalcitrant boycott violators, picketing also served as a deterrent against future offenses.[8]

What prompted the JBC to turn to picketing as a primary tactic? In its initial campaign the JBC learned what establishment black leaders had learned before them in their efforts to seek employment for those who had lost their jobs during the Great Depression: "Letters and committees sent to [businesses] are ineffectual. Firms are used to them and ignore them" (Gottlieb, 1967, p. 273).

The point was made dramatically clear when a young group of picketers achieved success against a Bronx, New York branch of the Kresge department store chain, which previously had not replied to letters sent to it asking that it stop importing German merchandise to sell to its customers. That the picketing made a difference is apparent from the group's account of its activities:

> But when two Jewish girls were placed in front of their stores wearing picket signs reading "For Humanity's sake, do not buy Nazi-made merchandise—this store continues to sell German goods," we could see how many people who were ready to enter the store refused to do so upon seeing the signs which the pickets wore. (Gottlieb, 1967, p. 274)

If a business reneged on its promise not to deal in German goods the boycotters sometimes went beyond picketing to more militant actions. A case in point was a needleworks business in New York whose Jewish owner had agreed not to handle German merchandise. When the owner was discovered to have violated the agreement by buying thousands of dollars worth of German goods, the JBC took action. First, the local JBC leader set up picket lines for two weeks in front of the owner's businesses. Second, as a further act of humiliation, the JBC leader had the offending owner's home picketed so his neighbors were made aware of his boycott violations. Third, having learned where the owner worshiped, the local JBC leader sent a passionate letter to the president of the synagogue, which began with a discussion of the boycott and its special significance to Jews. The letter noted that in similar circumstances, members of congregations had been expelled for dealing in German goods. The letter ended with the request that the synagogue's decision relating to the future status of the owner be communicated to the boycott group.

How did the boycott-defying owner of the needleworks business respond to all this pressure? According to Gottlieb (1967), his initial response was outrage. He declared that he would not be intimidated, nor would he be told how to operate his business. But in the end he yielded to the boycotters and stopped buying German goods.

Boycott Success

As the Nazi actions in Europe became more devastating, public opinion began to show increasing support for the boycott. By

April 1939 a Gallup survey revealed that 65 percent of the American people agreed "to join a movement to stop buying German-made goods" (Gottlieb, 1967, p. 338). And this figure had shown an increase from two earlier periods (56 percent in October 1938 and 61 percent in December 1938).

Major retailers in the United States also yielded to the boycott pressure. Among their ranks were such New York giants as Macys and Gimbels; also included were national chains such as Woolworth, Kresge, and Sears and Roebuck. German data also suggest an impact of the boycott on U.S. trade with Germany. In a memo prepared for Hitler by the Economic Policy Department of the German government on November 18, 1938, the value of imports from the United States in millions of Reichmarks is as follows: 1,729 in 1929, 592 in 1932, and 282 in 1937. The corresponding values for exports to the United States are as follows: 991 in 1929, 281 in 1932, and 209 in 1937 (Gottlieb, 1967).

Hitler himself on several occasions also conceded that the boycott was harming German economic interests. His most dramatic revelation came on April 28, 1939, in an address to the Reichstag. In responding to President Roosevelt's stated readiness to improve international trade relations, the German leader declared:

> It is likewise an unbearable burden for world economic relations that it should be possible in some countries for some ideological reason or other to let loose a wild boycott of agitation against other countries and their goods and so practically to eliminate them from the market.
>
> It is my belief, Mr. Roosevelt, that it would be a great service if you, with your great influence, would remove these barriers genuinely to free world trade beginning with the United States. For it is my conviction that if the leaders of nations are not even capable of regulating production in their own countries or of removing boycotts pursued for ideological reasons which can damage trade relations between countries to so great an extent, there is much less prospect of achieving by means of international agreements any really fruitful step toward improvement of economic relations. (Gottlieb, 1967, p. 441)

Ironically, this powerful view of the boycott was at variance with what many Jewish leaders saw as a tactic with rather limited influence, but one that had to be employed anyway for moral reasons. Rabbi Stephen S. Wise expressed these sentiments eloquently in February 1934:

> I have never for a moment held that the boycott is the solution of the problem of Hitlerism. Too many complicated and profound issues are involved in the Hitler revolt against civilization to permit any sane man to imagine that a simple device such as an economic boycott can solve that vast complex of problems. . . . I must say that my faith in the common people, if it could be deepened, has been deepened by the rightness of the mass reaction to Hitlerism primarily among the Jews, secondarily among all people. . . . We would not if we could, and we could not if we would, wield any weapon against Germany, but we cannot with self-respect continue to have dealings with that country which has decided we are outside the pale of decency.
>
> As a pacifist, I was hesitant about the boycott because it is an economic weapon, although from the beginning I believed and I still believe that its moral value is larger than its economic value. It was only after I heard from fellow Jews in other lands, in July and August, 1933, how deadly was the hurt inflicted upon Jews by Nazi Germany and that all the Jewish masses could do to express their disapproval was to boycott German goods and services that I felt it was our duty to join in the boycott. (Gottlieb, 1967, pp. 441–442)

We end this discussion of the anti-Nazi campaign by noting that the boycott may have succeeded more in its value-expressive goals than in its instrumental goals. Surely, as Wise observes, the boycott provided an opportunity for American Jews and others to express their sense of moral indignation and outrage at the actions of the Nazis. Surely, too, the boycott instrumentally was only a thorn, rather than a spear, in Hitler's side, in that it did not stop him from committing unspeakable acts of violence and brutality against humanity.

The Mexico Tourism Boycott of the Mid-1970s

American Jews initiated boycotts in the 1970s on international issues with events in Europe triggering two of the boycotts and a vote by Mexico in the United Nations prompting a third. Of the three boycotts, the Mexico action received the most attention and the largest grassroots participation by Jewish Americans.

Extensive news media reports of the boycott and its origins by Welles (1976) and, to a lesser extent, by Meisler (1975) provide a fairly complete story of what happened. The precipitating event occurred on November 10, 1975, when the United Nations General Assembly passed a resolution (72 in favor, 35 opposed, and 32 abstentions) equating Zionism with racism and racial discrimination. While passage of the resolution was not unexpected, the vote by Mexico in favor stunned many observers since Mexico had been an Israeli trading partner and longtime supporter.[9] Moreover, Mexico was not only home to a substantial and prosperous Jewish population but also a major tourist destination for hundreds of thousands of Jewish Americans.

Some observers believe that the UN vote represented a miscalculation by then-Mexican President Luis Echeverria, who was approaching the end of a seven-year nonrenewable term and seeking a leadership role on the international stage as a spokesperson for the nonaligned Third World nations (Welles, 1976). According to this reasoning Echeverria believed that a vote in favor of the UN resolution would demonstrate his independence of the United States and Israel as well as his allegiance to the values of the developing nations of the world. Welles (1976) noted that intimates of Echeverria believed that he was desirous of succeeding Kurt Waldheim as UN secretary-general or, should this not be possible, of becoming the head of some Third World organization. That the UN vote was a miscalculation became evident almost immediately after it was taken and, as Meisler (1975) observed, it is doubtful that Echeverria foresaw the magnitude of the reaction or its consequences.

According to Welles (1976), the response by American Jews to the Mexican vote was swift. The State Department reported that its phone lines were inundated with calls all day from "little people" all over the United States who swore they would never visit Mexico again. Also flooded with calls and mail were the Mexican Embassy and Mexican consulates around the country. The headquarters of American Jewish organizations were bombarded with calls; the B'nai B'rith's Anti-Defamation League reported that its switchboard was ablaze with lights. Moreover, in New York thousands of protesters demonstrated outside the United Nations headquarters.

As Welles (1976) observed, this was a grassroots protest with no central direction from the national Jewish American organizations. Moreover, what ensued next was a startling reversal of the usual pattern of organizational action in that the followers led and the leaders followed. And they followed with dramatic and forceful actions. The American Jewish Congress, which each year organized tours for some 15,000 members, canceled 22 15-day tours to Mexico for 1976. The B'nai B'rith dropped 20 for 1976 and 7 scheduled for 1975. Other Jewish American organizations which also responded vigorously by dropping scheduled tours to Mexico included the Jewish War Veterans, the Union of Hebrew Organizations, and the National Council of Jewish Women.

According to Meisler (1975), the first reaction of Mexican officials to the boycott initiative was one of bravado; the officials claimed they were "unconcerned and unintimidated." However, the response quickly changed when the full import of the boycott began to be appreciated. One indication of the damage being done came from the Mexico Hotel Association, which reported 30,000 cancellations in one week.

In retrospect, it should not have been unexpected that Mexico was selected as the boycott target rather than another one of the nations voting in favor of the UN resolution. Tourism, especially American tourism, accounted for 14 percent of foreign exchange earnings for Mexico in 1974 and was thus a major force in decreasing the $3.2 billion trade deficit in that year. To cope with this deficit Mexico needed a steady stream of American tourists.

And while Jewish Americans made up less than 3 percent of the U.S. population, their contribution to foreign travel to Mexican destinations far exceeded 3 percent. To illustrate, the most profitable tourist time for Mexico annually is the six-week

Christmas season. According to tourism officials in Mexico, most of these visitors are Jews, many of whom are traveling on tours arranged by the American Jewish Congress, the B'nai B'rith, and other Jewish American groups (Welles, 1976).

When the adverse effects of the boycott on Mexican tourism became apparent to President Echeverria he moved promptly to control damage by sending envoys on diplomatic missions to Israel and the United States. After a series of meetings with government officials and Jewish leaders the boycott was called off in 1976. A critical point in these communications was an interview in late May 1976 in which Echeverria conceded to the president of the B'nai B'rith that "Mexico should not have voted the way it did last November 10." After the boycott ended, tours to Mexico resumed under the auspices of American Jewish organizations.

Boycotts Triggered by European Events in the 1970s

European events led to Jewish American boycotts in 1970 and 1977. In 1970 Jewish groups boycotted performances of the Passion Play that was being staged in Oberammergau, Germany. The play, which was being performed for the 36th time since 1633, was believed by the boycotters to contain anti-Semitic passages. As a result, numerous block bookings were canceled by Americans, and a protest by the B'nai B'rith and the Jewish Defense League caused Luftansa, the national German airline, to cease its advertising of special Passion Play-related tours. Despite these efforts of the boycotters, the play was a sellout, with about 1.5 million requests for the 520,000 seats available over the course of the season's performances.

In 1977, an international travel boycott of France was called by American Jews and non-Jews to protest the French government's "indefensible, morally repugnant action" in releasing from custody the Palestinian leader Abu Daoud. Daoud was suspected of having planned the murderous attack on Israeli athletes at the 1972 Olympic Games in Munich. The American Jewish Congress announced that its members were canceling their travel programs with France. Support from non-Jewish Americans took the form of a resolution by 29 congressmen urging Americans to boycott French goods. This congressional action was led by then-Speaker of the House Thomas ("Tip") O'Neill; also expressing dismay at the French action were the Senate Foreign Relations Committee, the State Department, and then-President Elect Jimmy Carter.

Concluding Comments on Jewish American Boycotts

As noted earlier, Jewish American boycotts have dealt almost exclusively with international issues. Be it the actions of the Germans, the French, or the Mexicans, American Jews (and in some cases non-Jews as well) responded with deliberate attacks on businesses in these countries. These boycotts were surrogate in nature and often punitive as well in that they were usually designed to have a punishing effect on businesses in the targeted countries, even though the businesses may have been "innocent stand-ins" in that they had not participated in the offensive actions that triggered the boycott initiatives. Also noteworthy is the range of militancy expressed by the American Jewish organizations, with the Jewish War Veterans representing the far left (the first to declare a boycott against the Nazis and the last to call a halt to the boycott against the Mexicans), and a variety of others, such as the American Jewish Committee, representing the far right (this organization never joined the anti-Nazi boycott).

Finally, the absence of domestic issues prompting Jewish American boycotts is worthy of comment. This circumstance, which stands in sharp contrast to the situation over the years for African Americans, suggests that domestic conditions for American Jews, while perhaps not ideal, have been largely free of gross anti-Semitic behaviors, or sufficiently so to obviate such drastic actions as consumer boycotts.

Other Minority Groups

While it seems clear that African Americans and American Jews have made very extensive use of the boycott initiative in the twentieth century, other minority groups have employed the boycott initiative as well. In what follows we examine some of the more noteworthy of these efforts.

Italian Americans and *The Untouchables*

Negative images of minority groups on television shows are a frequent concern of the leaders of these groups, as Kathryn Montgomery has documented in her excellent historical study of network television's relations with minority groups (Montgomery, 1989). Among the early examples is the case of *The Untouchables*, a popular 1960s cops-and-robbers show set in the Roaring Twenties. Since the gangsters featured in this ABC network show often had Italian surnames, *The Untouchables* soon incurred the wrath of many Italian American groups. Prominent among them was the Federation of the Italian American Democratic Organizations of the State of New York, a group whose board of directors included three U.S. congressmen. According to Montgomery (1989), this group initiated a boycott against Liggett & Myers, the show's regular sponsor. The federation's boycott activities went far beyond issuing press releases: The group distributed some 250,000 posters to stores across the United States and apparently persuaded some 2,000 vending machine owners to stop stocking L&M cigarettes.

The boycott's impact was immediate and dramatic. Not only did Liggett & Myers stop sponsoring *The Untouchables*, but its producer, Desi Arnaz, together with concerned ABC executives, met with federation leaders to iron out a compromise (Montgomery, 1989). The compromise consisted of a new show policy banning the use of fictional characters with Italian names in the roles of hoodlums. Furthermore, the television executives agreed to balance the negative portrayals of Italian Americans with positive ones.

At least one prominent television critic (Jack Gould of the *New York Times*) found the television executives' action to be disturbing. Gould (1961) noted, "An outside group not professionally engaged in theater production has succeeded in imposing its will with respect to the naming of fictional characters, altering the importance of a leading characterization and in other particulars changing the story line" (p. 17). Gould worried that these concessions did not bode well for the autonomy of the television industry.

From the boycotter's perspective, however, the actions of the sponsor, the network, and the show's producer constituted a clear victory. And significantly, the victory was effected by the industry simply by fashioning a few changes in the hit television show's characters and plot which, according to Montgomery (1989), "were hardly noticeable to the show's general viewership." Not surprisingly, such industry concessions became more frequent in the years that followed.

Mexican Americans and *Nichols*

Some 10 years after the successful *Untouchables*-stimulated boycott by Italian Americans, Mexican Americans found themselves in a similar situation that prompted a boycott initiative. The organization responsible for the boycott was Justicia, one of several Mexican American groups active in media reform efforts in the late 1960s and early 1970s (Montgomery, 1989). One early success of these groups was the dropping of "Frito Bandito" by the Frito-Lay Company from its Fritos Corn Chips commercials. (Frito Bandito was the naughty Chicano cartoon character who "stole" the Frito Corn Chips in the commercials.) Another success was the purging from prime time of "Jose Jimenez," the pleasant but not-too-bright Hispanic character created by comedian Bill Dana with the signature line, "My name, Jose Jimenez." This line became familiar to millions of viewers of television variety shows (Montgomery, 1989).

Justicia, a small Latino community group with a storefront headquarters in East Los Angeles, had decided to concentrate its energies on prime-time television. The organization's location was ideal because the major production studios and the network's West Coast offices were only a few miles away. Also helpful was the pool of young dedicated Latino activists that Justicia drew to its ranks from local colleges and from the East L.A. community (Montgomery, 1989).

The Justicia-called boycott started when it heard about *Nichols*, an NBC series being developed that was set in the Southwest at the turn of the century. Since Mexican Americans were heavily represented in the Southwest population at that time, Justicia pressed NBC to incorporate a Latino in the show as a lead character. When this demand (as well as others) was rejected, Justicia decided to wait until the show had aired to see who the sponsors were so that Justicia could take action against them (Montgomery, 1989).

Upon learning that one of the sponsors was Chevrolet, Justicia complained to the automaker, but to no avail. So Justicia decided to boycott local Chevy dealers. According to Justicia President Ray Andrade, the boycott option seemed to make sense since it had been used successfully by Cesar Chavez against the California produce growers. However, since Justicia had very limited resources at its disposal, a national or state boycott was out of the question. The alternative, as the group's leaders saw it, was a local action. When Andrade noticed that many local Latinos were driving Chevys he decided to organize a boycott with picket lines at three Chevrolet dealerships in East L.A. The dealers responded by calling the headquarters for General Motors, which in turn called network executives, who arranged a meeting with Justicia at its storefront headquarters. Although the meeting failed to change the show's script, Montgomery (1989) found that it made a strong impression on the network executives.

That impression may well have set the stage for more responsive network programming decisions relating to Mexican Americans in the years ahead. Moreover, the negative immediate reaction to the Justicia boycott, according to Montgomery (1989), seems to be typical of punitive sponsor boycotts called after a show is aired in that by then "it was too late for a boycott" (p. 152).

Chinese Americans and Opium Perfume

When Yves Saint Laurent and its parent company, the Squibb Corporation, introduced Opium perfume in the 1970s, it quickly became one of the nation's best-selling fragrances. However, not all of the consumer reaction was positive. Indeed, an *ad hoc* committee of Chinese Americans quickly formed and demanded a change of name for the perfume and a public apology from Saint Laurent for "his insensitivity to Chinese history and Chinese American concerns" (Nemy, 1979). The *ad hoc* group, called the American Coalition Against "Opium" and Drug Abuse, expressed outrage at the choice of a name representing "a menace that destroyed many lives in China." Also upsetting to the coalition were the promotional materials for the fragrance featuring, as one coalition member put it, pictures of "a beautiful Caucasian woman obviously zonked out—in another world—amid a tracery of leaves strongly resembling cannabis" (Nemy, 1979).

At a planning meeting held on May 4, 1979, the coalition members considered several dramatic actions to highlight their concerns, including a funeral march demonstration to underscore the destructive powers of opium and a consumer boycott of Squibb and Yves Saint Laurent products. To underscore the boycott threat some coalition members attending the meeting wore buttons reading "Kill 'Opium', Boycott Squibb." The coalition and its boycott threat received welcome publicity when a sympathetic article with a large picture of the boycott button appeared in the *New York Times* (Nemy, 1979).

The threat of a boycott (indeed, some who looked superficially at the *Times* article with its prominent picture of the boycott button may have concluded that a boycott was not just threatened but actually under way) and the unfavorable publicity were apparently too much for Squibb; it decided to retain the Opium name but to tone down the "zonked-out" ads. The coalition concluded that this corporate action signified a partial success for its campaign.

Native Americans and Crazy Horse Malt Liquor

In March 1992 the Hornell Brewing Co. introduced Crazy Horse Malt Liquor as part of its new theme celebrating the American West and its traditions. Rather than produce the new malt liquor itself, Hornell decided to contract with G. Heileman Co., a major national brewer, to handle production.

Not surprisingly, many Native Americans took offense at the introduction of this product, which "demeans the name of revered Oglala Lakota Leader Tashunke Witco [Crazy Horse]." This statement reflects the feelings of the American Indian Movement (AIM) as well as two other organizations (the Wisconsin Greens and Honor, Inc.) that called for a boycott of the two brewers. Indeed, the Wisconsin Greens likened the Hornell action to naming a beer "Martin Luther King," an initiative they believed would be roundly condemned by African Americans and other

Americans. The Wisconsin Greens expressed their outrage with the Hornell action by picketing Hornell headquarters as well as its retail units.

According to Lyons (1995), former U.S. Surgeon General Antonia Novello denounced the new malt liquor as did leaders of the Oglala Sioux Tribe, who referred to it as a "slap in the face to the Native American people." A particular concern is the insensitivity to the pervasive alcohol problems of Native Americans, who suffer from the highest rate of alcoholism in the United States. A parallel concern is that Chief Crazy Horse was said to have adamantly opposed the consumption of alcohol among his people.

The boycott is supported by numerous Native American groups, human rights organizations, and members of Congress (Lyons, 1995). However, the beverage is now sold in some 40 states, and there is no evidence that the boycott has affected the corporate sales or image of either Hornell or G. Heileman.

Gay-Rights Boycotts

Gays and their supporters have been actively engaged in consumer boycotts, especially in the 1990s. Some of these have been surrogate boycotts because the parties that offended the gay groups were not directly reachable through marketplace actions.

The Philip Morris Boycott

This surrogate boycott, called in the early 1990s, was undertaken by the AIDS Coalition to Unleash Power (ACT UP) against the Philip Morris Company (Miller beer and Marlboro cigarettes) in the 1990s. While Philip Morris was the target, the party that offended ACT UP was U.S. Senator Jesse Helms of North Carolina, who has frequently taken public stands condemning homosexuality. Not only had Philip Morris contributed to Helms's campaigns, but it had also donated money to the Jesse Helms Museum (Lyons, 1991).

ACT UP lived up to its name with the tactics it used in its boycott campaign. For example, it reportedly dumped 15 cases of Miller beer into the gutter of a Washington, D.C., street in front of a popular bar. Six activists also unlawfully entered and demonstrated in Helms's Senate office; they were arrested and received six-month prison sentences and $500 fines (O'Neil, 1990).

Philip Morris responded to the boycott campaign by acknowledging that it had supported Helms but denying that this support meant that it agreed with Helms's stance on human rights issues. To illustrate their disagreement Philip Morris revealed that it had given generously to support many gay concerns and activities, including the Gay Games, the San Francisco Lesbian and Gay Freedom Day Parade, and many AIDS-related projects around the country.

The boycott ended as a partial success for ACT UP in June 1991. While Philip Morris announced that it planned to continue supporting Senator Helms through political contributions to his campaign, the company also made clear that it did not agree with his positions relating to homosexuality. Furthermore, Philip Morris pledged contributions of more than $2 million annually to gay and AIDS organizations.

The Colorado Boycott

In November 1992 Colorado voters approved an amendment to the state's constitution that overturned local laws banning discrimination against gays and lesbians. The reaction of national gay-rights organizations was swift and dramatic. They called for a boycott by convention delegates and independent travelers. Soon thereafter many groups signed on, including the National Organization for Women, the National Council for the Social Studies, the U.S. Conference of Mayors, along with municipal workers from Atlanta and Philadelphia (Wright, 1993).

Sen (1996) has written a case study of the boycott from a marketing perspective, and the following description of the boycott draws extensively from his report. At the outset it should be noted that although several groups participated in the boycott, the most prominent was Boycott Colorado. This organization, which was formed by gay-rights activists, initiated a call for a boycott just one day after the passage of the amendment. Although Boycott Colorado focused primarily on discouraging travel to Colorado, a second group, New York Boycott Colorado (NYBC), encouraged consumers not to buy goods produced by Colorado businesses, such as Celestial Seasonings, Coors, and Samsonite Luggage. While the Colorado boycotts had several objectives, a first priority was "to provide a visible deterrent to the institution of antigay civil rights initiatives in other cities and states of the United States" (Anderson, 1993, p. A12).

In just a few months a major boycott initiative was under way. And according to Sen (1996), it drew widespread support from many mainstream organizations. More than 100 official participants were identified by Boycott Colorado in 1993, including national educational, legal, political, and religious organizations; colleges and universities; companies and business associations; and entertainment celebrities.

Specific actions included cancellation of meetings and conventions by such national associations as the American Association of Law Libraries (which would have brought 5,000 people); the banning of official travel to Colorado by government workers in New York City and Los Angeles; the halting of production of a television miniseries; and the relocation of the NBC hit television series *Frasier* to Seattle from Denver.

The effect of these actions (as well as countless others) on Colorado was significant. According to Greenhouse (1995), the state determined that it had lost approximately $40 million in convention and tourism business. Denver was especially hard hit, having lost more than $30 million because of canceled conventions (Sahagun, 1995). Damage to the state's image was also considerable. According to Caudron (1993), more than 4,000 news items appeared in U.S. news media outlets within two months of the Colorado vote, and many of the items were negative. Indeed, some referred to Colorado as the "Hate State."

The Boycott Colorado campaign was suspended in late 1994 when the Colorado Supreme Court ruled that the amendment was unconstitutional. Like the Montgomery, Alabama, bus boycott led by Martin Luther King, it was a court decision that undid the offensive government action that a boycott had attempted to defy; however, in both instances a well-publicized groundswell of boycott support may have influenced the judicial decision.

The Cracker Barrel Campaign

While, as we have seen, gay-rights groups have often used surrogate boycotts to further their interests, nonsurrogate boycotts have also played a role. Perhaps the most publicized instance of such an initiative is the boycott called by the Tennessee Gay and Lesbian Alliance and the Queer Nation in 1991. This boycott, which was directed at the Cracker Barrel restaurant chain, was prompted by the firing of some gay and lesbian employees after the company issued a statement saying that Cracker Barrel would not hire employees "whose sexual preferences fail to demonstrate normal, heterosexual values."

The boycott leaders demanded an end to the antigay policy and the reinstatement of the fired employees with restitution of lost wages. They also demanded an apology to the gay and lesbian community (Zorc, 1991). Well-organized, well-attended demonstrations were held in front of Cracker Barrel restaurants, often on Sundays to affect brunch and lunch customers coming to dine after attending church. In addition, the boycotters engaged in what might be called "slow-down sit-ins"; large numbers of individual protesters entered the restaurants as "customers," filled as many tables as possible, placed a minimal order (e.g., a cup of coffee), and remained at the tables as long as possible (usually two to three hours). Needless to say, slow-down sit-ins can devastate restaurant revenues, especially if undertaken, as these were, at busy times such as lunchtime or dinnertime.

While Cracker Barrel did not issue an apology to the boycotters, it did concede that it may have overreacted (Cunningham, 1992). It also claimed to be an equal-opportunity employer that adheres to the laws regarding nondiscrimination in the workplace and hires employees solely on the basis of their qualifications (Kilborn, 1992).

Since all of the boycotters' concerns have not been addressed by Cracker Barrel, the boycott continues under the auspices of Queer Nation Atlanta (Lyons, 1998a).

ACT UP Boycott of Glaxo Wellcome

Another gay-rights boycott of a nonsurrogate type concerns the pharmaceutical company Glaxo Wellcome Inc., which ACT UP Golden Gate claimed was withholding its new antiviral AIDS drug, Abacavir (1592), from the marketplace. In the past, ACT UP chapters have called for boycotts of firms that were perceived as being slow to distribute new antiviral drugs for use by AIDS patients who have failed to respond to other treatments.

ACT UP contends that near-death AIDS patients should be included in final-stage testing of the drugs because the patients often have no alternative. According to ACT UP Golden Gate, Glaxo Wellcome first refused to cooperate with its request but after the boycott was initiated the company changed its policy to include these patients (Lyons, 1998b).

Women's Rights Boycotts

When this writer mentioned to women colleagues of the baby boom generation that a section of this book would examine boycotts relating to women's rights, many of them said that the ERA boycott must be included. The reasons for their insistence are not hard to understand. These women had lived through the battle led by the National Organization for Women (NOW) to persuade state legislatures in the 1970s to ratify the proposed Equal Rights Amendment (ERA) and had been supportive of the NOW effort. But as we shall see shortly, some of the "women's rights issues" are contentious among women, and the failure of the ERA to be adopted makes clear that many women saw it as a "right" they would prefer not to have their government provide. A related issue that has prompted calls for boycotts from women (as well as men) from both sides concerns the right of a woman to have an abortion. To illustrate, *Maude*, a popular 1970s CBS sitcom with a 47-year-old, married, middle-class woman as the lead, ran a two-part show in which Maude becomes pregnant, wrestles with the pros and cons of an abortion, and finally decides in favor. Not surprisingly, antiabortion groups were very upset with CBS for airing the show, and church leaders called for a punitive boycott against the corporations that had sponsored the two episodes (Montgomery, 1989). Moreover, upon hearing that the show was going to be aired again as a summer rerun, pro-choice groups announced plans to boycott any corporate sponsors that yielded to antiabortion forces by withdrawing their support of the show (Montgomery, 1989).[10]

In addition to the ERA boycott, women's rights boycotts have been called objecting to depictions of women being subjected to violent treatment in advertising and in the content of literary and musical works. Let us look at these various boycotts in turn.

The ERA Boycott

While the proposed ERA had three sections, it was the first that engendered the most controversy. It simply stated that equality of rights under the law "shall not be denied or abridged by the United States or by any State on account of sex." But the implications of this simple statement were a far-reaching mandate for equal treatment affecting domestic relations law, including rules for marriage, divorce, and child custody; public education programs from preschool through college; government employment criteria and benefits; labor and criminal justice laws; and Social Security and government pension laws (Whitney, 1984).

In 1972 Congress approved the proposed ERA, and it was sent to the states with a seven-year deadline for ratification by a minimum of 38 state legislatures. In just one year 30 states ratified the proposed ERA, and victory appeared to be in in sight for its proponents. However, in the mid-70s opposition forces led by Phyllis Schlafly, a conservative Republican leader from Illinois, stopped the ERA forces in their tracks. Calling the ERA the "extra responsibility amendment," Schlafly argued that it would create new, burdensome responsibilities for women while giving them no new rights and taking away existing ones. She was quoted by Wohl (1974, p. 55) as asking, "Why should we lower ourselves to 'equal rights' when we already have the status of special privilege?" Included here, in her view, were state laws requiring husbands to support their wives and families and to provide them with a home.

The Schlafly message and the successful campaign that it triggered prompted NOW to reconsider its ERA strategy. So in 1977, after a series of close defeats in the legislatures of Florida, Illinois, North Carolina, and Virginia, NOW leader Eleanor Smeal announced that the organization was launching national boycotts against states that had not yet ratified the proposed ERA.

The ERA initiative is an excellent example of a surrogate boycott that was successful in execution, in that some 200 organizations voted to hold their meetings only in states that had ratified the ERA, but unsuccessful in consequences, in that not one of the boycotted states voted to ratify the proposed ERA. Among the organizations signing on to support NOW's boycott were the Democratic National Committee, the National Council of

Churches, the United Auto Workers, the American Psychological Association, and the National Education Association.

In addition to those, NOW collected pledge cards in 1980 from 60,000 individuals who agreed to forgo vacations in Florida until the state's lawmakers ratified the proposed ERA. The boycott pledge cards had been distributed by NOW members in all 50 states. NOW leaders in Florida asked two things of Americans: that they not enter Florida as a tourist, but if they did enter anyway, that they avoid major tourist attractions such as Disney World and Sea World (DeSimone, 1981). Despite this threat to the livelihood of its its tourist industry, the Florida legislature did not ratify the proposed amendment.

The impact of the NOW boycott effort on travel to the targeted states was most apparent in losses of convention business. For example, Chicago estimated as of September 1977 that $15 million had been lost in convention business, and the Kansas City, Missouri, estimate was $1.1 million. The combined losses in convention business to one grouping of major cities in the unratified states—Chicago, Kansas City, Las Vegas, Miami, Atlanta, and New Orleans—was more than $100 million (Berry, 1988).

Why did the boycott campaigns fail to win over the state legislators? According to Berry (1988), the boycotts may have had an economic effect on the cities, but they did little to win the support of the more conservative legislators in the rural areas. Still another view is that the boycotts were declared too late to make a difference because the momentum had turned strongly against the ERA proponents by 1977. Indeed, even a three-year extension that was granted by the Congress to the seven-year ratification effort failed to add a single state to the ratification side of the ledger.

The WAVAW Boycotts

Starting at the time of the ERA boycott, many of the boycotts involving women's rights groups in the last quarter century have been concerned with mass-media depictions of women as victims of violence, many of which appeared in advertising text and graphics. One of the first groups to use the boycott as a tactic to combat the practice was the California based Women Against Violence Against Women (WAVAW). The WAVAW effort, which began in 1976, first targeted Warner Communications (now Time Warner) for depicting violence against women in pictures that appeared on the covers of record albums produced by Warner subsidiaries (Electra, Warner and Atlantic Records).[11]

A precipitating event was the 1976 release of the Rolling Stones album *Black and Blue,* with an advertising campaign featuring a picture of a woman who was tied, bound, and gagged, along with the caption, "I'm black and blue all over from the Rolling Stones, and I love it."

While graphic depictions of violence toward women had appeared in a variety of industries, WAVAW decided, in light of its limited resources, to focus on a single industry. WAVAW's choice of the music industry reflected the findings of preliminary research by the organization that revealed literally dozens of examples of record album covers depicting violence toward women.

Using photographs of these materials, WAVAW produced a slide show in 1976 for the California NOW convention. At the suggestion of WAVAW member Julia London, who had been an organizer for the United Farm Workers (a group that, as we have already seen, was very active in boycotts of grape and lettuce growers), WAVAW called for a boycott at the NOW meeting, and the call was endorsed by the NOW members in attendance. The boycott focused on Warner because many of its album covers were objectionable to WAVAW and because it was the largest company in the industry.

Now that it had a target, WAVAW took its slide show to meetings of various groups, and immediately after it was presented, WAVAW members borrowed a page from the UFW handbook ("give them something to do") by encouraging the audience members to write letters to Warner. To help with this task WAVAW came prepared with paper, envelopes, and mailing addresses. The strategy was successful in getting an effective letter-writing campaign under way.

The slide shows were also occasions for recruiting new WAVAW members as well as starting new WAVAW chapters. The success of these organizational efforts soon became evident in that more than 20 chapters of WAVAW were formed by 1978.

In response to this "critical mass" as well as extensive news media coverage, especially television coverage of WAVAW-staged dramatic events on Los Angeles's Sunset Strip, Warner Communications agreed not to use images portraying violence against women in its advertising materials. In addition, Warner agreed to have WAVAW develop and implement an all-day sensitivity training program for Warner advertising executives on violence against women, a program that drew upon the WAVAW slide show.

The successful conclusion of the WAVAW boycott in late 1979 was widely covered in the feminist press as well as local Los Angeles newspapers.

NOW Boycott of Knopf

As indicated earlier, women's rights groups were concerned about violence against women not only in advertising material but also in the texts of creative works. This concern became amply clear in 1990 when the Los Angeles chapter of NOW (LA-NOW) called for a boycott of Alfred Knopf Inc., a subsidiary of Random House. What sparked the boycott was a decision by Knopf to publish *American Psycho*, a novel by Bret Easton Ellis containing many passages that very graphically portrayed violence against women.[12]

LA-NOW President Tammy Bruce said in an extensive interview in May 1993 that the boycott was both instrumental and punitive—it was designed to last for all of the 1991 calendar year unless the publisher agreed to drop the book from its commercial offerings (which it did not do). LA-NOW hoped to cause financial damage to Knopf and to make clear to the company that there would be a price to be paid for publishing similar offensive material in the future. LA-NOW also hoped that the boycott would stimulate a public debate on the issue of violence against women in fiction.

With regard to boycott strategy, Bruce made clear that LA-NOW did not ask bookstores to refuse to sell the book. LA-NOW did, however, ask bookstores not to feature the book in in-store displays, not to do local marketing for it, and not to place the book on lower store shelves (under 4 feet high) where it would be accessible to children. In addition, LA-NOW asked its members to (1) pass out informational leaflets in front of bookstores,

(2) send letters to Knopf and Random House protesting the publication of *American Psycho*, (3) mount a petition drive against the book, and (4) post fliers about the boycott at local colleges, universities, and high schools.

Bruce claimed that she tried to meet with Knopf executives concerning the boycott only to find her overtures rebuked. Indeed, she claimed that Knopf President Sonny Mehta was said to have declared that he would "rather set himself on fire than meet with her."

There are conflicting reports regarding the boycott effects. A Knopf spokesperson said in a telephone interview that *American Psycho* sold well. The spokesperson speculated that some consumers "may have bought the book because of the boycott," suggesting that the boycott was not simply unproductive but counterproductive. However, Bruce claimed that many bookstores complied with LA-NOW's request to limit access to the book. She also noted that Knopf had not published any book with as much violence against women after *American Psycho*. The boycott officially ended on Dec. 31, 1991, but Bruce said in a January 1994 interview that many LA-NOW members continued to boycott Knopf.

Concluding Comments on Minority Boycotts

Upon looking back at the boycott activities reviewed in the last two chapters we find that several observations appear to be in order.

First, boycotts have been a key instrument of protest for minority groups over the course of the twentieth century, from the streetcar initiatives of African Americans in the South at the turn of the century to the current gay-rights initiatives in support of AIDS victims to secure the early release of new medications. One is struck not only by the diversity of these efforts but also by their association with some of the principal public figures and events of the century. On the one hand, we have such celebrated champions of people's rights as Martin Luther King Jr. and Cesar Chavez, and, on the other hand, such infamous enemies of minority rights as Adolf Hitler. And the boycott concerns have ranged from image issues, such as the television depictions of minorities, to substantive issues, the most critical of which was the anti-Nazi campaign to save the lives of millions of European Jews by implementing what Hitler referred to as "a wild boycott of agitation" (Gottlieb, 1967, p. 44).

Second, the minority boycotts have assumed a wide variety of forms, including surrogate and nonsurrogate boycotts, instrumental and value-expressive boycotts, and punitive and nonpunitive boycotts, as well as marketplace-oriented and media-oriented boycotts. And we have seen changes in the types used over the course of the century with a rise in media-oriented boycotts associated with the increasing importance of the news media in the last few decades. As one WAVAW representative put it in discussing its late-1970s boycott of Warner Communications for its depictions of violence against women in advertisements, "It was clear to me that we were never going to show a dip in sales, but we were going to be an embarrassment and that was just as important."[13]

Third, little is revealed in the minority boycotts accounts to permit an unequivocal answer to the question of boycott effectiveness. In many cases the boycott was one of many arrows selected from a minority group's quiver of resources, so it becomes difficult, if not impossible, to isolate its effects. To illustrate, the Montgomery boycott and the Colorado boycott may or may not have played a role in the successful court actions that followed them. Moreover, as we have repeatedly seen, a successfully executed boycott does not always lead to a successful consequence. The ERA boycott, for example, did generate helpful cooperation on the part of many individuals and national organizations, but their combined efforts were not enough to ensure passage of the proposed amendment. On the other hand, a failure at the execution or consequence level may be due to a less than fully appropriate use of the boycott tactic. To illustrate, there were those who believed that the ERA boycott would have been much more effective both at the execution and consequence levels had it been started earlier in the NOW campaign to ratify the amendment. According to this view, by 1977 the tide had turned almost irreversibly against ERA ratification, and the boycott was called in a desperate attempt to stop the momentum.

Finally, in the last few decades boycotts have become a tactic used to deal with minority image issues. In some instances a minority group is upset about negative images of itself in advertising and media program content, as we saw with women's rights groups, Italian Americans, Native Americans, and Mexican Americans. In other instances the issue has been the absence of positive images, as we saw with Mexican Americans. While these groups have had mixed success with boycotts as a tactic in confronting these issues, the various observations of Montgomery (1989) strongly question the effectiveness of calls for punitive boycotts to discipline sponsors of offensive episodes of television shows just after the episode has aired. Even boycott sympathizers, it would seem, may be unwilling to take punitive action against a sponsoring company for a single indiscretion.

◆7◆

BOYCOTTS BY RELIGIOUS GROUPS

For many years conservative religious groups as well as liberal religious groups have looked to the boycott as a tactic to further their goals. Often the concerns on the right have related to graphic depictions of sex and violence in film and television dramas. The concerns on the left, on the other hand, have often dealt with international humanitarian issues including mistreatment of various vulnerable populations such as women and children in developing countries of the world.

We look first at the boycotts on the right and then examine boycotts on the left.

Actions Initiated by Conservative Religious Groups

Although much current news media attention has focused on the boycott effort of the Reverend Donald Wildmon and his American Family Association (AFA) to ban "excessive" sex and violence from television programs, the reader should know that this was not the first attempt by a religious organization to use the boycott weapon to remove such depictions from public view. In this section we look first at the early efforts of the Catholic Church to boycott offensive feature films. Then we move on to the last few decades to examine the efforts of the religious right to boycott network television programs.

The Legion of Decency Campaign[1]

In the early days of the motion picture industry the major producers and distributors discerned a need for a public relations office to represent them to the public and to government, to help with such problems as averting censorship or regulation by external sources.[2] Will H. Hays was hired in 1922 to establish such an office, and it soon became very influential in guiding and representing the industry. The office's efforts led in 1927 to the establishment of an industry-sponsored "Don'ts and Be Careful" list for guiding film content, but the list was soon found to be inadequate.[3] So in 1930 the list was superseded by the Motion Picture Production Code. The idea for the code came from Martin Quigly, a Catholic layman and influential book publisher of the time who persuaded a prominent Catholic priest, Father Daniel A. Lord, S.J., to draft the code.

Within just a few years deficiencies in the code became apparent, and these were exacerbated by a changing environment in the early 1930s. Talking pictures became a commercially viable vehicle at the same time that the Great Depression was being felt by the motion picture industry in slumping box-office revenues. Matters went from bad to worse in 1933 when, according to Inglis (1947), the *New York Times* reported that "9,000 letters protesting the vulgarity and coarseness of current productions were received at the White House" that year (p. 120).

After years of working cooperatively with the movie industry to improve the moral integrity of films, Catholic leaders finally lost confidence in the industry's ability or desire to "clean its house." The first call for action came from Archbishop Cicognani, who noted a need "for the purification of the screen" while speaking at a Catholic charities conference in New York in October 1933. Just a month later the Catholic bishops of the United States decided at their annual meeting to establish the National Legion of Decency (NLD).

The relation between the NLD and consumer boycotts has been clearly articulated by Inglis:

In essence, the campaign of the Legion was an economic boycott against pictures which violated the Motion Picture Production Code. Unlike other efforts to improve movies, the Catholic pressure was exerted at the industry's most vulnerable spot—the box office. Senatorial investigation and threatened legislation could be postponed or circumvented in one way or another, and the Hays Office had shown itself to be adept at the techniques of exerting counterpressure, but a direct attack on the box office was another matter. (1947, p. 121)

In 1934 the NLD campaign got under way. The organization distributed to churches throughout the United States a pledge for reading by Catholic congregants. In many parishes the priest read the pledge aloud with the congregation repeating it. One estimate (Inglis, 1947) is that between 7 million and 9 million Catholics read the pledge (of a total of more than 20 million Catholics in the United States at the time).

The pledge itself, which consisted of eight sentences, not only condemned "vile and unwholesome" films, but also asked its spokespersons to recruit other members to join the NLD campaign. The actual wording of the pledge was as follows:

I wish to join the Legion of Decency, which condemns vile and unwholesome moving pictures. I unite with all who protest against them as a grave menace to youth, to home life, to country and to religion.

I condemn absolutely those salacious motion pictures which, with other degrading agencies, are corrupting public morals and promoting a sex mania in our land.

I shall do all that I can to arouse public opinion against the portrayal of vice as a normal condition of affairs, and against depicting criminals of any class as heroes and heroines, presenting their filthy philosophy of life as something acceptable to decent men and women.

I unite with all who condemn the display of suggestive advertisements on billboards, at theater entrances and the favorable notices given to immoral motion pictures.

Considering these evils, I hereby promise to remain away from all motion pictures except those which do not offend decency and Christian morality. I promise further to secure as many members as possible for the Legion of Decency.

I make this protest in a spirit of self-respect, and with the conviction that the American public does not demand filthy pictures, but clean entertainment and educational features. (Inglis, 1947, p. 122)

The NLD campaign received widespread support from non-Catholics as well as Catholics. The campaign was also backed by the Federal Council of Churches of Christ in America and representatives of such fraternal organizations as the B'nai Brith, the Elks, the Knights of Columbus, the Masons, and the Odd Fellows.

Specific campaign actions of the time have been documented by Inglis:

Speeches were made at gatherings of Catholics and affiliated groups and over the radio. Publicity about the campaign appeared not only in Catholic publications but in the press of the nation. Parochial school children paraded with banners like "An Admission to an Indecent Movie Is a Ticket to Hell." In some cities theaters were picketed. Lists of condemned pictures were published and posted. (1947, p. 124)

Inglis concludes that the NLD campaign was successful. She attributes its success to multiple factors, not the least of which was the consumer boycott:

The pressure ... was well aimed and well timed, and it was exerted by a powerful organization which enlisted the cooperation of its followers through an appeal to conscience. The objective was generally acceptable to non-Catholics, and their support made the movement a national one. The industry could resist or evade the issue no longer. The device of a consumers' boycott proved to be a more effective threat than the threat of governmental regulation. (1947, p. 125)

The Early Wildmon Campaigns

Almost a half century after the League of Decency campaign got under way in the early 1930s with its focus on "vulgarity and coarseness" in feature films, a parallel effort with similar concerns about prime-time television was getting started in the South. This effort has been led for more than 20 years by Donald Wildmon, a Tupelo, Mississippi, minister who became enraged one evening in 1976 when he watched television with his family and found his senses bombarded with explicit sex scenes, earthy language, and acts of brutality. His reactions has been noted by Montgomery (1989) who, with Gitlin (1983), have presented perceptive descriptions and analyses of the movement spawned by Wildmon:

> I sat there and I recalled the changes that I'd seen in my society in the last twenty years: the magazines at the check-out stands, the movies, and other changes. And I sat there and said to myself, "You know, they're going to bring this into my home." And I became mad. I experienced some righteous indignation. . . . I became upset. And I said, "Look, this medium has the potential to be the most constructive medium in the history of mankind, but look where it's going. . . . Television is out of whack, it's out of bounds" (Montgomery, 1989, p. 154).

How Wildmon channeled his sense of outrage into a powerful moral movement is a fascinating story. The first few years of the story have been insightfully analyzed in a report by Montgomery (1989), and the treatment of this period that follows here draws extensively from her detailed account. Especially compelling from the perspective of this book is Wildmon's skillful use of the boycott tactic, particularly in the early stages of movement activity.

The first organizational step for Wildmon was establishing the National Federation of Decency (NFD). He recruited volunteers to monitor prime-time television shows and started informing sponsors about NFD concerns through letter-writing campaigns. A major NFD initiative occurred in 1979 in response to CBS's plan to air a TV movie, *Flesh and Blood*, about an incestuous relationship between a young man and his mother. NFD organized a public protest against the project consisting of pickets at CBS headquarters and letters sent to leading television advertisers warning them not to sponsor the controversial film. CBS postponed the air date for the film, and when it was later broadcast, the most explicit sexual scene had been deleted (Montgomery, 1989). Although this might be seen as a victory of sorts for the fledgling NFD, the organization was dismissed by a *TV Guide* article as largely a one-man operation that was more of a nuisance than a serious threat to the television industry (Weisman, 1979).

The next step for Wildmon derived from an accident of timing. Just as the Legion of Decency campaign was helped by the Great Depression and the pressure it exerted on the movie industry, so, a half century later, was the religious right and its television campaign aided by the November 1980 national election, which produced a major victory for conservative Republicans signaling a public opinion shift to the right. Coming into prominence at the time was the Moral Majority, a national conservative organization. Led by television evangelist Jerry Falwell, the Moral Majority was founded as a coalition of political and religious organizations to generate public support and raise money for its conservative causes (Montgomery, 1989).

Entertainment television soon became a target of conservatives, who alleged that it was controlled by liberals with loose morals who were intent upon undermining core American values by piping sexually explicit, anti-Christian programs into the living rooms of the nation (Sterling & Kittross, 1978). Acting on these concerns the Moral Majority announced on Election Day that it was committing a half-million dollars to a national campaign against "excessive TV sex and violence." And just a few months later (February 1981) the NFD joined forces with the Moral Majority to form a new organization, the Coalition for Better Television (CBTV), with Donald Wildmon as its leader. Coalition members included a host of familiar "New Right" organizations, such as the Christian Voice, the Eagle Forum, and the American Life Lobby. While CBTV leaders saw themselves as reformers acting in the public interest, Montgomery (1989) noted that this characterization is not the whole story:

> The cause was also framed in fervently religious terms. This was no less than a holy war, CBTV leaders proclaimed. "The ugliest mark," said Wildmon, "that will be written against the institutional church in this century will be its silence in the face of immorality and the decline of public morals. Our society promotes hedonism, heathenism, materialism, greed—every-

thing that's destructively different from Christian values. Yet the Church is silent" (p. 157).

In his new position as head of the well-funded coalition, Wildmon showed himself to be an accomplished strategist and tactician. Unlike earlier leaders who had campaigned against alleged television shortcomings, Wildmon decided to focus CBTV energies not on the networks but on the advertisers. He told his followers to forget the networks, saying they did not care what CBTV thought. He claimed that the coalition's real clout was with the organizations that paid the bills—the commercial sponsors. To document what kinds of shows these companies were sponsoring, CBTV mounted a vast nationwide operation of 4,000 volunteers to monitor prime-time shows for offensive behaviors (Gitlin, 1983).

While this strategy showed sophistication in its conceptualization, it also exhibited shrewdness in its tactical details. Wildmon proved to be a master dramatist with a dual focus on secrecy and suspense (Montgomery, 1989). He declined to explain the particulars of his monitoring system so it was virtually impossible for advertisers to know what the monitors were noting as offensive behavior. To keep them in suspense, CBTV announced a two-step plan: The coalition would continue its television monitoring for several months, and at the end of this period (June 1981), CBTV would publicly identify the sponsor of the most offensive programming. And after identifying the "guilty corporation," CBTV would initiate a nationwide boycott against it.

Jerry Falwell described how the boycott would work:

> We have made a commitment . . . to put two million dollars at least into the boycott. For example, if we [the Moral Majority] were called and told, "Okay, the boycott begins X date," we would write to four and a half million families, instantly, saying, "Here are the facts, here are the people, here are the products, here are the things we don't want to buy anymore, here's why," and so forth. So would all the other three hundred organizations. We would buy full-page ads across the nation, listing the Public Enemy Number One and his products, and urging the boycott. And we would get on TV and radio and

press conferences everywhere and eighty thousand pastors next Sunday would preach on it, and would put it in the Church bulletins and within thirty days the dust would be flying. (Montgomery, 1989, p. 159)

This provocative message and others like it were not easily dismissed by televison advertisers and network executives. Conservative leaders like Jerry Falwell had just shown in the November election that they were a force to be reckoned with. And while television boycotts had been threatened before and a few isolated actions had actually gotten under way, no nationwide coordinated action had ever been previously launched (Montgomery, 1989).

What made the CBTV threat all the more unsettling for the television industry and its corporate advertisers was that the coalition appeared to have the wherewithal to carry out a successful boycott. And what made the threat all the more credible was the CBTV decision to concentrate on a single corporation, the "worst offender" as determined by CBTV acting as judge and jury (Montgomery, 1989).

The networks decided to fight back. Calling CBTV "unscrupulous" and "formidable," CBS senior vice president Gene Maher weighed in with particulars:

[Their] idea is not to attract sympathy and support [for their cause] but to compel concessions. This involves the violation of rights, not the exercise of them. The advertiser is the pressure point. The concession comes down to making TV do and say what [the coalition] thinks TV should do and say and show. We have no problem with a teacher teaching or a preacher preaching not to watch a particular program, but we have problems with a threatened boycott. . . . No matter how you couch it, and no matter how well intentioned it is, that's censorship. (Montgomery, 1989, p. 160)

Wildmon and such prominent CBTV supporters as conservative columnist George Will responded to the censorship charges. Wildmon called the boycott initiative a type of "militant conservatism." He went on to say:

The network has the right to spend its money where it wants to; the advertiser has the right to spend its money where it wants to; and the consumer has the right to spend his money where he wants to. The clearest expression of the first amendment is the right of a corporation or an individual to spend money where they want to. . . . It's the responsibility of every Christian to be a good steward of all his money.

Censorship has existed ever since man learned to communicate. It has to exist of necessity. It exists right now. Everything you see on television has been censored; but the question is, who is doing the censoring? When the networks cry censorship, they're usually speaking of an official act. We're not official, not a government organization. We're a citizens' group. The only clout we have is with personal economics, and that's a perfectly legitimate clout. (Montgomery, 1989, p. 162)

By May 1981, with the June CBTV decision date just a month away, it became clear that despite their protestations to the contrary, many corporate advertisers were growing uneasy. A senior executive of General Foods indicated that he and his colleagues were nervous, and a Procter & Gamble senior official observed that while many Americans may not agree completely with Wildmon, they think he has a legitimate point. Moreover, Grant Tinker, who was soon to be named president of CBS, observed that the CBTV effort would not have been necessary if the networks had "kept their houses clean" (Montgomery, 1989).[4]

Finally, on June 15, a major crack occurred in the "united front" of the television advertisers with a dramatic announcement by Procter & Gamble that it had pulled out of 50 network television programs during the preceding season because the shows contained excessive violence, profanity, or sex. It went on to commend CBTV for expressing what Procter & Gamble considered to be important and widely held views.

Wildmon, of course, expressed delight at the announcement for two reasons. First, Procter & Gamble, which had a conservative reputation, had left the field, so to speak, by sponsoring a television program in 1977 that Wildmon's National Federation of Decency (NFD) had found to be offensive. He vowed in 1980 that NFD would keep the company "in its prayers and off its shopping lists." Procter & Gamble's announcement was greeted with all the grace of a compassionate father welcoming home his wayward son. Second, Procter & Gamble was one of television's major advertisers, and CBTV believed that as an industry leader the company would attract other advertisers to its position (Montgomery, 1989).

The domino effect that CBTV had hoped for did indeed occur, with many major corporations agreeing to reevaluate their advertising campaigns with the objective of excluding programs with offensive content. One casualty of the movement was sexual explicitness. As Todd Gitlin put it in referring to the shows being considered for the 1981–82 season: "The fall schedule does not include a new crop of jiggle shows (and *Charlie's Angels*, the mother of all jiggle shows, is gone)" (Montgomery, 1989, p. 168).

With major corporations following the Procter & Gamble lead by capitulating to CBTV pressure, the Moral Majority announced that the planned CBTV boycott was being called off. While many advertisers were obviously relieved to hear this news, some observers suggested that CBTV had taken the action because the organization was afraid that its members and supporters would not participate in the boycott.

The CBTV monitoring campaign continued in the 1981–82 television season with the scope of concern extended first to include "sex-oriented" TV commercials and then later to include "fairer treatment of Christians in prime-time programming." In January 1982, a March 2 date was announced for a boycott of advertisers that had not yielded to CBTV's demands. However, a bombshell suddenly dropped upon CBTV of Procter & Gamble proportions when the Moral Majority, the principal member of the coalition, announced that it would not participate in the planned boycott. The Moral Majority gave as its reason its belief that the television industry had made a good-faith effort to respond to CBTV concerns and should not be threatened with another boycott action.[5]

Nonetheless, CBTV kept on course by calling a boycott in early March. What was surprising to some observers was the target selected for this action. Instead of an advertiser CBTV picked a network, NBC, and its owner, RCA. Wildmon claimed that they were selected because of the offensive nature of so many

NBC shows. Other observers, however, speculated that the selection of RCA/NBC may have been influenced by declining NBC ratings and the financial difficulties recently experienced by RCA. In any case the complexities of operating a boycott against a megaconglomerate the size of RCA became immediately evident when the CBTV boycott campaigners mistakenly included Gibson Greeting Cards on their don't-buy list. The Gibson subsidiary had been sold by RCA several months earlier, and an embarrassed CBTV had to issue a public apology.

A second embarrassment occurred a few months later when CBTV selected an NBC-TV movie, *Sister, Sister,* for attack. The film, about three black sisters in the modern South who were torn with emotional conflict, featured a black minister who has affairs with two of the sisters. Although Wildmon had not seen the film he accused it of being anti-Christian and antireligious based upon what he had heard about it. Moreover, he urged hundreds of major advertisers not to sponsor the film. NBC counterattacked by enlisting the help of African American activists who supported the film. These activists were successful in retaining some advertisers as sponsors of the TV film.

Why had the African American activists been so willing to work with the network? The answer appears to be that the film was not simply a black exploitation work, as Wildmon had suggested, but a serious drama authored by Maya Angelou, a distinguished African American writer. Wildmon and CBTV, it seems, had picked an inappropriate program to attack, and the coalition suffered a loss of credibility as a result.[6]

Finally, a critical question remains concerning the impact of the CBTV boycott on RCA business. While Wildmon claimed that RCA's consumer electronics business had suffered because of the boycott, evidence provided by RCA and by the *Los Angeles Times* indicated that RCA and NBC had dramatic increases in profits during the boycott period (Montgomery, 1989).

The Later Wildmon Campaigns

The Wildmon-led boycott campaigns have continued over the decades of the 1980s and 1990s through the efforts of the American Family Association (AFA) and its companion organization,

Christian Leaders for Responsible Television (CLear-TV). The organizations are large and influential with AFA's newsletter circulation reportedly numbering around 1 million readers (Lyons, 1996) and with CLear-TV's coalition consisting of some 1,600 church leaders representing more than 70 denominations (Putnam, 1994).

According to Putnam, the former editor of the *National Boycott News*, the Wildmon-led groups have been responsible for an "impressive list of boycott victories" over the years. To illustrate, in 1989 boycotts called by AFA and CLear-TV that targeted Clorox and Mennen were, according to the two groups, successful in persuading the two firms to markedly reduce the extent to which the programs they sponsored used sex, violence, and profanity in their scripts. The next year, according to Putnam (1994), Burger King became a boycott target of AFA and CLear-TV. Just a few weeks after the boycott announcement Burger King worked out an agreement with the boycotters that featured a greater emphasis on "traditional family values" in the programs sponsored by Burger King. More recent boycott efforts targeting Johnson Wax and Pfizer have also succeeded in shifting the programs sponsored by these corporations in a "family values" direction (Putnam, 1994). Still other advertisers who have yielded to pressure from AFA and/or CLear-TV, according to Putnam (1994), include Domino's Pizza, General Mills, Marathon Oil, McDonald's, Procter & Gamble, and Purina.

Perhaps the best known of the AFA boycotts has been its campaign against the Walt Disney Company for a multitude of offensive behaviors attributed to the giant entertainment firm. This AFA initiative, started in 1996, was first called to protest such "gay-friendly" policies as extending insurance benefits to the partners of Disney's gay employees and permitting gay groups to hold exclusive events at Disney theme parks. Later AFA objected to *Ellen*, a program offered by the Disney-owned ABC television network featuring a lead character who reveals that she is a lesbian.

The AFA boycott of Disney received support in June 1996 from the Southern Baptist Conference, which announced that it was joining the AFA boycott forces to demand that Disney discontinue its "gay-friendly" policies. The strength of this religious right organization should not be underestimated. According to

Goodstein (1998), the Southern Baptists, with almost 16 million members, have recently emerged as the nation's largest Protestant denomination. Also endorsing the Disney boycott was the 2.5 million member Assemblies of God church, which announced its support in August 1996.

Disney has vowed to stand by its past policies relating to gay issues. Its action is consistent with one taken by the major television networks, which moved in 1990 to establish the National Television Association, an organization that attacked AFA-type boycott initiatives as "attempts to manipulate our free society and democratic process." According to Putnam (1994), the American Association of Advertisers has also been supportive of controversial television network programming, claiming that it reflects the complexity and realism of the larger society.

In addition to the philosophical issues dividing the boycotters and the television industry are the economic losses generated by the "family values" pressures. Putnam (1994) cites a speech delivered by Robert Iger, president of ABC Entertainment, to a meeting of the Association of National Advertisers in which he claims that "advertiser pullout" stemming from such boycott pressures is causing ABC to lose millions of dollars each year.

All of these developments attest to the long-standing influence of the AFA, which Zachary Lyons, former editor of the *Boycott Quarterly*, recently referred to as "perhaps the most successful boycotting organization on Earth" (1996, p. 6). And they also demonstrate the impact that one individual, Donald Wildmon, has had using boycotts and the threats of boycotts to move the media in a "family values" direction.

Actions Initiated by Liberal Religious Groups

Paralleling the leadership actions of Donald Wildmon and his American Family Association on the religious right over the last two decades have been the leadership actions of Timothy Smith and the Interfaith Center on Corporate Responsibility (ICCR) on what might be called the religious left. Smith, a longtime social activist and Union Theological Seminary graduate, has served as ICCR executive director since 1976.

The origins of ICCR go back to 1971 when the Episcopal Church initiated a stockholders' resolution requesting General Motors to withdraw from South Africa.[7] When the resolution failed, the Episcopalians and several other Protestant groups decided to start ICCR. Its mandate initially was to coordinate the proxy activities and resolutions of these groups with a special focus on "urging Goodyear, Gulf Oil, International Business Machines, and Mobil to stop doing business in the white-ruled nations of Angola, Guinea, Mozambique, Rhodesia, and South Africa" (O'Toole, 1998, p. 305). All of these nations had records on human rights that the Protestant groups considered to be deplorable, and it was this judgment that prompted the ICCR action.

While, as we shall see presently, ICCR has sometimes supported consumer boycotts relating to human rights issues, more often it has focused its energies on changing corporate behavior through the use of proxy statements. How this works has been succinctly summarized by O'Toole:

> Mailed to shareholders each year in advance of a company's annual meeting, the proxy typically solicits votes on such routine affairs as the election of directors and ratification of management's choice of auditors. Most proxy resolutions are put forward by management, but any investor who has owned at least $1,000 worth of a company's stock for a year has the right to sponsor a resolution for inclusion in the proxy and bring it to a vote at the annual stockholder's meeting. There are deadlines to be met, and the rules of engagement, set by the Securities and Exchange Commission, do not allow resolutions on "ordinary business"—areas deemed the exclusive domain of management. Beyond ordinary business lies a vast territory in which managements set company policy on social issues. (1988, p. 303)

The use of the proxy vote as a social change agent goes back to the 1960s when Eastman Kodak rescinded its commitment to employ and train young blacks in Rochester, New York. Social activist Saul Alinsky decided not to call for a boycott in response to this turnabout action because it was unlikely to suceed, given Kodak's virtual monopoly on photographic film. Instead, Alinsky made a nationwide tour stopping at churches along the way to ask congregations with Kodak stock in their portfolios to assign their proxy votes to an Alinsky coalition called FIGHT consisting of community groups in the poorest areas of Rochester. Despite the efforts of a FIGHT representative at the Kodak annual meeting, the proxy tactic failed, but the battle was widely reported in the news media, and shortly thereafter Kodak negotiated a new agreement with FIGHT.

Although a renowned veteran of many skirmishes with corporations, social activist Alinsky was surprised at the reactions of business leaders to the use of the proxy:

> Their anxious questions convinced me that we had the razor to cut through the golden curtain that protected the so-called private sector from facing its public responsibilities. . . . In all my wars with the establishment I had never seen it so uptight. I knew there was dynamite in the proxy scare. (Alinsky, 1972, p. 175)

Taking a page from the Alinsky manual, ICCR has made extensive use of proxies to urge corporations to reduce pollution, end discrimination in employment, pay Third World employees a decent wage, and end human rights abuses in Burma and other nations. And ICCR has often been successful, with perhaps its most significant accomplishment consisting of its antiapartheid victory in South Africa. While others led the consumer boycott campaign to get more than 160 U.S. corporations to leave South Africa in the 1980s, it was ICCR that led the shareholder proxy campaign to hasten their departure. The importance of the latter campaign has been noted by Paul Neuhauser, a law professor and ICCR adviser who contends that shareholder resolutions were a primary reason for apartheid becoming a major issue in the United States in the 1980s (O'Toole, 1998).

Despite opposition from some corporate boardrooms, ICCR has grown steadily in the last two decades and by 1996, its 25th anniversary year, it had become a federation of 275 Catholic, Jewish, and Protestant organizations with an aggregate portfolio valued at more than $70 billion. And its shareholder resolutions have regularly won the support of foundations and universities, as well as municipal and state pension funds.

In 1996, ICCR celebrated its 25th anniversary with a special issue of its publication, *The Corporate Examiner*, which documented its leadership activities since its beginnings in 1971. In a summary paragraph, Tim Smith (1996) pointed out the many accomplishments of ICCR during this period.

> Through twenty-five years the voice of the faith community has been strong, consistent, persistent in identifying the role of corporations in society's problems and challenging them to change harmful policies and practices. ICCR and its members have charged that banks lending to South Africa during apartheid supported racism and repression with those loans; companies promoting infant formula have contributed to the illness of millions of infants; companies generating and improperly disposing of toxic waste are destroying God's creation; companies pursuing the lowest achievable labor costs in their international operations are operating sweatshops and impoverishing their employees; arms manufacturers selling on the world market share responsibility for the wars in which their weapons are used. The list goes on but the message is the same: Corporate decisions must serve the social as well as the financial bottom line. (Smith, 1996, pp. 3–4)

Among the boycott-related milestones noted in the special publication are the following (listed by topical area):

Labor Issues

1976 Church groups joined the corporate campaign to persuade J.P. Stevens, a large Southern textile manufacturer, to sign a collective bargaining agreement. The church groups filed shareholder resolutions with J.P. Stevens, and they also endorsed and supported a nationwide consumer boycott of the firm's products. J.P. Stevens signed the agreement in 1980.

1985 A consumer boycott was called of Campbell Soup Company products in support of an effort to unionize farm workers in Ohio and Michigan. The boycott, which was supported by various labor, church, and community groups, received formal support from the Ohio Catholic Bishops in 1985. One year later a collective bargaining agreement was signed securing first-time rights for the farmworkers.

1987 A new boycott of California table grapes, which was called by the United Farmworkers of America, received formal endorsement by the National Council of Churches. Among the union concerns were fair union representation and the use by the growers of dangerous pesticides on the crops to be harvested by the farmworkers.

International Issues

1976 Investors representing the religious community took Coca-Cola to task because of the actions of its franchise bottler in Guatemala. The major concerns were the bottler's "repressive actions and interference with worker efforts to organize." These registered concerns led to strikes and consumer boycotts as well as demonstrations and publicity campaigns. Finally, in 1980, Coca-Cola took corrective action by replacing the bottling plant's management and by formally recognizing an employees union.

1991 Neighbor-to-Neighbor, a U.S.-based protest group, initiated a consumer boycott of Procter & Gamble products in an effort to persuade the company to facilitate a settlement of the civil war in El Salvador. ICCR members helped in 1991 by sponsoring a shareholder resolution critical of the company's ties to local coffee growers who supported an extreme right-wing political party in El Salvador. The boycott was lifted after a cease-fire ended the civil war in 1992.

1993 Religious investors introduced four shareholder resolutions critical of companies that were doing business in Burma, a country well known for its "illegal and repressive" military government, which had taken over power after a successful 1988 coup. Three years later Pepsico divested its stake in its Burma franchise company in response to an international consumer boycott. Other corporations soon followed suit.

Health Issues

1975 Religious investors started taking actions that eventually led to the Nestle boycott. A first action was the filing of resolutions criticizing the marketing of infant formula in developing countries by large transnational corporations such as Nestle. Thus began what later became known as the "corporate responsibility movement's first successful worldwide campaign." Indeed, a partnership formed among religious investors and faith communities, on the one hand, and health and consumer activists, on the other, to challenge the marketing practices of multinational corporations.

1976 The infant formula concerns intensified when Sisters of the Precious Blood sued Bristol-Myers for alleged distortions about infant formula marketing that were contained in the firm's proxy statements. The company agreed to an out-of-court settlement that required the issuance of a corrected report to shareholders and also provided an opportunity for ICCR members to meet with the Bristol-Myers board of director to share ICCR's concerns.

1977 In an effort to bring a halt to objectionable corporate marketing practices for infant formula, a consumer boycott was called on July 4 by the Infant Formula Action Coalition (INFACT), a grassroots organization that came together as a result of discussions held by the Third World Institute of the Newman Center of the University of Minnesota.

1978 The Presbyterian Church endorsed the INFACT boycott, and soon thereafter so did dozens of other religious groups. Demonstrations by religious groups took place at Nestle-owned Stouffer restaurants across the nation.

1981 At the urging of ICCR and an international consortium of infant health and nutrition advocates, the World Health Organization (WHO) adopted the "Code of Marketing for Breastmilk Substitutes," a landmark document that became the policy foundation for the national and international regulation of infant formula marketing practices. At the same time, the Nestle boycott spread beyond the

United States to Australia, Britain, Canada, France, Germany, New Zealand, and Sweden.

1982 ICCR members filed investor resolutions calling on Abbott Laboratories, American Home Products, and Bristol-Myers to adopt the WHO code on marketing practices for infant formula.

1984 An agreement was reached between Nestle and the international team of boycotters. The protesters agreed to suspend the seven-year boycott action, and Nestle, in turn, agreed to implement the WHO code in developing countries.

1988 After four years of watching and waiting, a new infant formula boycott group, Action for Corporate Accountability (ACT), announced that it was resuming the Nestle boycott. According to ACT, Nestle had engaged in "broken promises and legislative hair splitting," the result being that it had failed to adopt the provisions of the WHO code.[8]

Militarism Issues

1986 A consumer boycott of General Electric products was launched by INFACT, which had initiated the 1977 Nestle boycott. The action was taken to protest GE's production of nuclear weapons.

1992 The GE boycott received media attention when the INFACT-produced documentary film *Deadly Deception*, which provides a critical look at GE's nuclear weapons business, received the Academy Award for best documentary short.

1993 INFACT terminated the seven-year GE boycott after the company ended its production of nuclear weapons. The boycott had attracted four million supporters in 14 countries.

Perhaps the potential power of the religious left to affect the fate of boycotts is best seen not in the near-celebrative anniversary statements of its ICCR supporters, but in the respectful criticisms of its boycott targets. To illustrate, in the context of the Nestle boycott, Nestle executive Rafael Pagan discussed Nestle's strategy for dealing with the religious leaders of the boycott in a speech delivered to the Public Affairs Council in New York on April 22, 1982:

> Our primary goal is survival. Our secondary goal must be to separate the fanatic activist leaders—people who deny that free wealth-creating institutions have any legitimate role to play in helping the third world to develop—from the overwhelming majority of their followers—decent, concerned people who are willing to judge us on the basis of our openness and our usefulness. In particular, we must strip the activists of the moral authority they receive from their alliances with religious organizations.
>
> When I came to Nestle last year, I realized that the company's highest priority was to establish a dialogue with those church leaders who were supporting, or who might support, the activists' boycott against us. (Pagan, 1982, p. 19)

This strategy of splitting the boycott movement apart by appealing to its church leaders was somewhat successful. To illustrate, the strategy led the United Methodist Church to conclude in April 1983, after a two-year investigation, that it would not formally endorse the boycott. Moreover, at the end of 1983 the General Council of Ministries of the United Methodist Church approved a report recommending that it would not be appropriate for any agency of the church to participate in the boycott. And the Methodist Church was joined in their dissociation from the boycott by the Church of the Brethren, which in late 1983 decided to withdraw its support from the boycott.

Needless to say, however, the majority of church sponsors of the Nestle boycott followed the ICCR lead by staying with the boycott until an agreement was reached the following year. Actions such as these illustrate the power of ICCR as an instrument of social change.

Concluding Comments

This brief overview of the role of the religious right and left in consumer boycott activities reveals some striking similarities and differences. The similarities concern the dominant roles played by two organizations, one on the right and the other on the left, and the respected position of each of their leaders among his organization's followers. It is as hard to imagine AFA without Donald Wildmon as it is to imagine ICCR without Timothy Smith. Both men and their organizations have been very effective in doing their jobs.

The difference between the two organizations and their leaders is to a great extent one of style. Donald Wildmon and his AFA constituents represent a blue-collar, in-the-trenches approach to righting what they have identified as social and moral wrongs. The consumer boycott tactic with its direct-action, no-holds-barred approach to problem solving seems to be a good fit for these working-class warriors. Timothy Smith and ICCR, on the other hand, represent a middle- or upper-middle class approach to coping with social and moral problems. Their white-collar legalistic approach consists of working inside the system to effect change through proxy votes and resolutions. This is not to say that ICCR has not engaged in boycotts or strikes; as we have seen, they have participated in such direct actions, but almost always as a follower rather than a leader.

Needless to say, both styles of social action can be, and indeed have been, effective. And Smith's ICCR and Wildmon's AFA present excellent models of the two approaches. Indeed, when the ICCR and AFA efforts are examined in the historical context of the civil rights struggles in the South, which were led, as we saw in Chapter 5, by black ministers and churches in such cities as Montgomery, Baton Rouge, and Tallahassee, we see that the religious tradition of effective boycott leadership has a long and distinguished past.

◆8◆

ECOLOGICAL
BOYCOTTS

A concern with perceived threats to environmental quality, for humans and nonhumans alike, has prompted new groups to form to vigorously protest offending actions of corporations. Organizations such as Earth Island Institute, People for the Ethical Treatment of Animals, Earth First!, and the Rainforest Action Network did not exist a generation ago, but they now are major players in consumer protest actions against perceived corporate abuses of the environment.[1] This chapter reports a study of some 24 efforts by these groups and others to promote a sustainable future through organized consumer boycotts against major corporations.

The chapter represents a shift in substance and style from the previous chapters on protest groups and the boycotts they initiated to further their objectives. Because ecological boycotts are a relatively new phenomenon, an extensive scholarly literature on these initiatives does not exist to serve as a foundation for the historical analysis and evaluation that characterized the earlier chapters. This being the case, we decided to conduct our own survey study of recently initiated ecological boycotts by interviewing the boycotters and their targets. This chapter presents the procedures and results of the interview investigation in an empirical social science study format.

The participants in the boycotts included environmental protection (EP) groups as well as animal rights (AR) groups. The concerns of the EP groups have included destruction of the rain forest, biodegradability of consumer product packaging, recycling of oil in the production of automobiles, and the destruction of wildlife in natural settings (e.g., dolphins). AR activists have shared the environmentalists' focus on wildlife, but they have also concerned themselves with the treatment of animals in captivity. Particularly offensive to these groups is the use of laboratory animals in consumer product development and testing (e.g., cosmetics), especially if this practice results in cruel treatment or death to the animals.

The primary objective of the empirical study reported here was to secure an understanding of contemporary consumer boycotts dealing with EP and AR issues. While many issues have served as the focus of consumer boycotts, it is these two, more than others, such as women's rights and censorship, which are associated with efforts to secure a sustainable future for life on earth. These two issues, while relatively absent in the boycott agendas of the 1970s (Friedman, 1985) and the early 1980s (Garrett, 1987), have emerged as major concerns of boycott efforts in the late 1980s and 1990s, reflecting the larger contemporary role assumed by the EP and AR movements.

Three key research questions posed in the study were as follows:

1. What prompted the boycott groups to act?
2. What actions did they take and how did these actions affect consumers, the media, and the targets themselves?
3. What lessons can be learned from these experiences to help activists work more effectively toward the goal of a sustainable future?

The discussion that follows describes the study procedures and delineates the research results.

Defining Consumer Boycotts

To guide the data collection, we needed a working definition of consumer boycotts. As in Chapter 1, a *consumer boycott* was defined as an attempt by one or more parties to achieve certain objectives by urging individual consumers to refrain from making selected purchases in the marketplace. Consumer boycotts use marketplace means to accomplish what may or may not be marketplace ends. Thus a variety of objectives external to the marketplace, such as preservation of the rain forest, were considered.

Data Collection Procedure

The data collection procedure consisted of three stages.

Stage 1: Literature Review

A major effort was made to secure information pertaining to EP and AR boycotts from 1987 to 1992. This time period was selected when the study data were originally collected in mid-1993 because boycotts occurring prior to it were likely to be too dated to yield much useful information, and boycotts occurring later were likely to be too recent to assess with appropriate perspective. Just recently (early 1998), EP and AR boycotts in the original sample that continued beyond mid-1993 were scrutinized, so the results reported here provide a contemporary update on these older boycotts.

The data sources for the study included 15 literature retrieval indexes for newspapers and magazines. Also included were file materials from two major boycott resource centers, the Institute for Consumer Responsibility and Co-op America. The literature search identified more than 100 EP and AR boycotts.

Stage 2: Mail Survey

To secure more information about these boycotts, a brief screening questionnaire was prepared and mailed to the principals representing the boycotting groups and their targets. Accompanying each screening questionnaire were copies of materials secured in Stage 1 describing the particular boycott. We asked the parties to check the materials for accuracy and completeness and to provide, where appropriate, the necessary corrections and additions. We also requested a current address and phone number for the individual most knowledgeable about the boycott in the boycott group or targeted organization who could serve as a contact person for additional questions.

Stage 2 yielded 32 instances of matches: cases in which the two parties to a boycott (boycotter and target) both responded to the survey and included information on contact persons.

Stage 3: Personal Interviews

The goal at this stage was to interview each member of the 32 pairs, either in person or by telephone. We developed and pretested two interview forms, one for the boycott group and one for the target corporation. In mid-1993 both members of 24 matched pairs, boycotter and target, were interviewed. Of the 24 boycotts, 12 dealt with EP issues and 12 with AR issues.

The Stage 3 interviews varied in length from one hour to several hours. Detailed information was sought about the boycott particulars from boycott group representatives and from corporate target representatives. The latter were typically executives in the corporate office of public information, although two were presidents of their companies.

Data Analysis Dimensions

Because the total number of boycotts of each type was small, the data analysis was primarily descriptive, with attention given to many of the boycott dimensions delineated in Chapter 1.

Results

In what follows, the results of the interviews are presented and briefly discussed. This section starts with a focus on tabular summaries of the data and continues with brief narrative accounts of some of the boycotts.

As indicated earlier, the 24 boycotts split evenly into EP and AR actions. The boycott groups, targets, and issues associated with each action are presented in Tables 8.1 and 8.2.

General Boycott Characteristics

At the outset two characteristics found in all 24 boycotts should be noted briefly. First, the 24 boycott leaders interviewed all saw their efforts as more "instrumental" (oriented toward practical ends) than "expressive" (oriented toward venting frustrations) in that they each made concrete demands on the targets. Second, each of the 24 boycotts was viewed as a "conscience" boycott rather than a "beneficiary" boycott; as noted in Chapter 1, the former is initiated to help the public at large, while the latter is launched primarily to aid the boycotters.

Four other differences in boycott characteristics were found within the AR and EP groups. In particular, most of the boycotts were national in scope (11 of 12 EP actions and 8 of 12 AR actions), and the remainder were international efforts.

A second noteworthy characteristic of the boycotts is their time duration. Most boycotts of each type extended beyond a year (11 EP and 10 AR actions). This finding may be somewhat artifactual in that after a year without progress, boycott groups sometimes insist that a boycott is continuing despite the fact that little in the way of action is evident to impartial observers. Several of the boycotts in the study sample appeared to fit this characterization. Also of interest is that all three boycotts that

Table 8.1 Environmental Protection Boycotts: Boycott Targets, Groups, and Issues

Target Firm	Boycott Group	Boycott Issue
American Express	Colorado Earth First!	Ski resort development
Bumble Bee Seafoods	Earth Island Institute	Dolphin-safe tuna
Chrysler	Waste Oil Action	Recycled oil
Dixon-Ticonderoga (pencils)	Rainforest Action Network	Tropical timber
Dow Chemical	Environmental Action Foundation and Environmental Defense Fund	"Photodegradable labels"
Empire-Berol (pencils)	Rainforest Action Network	Tropical timber
General Motors	Waste Oil Action	Recycled oil
Georgia-Pacific	Rainforest Action Network	Tropical timber
Heinz (Starkist tuna)	Earth Island Institute	Dolphin-safe tuna
Mitsubishi	Rainforest Action Network	Tropical timber
Ralston Purina (tuna)[a]	Earth Island Institute	Dolphin-safe tuna
Weyerhaeuser	Rainforest Action Network	Tropical timber

[a] During the course of the boycott, the Chicken of the Sea subsidiary of Ralston Purina was sold to Van Kamp, an Indonesian firm.

Table 8.2 Animal Rights Boycotts:
Boycott Targets, Groups, and Issues

Target Firm	Boycott Group	Boycott Issue
American Express	PETAª	Fur sales in catalogs
Avon	PETA	Animal testing
Benetton	PETA	Animal testing
Bristol-Myers Squibb	PETA	Animal testing
Chesebrough-Pond's	PETA	Animal testing
Dow Chemical	PETA	Animal testing
General Motors	PETA	Animal testing
Gillette	PETA	Animal testing
Mary Kay Cosmetics	PETA	Animal testing
Neutrogena	PETA	Animal testing
Procter & Gamble	IDAᵇ	Animal testing
Smith Kline Beecham	PETA	Animal testing

ª People for the Ethical Treatment of Animals
ᵇ In Defense of Animals

extended for less than one year (Avon, Benetton, and Empire-Berol) were ended because their leaders claimed that the boycott objectives had been met.

Two additional general boycott descriptors concern the boycotters' actions and their orientation. In Chapter 1, we distinguished among four stages of escalation or militancy for boycott actions ranging from the very mild (action considered) to the very militant (action taken). Most of the EP boycotts (9 of 12) and the AR boycotts (7 of 12) had escalated to the most militant fourth stage, with the remainder found at one of the two intermediate stages (action requested or action organized).

Also interesting were the results regarding boycott orientation. Almost all of the boycott groups focused on the media rather than the marketplace (11 EP and 11 AR boycotts). The difference between the two emphases is illustrated by the site a boycott group picks for a protest demonstration. A marketplace-oriented boycott group would be likely to demonstrate in front of a store selling a boycotted product, urging consumers not to buy the item. A media-oriented boycott group, on the other hand, would be more likely to select the target headquarters, making sure that demonstrators were positioned in front of a company sign or logo, so that television cameras would be able to link these identifying visuals with the boycotters' publicity materials.

Boycotted Goods and Companies

As shown in Table 8.3, most of the targets were producers or processors (11 of 12 EP and 8 of 12 AR boycotts). Three of the AR boycotts targeted firms that were both producers and retailers (Benetton, Avon, and Mary Kay).

When the boycott representatives were asked why they had picked their targets, all 24 focused on the target's offensive actions. Several offered additional reasons, however. Chief among these was the fact that the target or its brands were well-known to the boycott audience; four EP and four AR boycott spokespersons talked about high visibility as a factor.

Noted next in Table 8.3 are four items that relate more to a marketplace-oriented boycott than to a media-related boycott in that they describe circumstances relating to the nature of the consumer products and services being boycotted. First is the number of major brands being marketed by each target. As we saw in Chapter 2, the smaller the number of brands offered by a target, the easier it is for a marketplace-oriented boycott to achieve success (Friedman, 1991). As shown in Table 8.3, a wide range of values was found here reflecting such single brand-name companies as Weyerhaeuser and Mary Kay, on the one hand, and such multiple brand-name companies as Gillette and Procter & Gamble on the other. In general, though, the EP targets offered far fewer brands to be boycotted than the AR targets.

The next entry in Table 8.3 examines the ease with which consumers could identify the targeted firm's brands in the marketplace. The importance of this entry to marketplace-oriented boycotts was made clear in Chapter 2: Consumers need to be able to identify boycotted goods if they are to refrain from buying them. Almost all of the targeted goods were considered easy to identify (11 of the 12 EP boycotts and 10 of the 12 AR boycotts). Weyerhaeuser was thought to be difficult because it manufactures disposable diapers for major retailers but under the retailer's name rather than its own.

**Table 8.3 Frequency Distributions of Characteristics
of Boycotted Firms and Goods**

Characteristic	EP	AR
Nature of target business		
Producer/processor	11	8
Retailer	1	1
Both	0	3
Total	12	12
Why was target company selected as focus of boycott?		
The company's behavior was offensive to boycotters.	12	12
The company or its brands were well known to boycott audience.	4	4
The company had attempted to project a responsible image that the boycotters thought was inconsistent with its practices.	1	0
The company was the leader (in sales) in its field.	1	0
The company was vulnerable due to a recent drop in sales/profits.	0	1
The company was vulnerable since its goods were sold in retail stores with the same name as the firm.	1	1
The company seemed to be amenable to change since it did not have a long-term commitment to the policies being challenged.	0	1
The company was American owned while others were not.	1	0
Total	20[a]	19[a]
Number of brands marketed by target firm		
1	5	4
2–5	4	0
6–20	1	3
More than 20	2	5
Total	12	12
How easy/difficult for consumers to identify boycotted goods?		
Easy	11	10
Difficult	1	0
Neither easy nor difficult	0	2
Total	12	12
Were acceptable substitutes for boycotted goods readily available to consumers at comparable prices?		
Yes	10	12
No	2	0
Total	12	12
Were consumer violations of the boycott visible to the public?		
Yes, publicly visible	3	2
Yes, but only in retail stores	9	8
No, only in the home	0	2
Total	12	12

[a] Some boycott targets were selected for more than one reason; thus totals exceed 12 for both columns.

Also of interest was whether acceptable substitutes for the goods being boycotted were readily available to consumers and at a comparable price. This question, which was discussed in Chapter 2, is often more relevant to commodity boycotts (e.g., coffee) because committed users of the commodity often have difficulty finding an attractive alternative. For many brand-name goods, however, acceptable substitutes are often available at a comparable price, and this is what was found for this study. With the exception of the tuna boycott, where all three major producers of tuna were boycotted (making it, in effect, a commodity boycott), all of the EP and AR boycotts targeted goods that were available in nonboycotted form at comparable prices.

A final concern of Table 8.3 is the visibility of consumer violations of the boycott. The logic here, which was explained in Chapter 2, is that a marketplace-oriented boycott is more likely to be effective if it targets products whose purchase or use is done openly, thus assuring that others will be aware of the transgressor's actions. As indicated in Table 8.3, most of the boycotts targeted retail goods of the sort that public exposure of the violator's transgression would be limited primarily to the retail store environment (9 EP and 8 AR boycotts). Some boycotts, however, featured products whose identities would be apparent to observers outside the store environment (e.g., furs in general, and Chrysler and General Motors cars in particular). Still other boycotts targeted products that are usually purchased in the privacy of one's home or office, and that, when used, do not carry with them telltale indicators of the company name.[2]

Boycott Communications

In light of the media orientation of the boycotts, one might think that their leaders would attempt to dramatize their causes in the hopes of attracting the attention of the media. And this is indeed what was found both with regard to the boycott announcements and follow-on activity. Boycotters produced protest demonstrations, press conferences featuring disenchanted former employees of target companies, celebrity dramatizations of boycott issues, the unfurling of giant banners in public places, disruptions of stockholder meetings, and mass picketing at the homes and offices of corporate leaders. As indicated in Table 8.4, 10 of the boycott groups made use of such tactics in their boycott announcements (6 EP and 4 AR boycotts), and 17 did so in follow-on pursuits (10 EP and 7 AR boycotts). Especially active here were the Rainforest Action Network (RAN) and People for the Ethical Treatment of Animals (PETA).

While the boycott groups communicated with the media, in many instances they did not communicate with the targets of their actions prior to the start of the boycott (see Table 8.4). Indeed, in only 4 EP and 6 AR actions did such communication occur. And while more communications between boycott groups and their targets occurred for EP actions after the boycott began (10 as compared to 4), the number (6) stays the same for AR boycotts.

Why the lack of communication for so many AR boycotts? It appears that PETA, the group primarily responsible for most of the animal rights boycotts, had made its demands known early to target companies, asking them to sign a statement indicating that

Table 8.4 Frequency Distributions for Boycott Communications

Communication Aspect	EP	AR
Was drama employed in making the boycott announcement?		
Yes	6	4
No	6	7
Don't Know	0	1
Total	12	12
Was drama employed in subsequent boycott actions?		
Yes	10	7
No	2	3
Don't Know	0	2
Total	12	12
Was there communication between boycotters and target prior to call for boycott?		
Yes	4	6
No	8	6
Total	12	12
Was there communication between boycotters and target after call for boycott?		
Yes	10	6
No	0	6
Don't Know	2	0
Total	12	12

they would cease using animals in product tests and would not use animals for this purpose in the future. Since PETA had made clear that its position was not negotiable, it apparently saw little reason for communication to occur (unless, of course, a target wished to capitulate).

Boycott Outcomes

Though a boycott might have many outcomes, most observers focus primarily on its success or failure. Here we apply to the AR and EP boycotts the criteria for measuring success (consequence and execution) that we presented in Chapter 1.

The first item of Table 8.5 considers the consequence criterion. At the outset it should be noted that slightly more than a third of the boycotts realized their objectives either completely or partly. Four of the PETA boycotts were successful in securing commitments to end animal testing (from Avon, Benetton, General Motors, and Neutrogena), while other animal rights boycotts directed at drug companies did not secure such commitments. Five of the EP boycotts were successful in whole or in part. Let us examine them in turn.

First, Heinz, Bumble Bee Seafoods, and Van Kamp agreed to Earth Island Institute's conditions for ending the tuna boycott in a manner that would halt the wholesale killing of dolphins by tuna fishing interests. Also, Dow agreed to the demand of the Environmental Action Foundation and the Environmental Defense Fund that it stop using the term "photodegradable" in the labeling and advertising of its plastic bags. (The bags are photodegradable only under very special environmental conditions that are not likely to be met in the daily life of the American consumer.) Moreover, Empire-Berol yielded to the Rainforest Action Network's demand that it stop importing tropical timber from rain forests to use in the manufacture of its pencils. Empire-Berol indicated that it had assumed that its suppliers secured the timber from sources employing sustained-yield management practices; when further inquiries by Empire-Berol found otherwise, the company discontinued importing the tropical timber.

As to execution criteria, we find little or no evidence in Table 8.5 of an overall effect on consumer purchases during the boycott

Table 8.5 Frequency Distributions for Boycott Outcomes

Outcome	EP	AR
Consequences/effects of boycott		
Terminated as a complete success (all objectives met)	5	4
Terminated as a partial success (some objectives met)	0	0
Terminated as a failure (no objectives met)	0	0
Ongoing (active)	6	3
Ongoing (inactive)	1	5
Total	12	12
Estimated execution effect of boycott on target's sales during boycott period		
A somewhat positive effect	0	0
A somewhat negative effect	1	1
No evidence of an effect	11	11
Total	12	12
Estimated execution effect of boycott on target's sales in postboycott period		
A somewhat positive effect	0	0
A somewhat negative effect	0	0
No evidence of an effect	5	4
Total	5	4
Estimated execution effect of boycott on target's image during boycott period		
A somewhat positive effect	0	0
A somewhat negative effect	3	4
No evidence of an effect	9	8
Total	12	12
Estimated execution effect of boycott on target's image in postboycott period		
A somewhat positive effect	1	1
A somewhat negative effect	1	0
No evidence of an effect	3	2
Total	5	3
Did boycott result in organizational/procedural changes being made by target company to make boycotts less likely (or less damaging) in the future?		
Yes	1	2
No	11	10
Total	12	12

period or after the boycott was settled (in the cases for which a settlement occurred). Perhaps not surprisingly due to their media orientation, boycott groups generally tended not to claim that their efforts had affected sales, and this lack of impact was also reported by the corporate respondents in the study.

The situation for image effects reported in Table 8.5 was somewhat stronger. In 7 of the boycotts (3 EP and 4 AR boycotts), the target's image was hurt, as indicated by the respondent's comments and by news articles covering the boycotts. Affected somewhat negatively on the EP side were Heinz, Bumble Bee, and Ralston Purina. Affected somewhat negatively on the AR side were Avon, Benetton, General Motors, and Gillette.

At the conclusion of the boycotts, most of the targeted companies found themselves in a neutral image zone since they were no longer the subjects of image-threatening stories in the news media. Two exceptions appear to be Heinz and Benetton. Each company did a complete about-face at the end of the boycott, using to advantage its new position as the first major company to adopt the boycotters' platform as its own. Heinz used this turnabout in its advertising, claiming that it was the corporate leader of the dolphin-safe campaign and praising Earth Island Institute for its contributions to this effort. Moreover, Benetton became a "friend" of the animal rights movement by contributing significantly to PETA's fund-raising efforts.

One last data question in Table 8.5 is worthy of note: Did the boycotts prompt the companies to make organizational or procedural changes so that boycotts would be less likely or less damaging in the future? As indicated in Table 8.5, almost all of the companies answered this question in the negative. The two exceptions on the AR side spoke of internal efforts to take a broader view of their corporate mandate so as to include environmental and social concerns. The one exception on the EP side noted that it had dropped its local public relations firm in favor of a national firm with experience in crisis management.

Boycotts as Dynamic Entities

In the preceding discussion, boycotts have been treated as static entities that occur in virtually context-free environments. Also suggested by the tables, with their frequency distributions, is that a boycott's occurrence and outcome are independent phenomena, uninfluenced by the behavior of other boycotts. In this brief section we see that this simple picture of boycotts is more myth than reality.

At the outset the reader should note that several of the boycotts discussed here fit together into two networks (an animal testing network and a dolphin-safe network). Within each network a boycott group looked initially for an Achilles' heel, a company that could serve as a promising first target. "Promising" here means that (a) the company would be relatively easy for the boycotters to defeat, and (b) once defeated, its demise would influence other targets in the network to yield as well.

Interestingly, the Achilles' heels selected for these domino-effect roles were Heinz for the dolphin-safe network and Benetton for the animal testing network. In both cases the boycott groups made excellent strategic choices in that these two targets not only yielded to the boycott pressure, but their yielding generated the desired domino effect. Indeed, as a result, most cosmetics sold in the U.S. are no longer tested on animals, and virtually all canned tuna sold in American markets is "dolphin-safe."

For the AR network, PETA focused first on Benetton for several reasons. First, the international women's clothier had hundreds of stores throughout the United States to serve as convenient targets for picketing and demonstrations. Second, PETA had support groups in England and Italy that would help by participating in a coordinated international protest at Benetton stores. Third, Benetton had just started to broaden its merchandise line to include its own brand of cosmetics, so its policies with regard to animal testing of these products were newly formed and thus more amenable to change than the policies of more established cosmetics companies.

PETA launched the Benetton boycott in 1988 as part of its "Compassion Campaign." Two months later Benetton yielded, and shortly thereafter Avon, Revlon, and many other smaller cosmetic firms followed suit.

The Heinz Starkist story followed a similar pattern. The dolphin-safe campaign was initiated by Earth Island Institute in

1988 with a commodity boycott of all canned tuna because none of it was dolphin-safe. Three brands dominated the tuna industry at the time of the boycott: Starkist (the Heinz brand), Bumble Bee, and Chicken of the Sea. Shortly after the tuna boycott began, Earth Island Institute concentrated its boycott efforts on Heinz, targeting all Heinz products including nontuna items. Why Heinz? According to an Earth Island Institute spokesperson,

> We chose Heinz because they were the largest and they were American-owned so consumers communicating to an American company made a lot of sense. They were a company that had a reputation for being interested in life enhancement, so they had a public posture that was important to them.

In the months that followed the Earth Island Institute decision to target Heinz, pressure was exerted on the company by a diverse cast of characters including ecology-minded schoolchildren and celebrities from the entertainment business. When, on April 12, 1990, Heinz announced that it would yield to all of the demands of the boycotters, the ensuing domino effect could hardly have been more immediate; within hours Heinz's two corporate competitors (the producers of Chicken of the Sea and Bumble Bee tuna) announced their intentions to implement similar dolphin-safe policies. Despite some glitches in the adoption of these policies, they were eventually implemented, and the boycott ended.[3]

Discussion

Study Limitations

All empirical research studies have limitations, and this study is no exception. Among the limitations are the small sample size and the lack of independence of some members of the sample, a lack that became apparent in the foregoing discussion of domino effects.

Related to the small sample problem is that of sample bias. Some major corporations (e.g., Exxon) declined to participate in the study and one boycott group did as well. And while one may speculate about the reasons for their nonparticipation, the fact remains that the sample may be unrepresentative of contemporary EP and AR boycotts.

Other study limitations concern the use of interviews. In this context, the people interviewed, especially those representing large organizations, tended to be public relations specialists whose job it is to present their organizations in the best possible light. This objective may well have colored the statements they provided. In addition, interviews are subject to such obvious factors as memory lapses (some of the boycotts were five years old) and lack of information (some of the people interviewed came on the job after the boycott began).

A final limitation concerns the external validity of the findings. Since many of the boycotts occurred while the economy was in a recession, placing severe pressure on many consumers and corporations, the boycott actions may not generalize to time periods in which the economy is in a healthier state.

Interpreting the Study Findings

In light of the serious limitations inherent in the study design, the findings should be viewed with considerable caution. Indeed, it would seem prudent to view trends in the data not as firm foundations for definitive empirical generalizations, but merely as suggestions of such generalizations. Should additional research using different samples and methodologies yield similar findings to those uncovered here, then, of course, the generalizations could and should be voiced more strongly. But until such circumstances occur, a modest close-to-the-data approach would seem very much in order.

With these caveats in mind it is well to ask what generalizations are suggested by the data. Of special interest are generalizations that are consistent with past research findings on consumer activism (e.g., Berry, 1977; Brobeck, 1991, 1997; Herrmann and Mayer, 1997; Mayer, 1989; Smith, 1990; Vogel, 1970) and past boycott practice (e.g., Adams, 1991; Clarkson, 1984; Friedman, 1971, 1985, 1991; Garrett, 1987; Pruitt & Friedman, 1986; and Putnam & Muck, 1991). Among the data suggestions of interest are the following:

1. Contemporary EP and AR boycotts tend to be national in scope.
2. Contemporary EP and AR boycotts tend to be more instrumental than expressive in character.
3. Contemporary EP and AR boycotts tend to be of long duration with many lasting for a year or more.
4. Contemporary EP and AR boycotts tend to assume a militant stance, featuring such actions as pickets and demonstrations.
5. Contemporary EP and AR boycotts tend to target producers and processors rather than retailers.
6. Contemporary EP and AR boycotts tend to be more media-oriented than marketplace-oriented.
7. In seeking targets for their actions, the largely media-oriented EP and AR boycott groups tend to look for image-related weaknesses to exploit through the skillful use of dramatic devices and techniques.
8. However, marketplace-oriented boycott considerations, such as product characteristics, are not ignored in EP and AR actions.
9. Communications between boycotters and targets in contemporary EP and AR actions follow no simple pattern.
10. Whether measured by execution or consequence criteria, the success rate for EP and AR boycotts tends to be modest.
11. Postboycott periods see few organizational changes by targets to make boycotts less likely or damaging in the future.
12. While some boycotts may be productively studied as static entities in isolation from each other, other boycotts are more profitably viewed as dynamic interdependent entities, and these boycotts defy understanding unless studied as networks of actions in the context of a larger unfolding boycott campaign.

The Role of Consumer Activism in Securing a Sustainable Future

As noted earlier, a key concern of the interview study was to determine what lessons could be learned from the boycott experiences to help activists work more effectively to secure the goal of a sustainable future. In this section we address this concern.

First it should be noted that many observers believe a major societal transformation will be required to realize the goal of a sustainable future. Further, this transformation, which will affect such critical areas as energy utilization, pollution control, and waste disposal, cannot succeed without the help of major corporations (Davis, 1991). There are many ways to secure their participation (government regulation, tax incentives, etc.), and consumer activism in general—and consumer boycotts in particular—would appear to be one of them. Indeed, a case could be made for organized consumer action in the form of boycotts as one of the more attractive tactics available to ordinary people seeking to secure a sustainable future. For, in theory, the boycott permits such individuals to exercise "economic democracy" every day with their purchases in the marketplace by rewarding companies whose actions are ecologically sound and by punishing companies whose actions are not. By joining a boycott campaign, consumers are able, in theory, to exert economic pressure on corporations to influence their actions in ecologically desirable directions.

The critical question that naturally arises is how well economic democracy theory translates into practice. The findings of this modest study suggest that what works in theory may not work in practice. While it is true that some of the boycotts were effective, most were not. And those that were effective were characterized by certain psychological properties that may limit the usefulness of the consumer boycott tactic to the promoters of a sustainable future. In particular, the objectives of the successful boycotts tended to be cognitively simple and emotionally appealing. Indeed, some of these objectives took on the character of catchy slogans, such as "Save the dolphins" (from the nets of the tuna fishermen) or "Save the rabbits" (from the tests of the cosmetics developers). Unfortunately, the complexities inherent in many ecological recommendations for corporate practices are not likely to be reducible to simple slogans for energizing and directing boycott campaigns.

The successful boycotts apparently worked not because consumers stopped buying the boycotted goods but because the boycotters were able to secure news media coverage of the offending practices of the targeted companies. This suggests that ecological change agents, intent upon securing a sustainable future through changes in corporate behavior, may wish to consider mounting major media-oriented boycott campaigns, especially if the boycott objectives can be reduced to simple slogans. Such campaigns are often expensive and indeed, it was relatively large and well-funded organizations, such as PETA and RAN, that were able to initiate and sustain them. By contrast, smaller organizations, such as Waste Oil Action, with more complex boycott objectives (increase the use of certain recycled oil in the manufacture of automobiles) were not able to mount major publicity campaigns, and this may be why their efforts did not succeed.

While the complexities of ecological change objectives may not lend themselves very easily to the consumer boycott tactic, occasions may arise that suggest the boycott as the approach to take. A circumstance that comes to mind is a new corporate initiative that demonstrates insensitivity to ecological considerations. This is what happened when Dow referred to its plastic bags as "photodegradable" despite the fact that under normal consumer use and disposal the materials did not readily degrade. The publicity resulting from the boycott call by two environmental groups led to government inquiries and eventually to an end of the mislabeling practice.

To sum up, while in theory consumer boycotts offer the ecological strategist a powerful weapon for prompting corporations to work toward the realization of a sustainable future, in practice, the boycott tactic may have limited usefulness. The tactic would appear to work most effectively under circumstances that permit the ecological objectives of a boycott to be reduced to a simple message with wide appeal to American consumers. Even in such instances, a major publicity campaign may well be required, one that focuses on the media at least as much, if not more, than it focuses on the marketplace. While these circumstances are likely to be uncommon, given the complexities of ecological change policy, this is not to say that they are nonexistent. Indeed, the occurrence of major visible corporate errors in ecological policy may be the circumstance most likely to be successfully dealt with by a boycott initiative.

Closing Comments

While its methodology may be less than ideal, this interview study of contemporary EP and AR boycotts suggests several generalizations about these actions. Perhaps most significant is the media orientation of these various protest efforts with their emphasis on dramatic actions. Also significant are the modest success rates for these efforts and the frequent linkage of success to a larger interconnected boycott campaign. Domino effects were responsible for many of the successes tied to these larger campaigns, and such campaigns may offer a model for boycott efforts of the future. Finally, it is suggested that these efforts may work best for ecological strategists, if boycott objectives can be reduced to cognitively simple messages with wide appeal to American consumers.

◆9◆

CONSUMER "BUYCOTTS"

Readers of the consumer affairs literature are often struck by its accent on the negative. Much has been said, for example, about irresponsible actions of corporations in the marketplace; also frequently criticized are the impulsive behaviors of consumers, especially those who have been duped out of their savings by confidence swindlers.

In this chapter the other side of the coin is explored in that a project report is presented of an effort to identify and evaluate a positive behavioral model for consumer activism. In what follows, the background of this research project is presented along with the project goal. Next the research procedure is described, and a brief summary is presented of the research findings and their implications.

Some activists see a promising alternative to consumer boycotts in their "flip side," consumer buycotts, which attempt to induce shoppers to buy the products or services of selected companies in order to reward them for behavior consistent with the goals of the activists. While boycotts often aim to punish firms for past misdeeds, buycotts commonly endeavor to reward them for past good deeds, and the reward approach is generally favored by behavioral theorists and practitioners (e.g., Bandura, 1969, 1987).

Although buycotts have not enjoyed the popularity of their boycott counterparts among consumer activists, given the limited success of boycotts and the behavioral science promise of buycotts, this research project had as its goal an extensive study of consumer buycotts with recommendations concerning how this tactic might be effectively used by activists.

Before pursuing consumer buycotts further, two caveats should be noted. First, these actions, like their consumer boycott counterparts, should be viewed as marketplace means to secure what may or may not be marketplace ends. Thus, in addition to such usual consumer economic concerns as lower prices and higher quality goods, a multitude of other considerations, such as minority rights, environmental quality, and fairness of labor practices, may assume significant roles in buycott actions. The second caveat is that to avoid confusion with commercial advertising, the consumer buycott term should not be used to refer to pro-buying initiatives with a profit-making orientation.

Project Procedures and Results

To study ongoing consumer buycotts a three-step procedure was envisioned consisting of identifying such initiatives through a literature review, conducting interviews with their principals, and analyzing the data generated by the interviews. This effort was to be supplemented by trips to special boycott resource centers in Washington, D.C. (Co-op America), and Seattle, Washington (the Institute for Corporate Responsibility), since these centers' files contain private correspondence and internal reports not generally available in university libraries.

The literature review focused primarily on American news sources such as *Newsbank*, which, since the mid-1970s, has been indexing news stories on microfiche for more than 100 American newspapers. Also examined were magazines and academic publications by searching through available hard copy and computerized sources (e.g., CD-ROMs for *Psychological Abstracts, Sociological Abstracts*, and *ABI-INFORM*).

These various initiatives were all undertaken, but unfortunately they produced few instances of documented buycott campaigns (e.g., Bird and Robinson, 1972). Suggestions regarding the reasons for the paucity of buycott campaigns were offered in interviews with the two boycott resource center coordinators in Seattle and Washington, D.C. (as well as a third interview with the coordinator of a relatively new boycott resource center, the Center for Economic Democracy in Seattle, which published *The Boycott Quarterly*). The reason most often noted was that organized activist groups tend to favor protest (boycotts) over praise (buycotts) as a means for effecting change. In addition, one coordinator noted that the name "buycott" was too new and unfamiliar to be widely employed, and thus it is not likely to show up in a literature review. Indeed, the lack of universal agreement on a term to represent the buycott practice was made evident by such alternatives to buycott as "girlcott," "procott," "reverse boycott," and "antiboycott," all of which were found in the popular and scholarly literature. "White list" was also used in association with buycott actions in sharp contrast to the boycott-related "black list." Indeed, at the turn of the century the National Consumers League white-listed department stores with personnel policies that demonstrated concern for the working conditions of women and child employees.

The dearth of buycott cases to scrutinize in the current literature prompted a broadening of the study objectives to (1) include historical and foreign material and (2) develop a conceptual framework for understanding the place of buycotts, both descriptively and prescriptively, on a consumer activist agenda. The historical and foreign material focused on such initiatives as early consumer buycotts in the United States of union goods and black business offerings as well as contemporary Dutch and Belgian consumer initiatives to buy coffee grown by small Third World producers.[1] Also included were such historical *and* foreign initiatives as the Nazi Party campaign in the 1930s to encourage German consumers to buy from German businesses, rather that Jewish businesses.[2] (All non-Jewish stores were urged to bear an identifying sign stating "German Shop.") A more recent historical initiative including domestic and foreign interests was the campaign launched in 1985 by nuclear abolitionists in Australia and the United States; this campaign urged consumers to buy products from New Zealand in support of its government's refusal to allow American ships carrying nuclear weapons to dock in its harbors.

While information on many of these buycott initiatives might best be described as fragmentary, what there is, in conjunction with the much more comprehensive material available on boycotts and other consumer initiatives (e.g., Friedman, 1991; Smith, 1990), has sparked the first steps in the development of a conceptual framework for buycotts that may prove of interest to scholars as well as practitioners.

Perhaps the most fundamental distinction drawn by this framework is between *calls for buycotts* and *actual buycotts*.

Calls for Buycotts

Calls for buycotts are typically public pleas made in the news media by individuals or by organizations although they are usually made by organizations. (The public character of the call is important in that a private recommendation to make a particular consumer purchase communicated to one individual by another, say a friend or a neighbor, would not be considered a call for a consumer buycott.) And consistent with our earlier definition, the parties calling for a buycott would have no profit motive for doing so.

In addition, a buycott call may be direct or indirect. A direct call would take the form of a public announcement requesting consumers to purchase one or more products or services. An indirect call could take several forms. Most typically, such calls consist of published lists or seals of approval that identify available products, services, and/or retailers being recommended to consumers. Lists may take such forms as green pages (ecologically oriented companies recommended by environmental groups such as Co-op America), "best buys" (product brands and models recommended for purchase by *Consumer Reports* and other consumer testing publications), and "cruelty-free" products (product brands and models for, say, cosmetics developed by using a process that does not endanger the health or well-being of laboratory animals).

Seals of approval are also diverse in nature, including traditional union labels, the RUGMARK seal of the National Consumers League indicating that a carpet has not been made with child labor, and various environmental seals of approval, such as

Green Cross and Green Seal and the dolphin-safe symbol now appearing on canned tuna.

Actual Buycotts

Actual buycotts go beyond such published lists and seals of approval to launch organized campaigns for the purpose of persuading consumers to purchase the one or more items identified by the buycott. The Buy American campaign is an example of such an actual buycott; this campaign generated television commercials featuring such celebrities as Bob Hope highlighting "Made in America" labels on items of clothing in a retail context. This particular buycott campaign illustrates some of the parallels between modern-day buycott and boycott campaigns. A key similarity is the focus of both campaigns on the media rather than the marketplace in that a television ad rather than a retail store picket line was employed to spread the campaign message (Friedman, 1991). The Buy American campaign also illustrates a couple of substantive problems often associated with buycott campaigns. One is identification: In today's complex manufacturing environment, it is often not clear if a consumer product is of domestic or foreign origin. Another is long-term consequence: Many economists believe that an effective Buy American campaign could hurt rather than help the American economy (Lohr, 1993).

Many so-called buycotts appear to be calls for buycotts rather than actual buycotts. And this being the case, it is questionable whether they can really be considered to be true buycotts. For as every advertiser knows well from experience, published lists or seals of approval are often a necessary but insufficient step to alter well-established consumer purchase behaviors; an advertising or promotional campaign is usually needed to make the message actionable.

Other Conceptual Distinctions among Buycotts

A second fundamental conceptual distinction among buycotts is between the parties serving as the target of the buycott and the parties whose actions are being heralded by the buycotters. Sometimes they are one and the same, as in the case of a buycott being called to reward a retailer who has donated a substantial percentage of its profit to charity. In other instances the heralded party may not be directly accessible to the buycotters so they choose a proxy to reward instead. An illustration of this kind of indirect action is the case of a group that finds itself favorably impressed by the government policies of a city, state, or foreign nation and acts upon its feelings by buycotting the businesses operating in the affected geographic area. Thus we find that buycotts may be viewed as direct or indirect with regard to the targets they endeavor to reward. Since indirect buycotts have a "stand-in" quality to their targets we borrow a page from the boycott taxonomy of Chapter 1 and refer to them as *surrogate buycotts* (the New Zealand buycott referred to earlier is an example), and to complete the analogy, we refer to direct buycotts as *nonsurrogate buycotts*.

Yet a third conceptual distinction among buycotts draws upon the terminology of McCarthy and Zald (1973) and its application to consumer boycotts by Friedman (1991). This distinction, which was introduced in Chapter 1, is between *beneficiary buycotts* and *conscience buycotts*. The former refers to a buycott initiative in which the sponsors and beneficiaries are of the same constituency, such as an organized labor action to encourage the purchase of union-labeled products. The latter refers to buycott efforts, such as an animal rights campaign, in which the sponsors and beneficiaries are of different constituencies (in this case, human sponsors and animal beneficiaries). Some observers believe the beneficiary and conscience categories provide a potentially useful distinction between selfish and selfless actions; in practice, however, the distinction is often difficult to draw and maintain.

A fourth fundamental distinction among buycotts drawn by the conceptual framework is between *single-target buycotts* and *multiple-target buycotts*. Among actual buycotts (those with campaigns) the multiple-target varieties appear to be the more common (e.g., consumers being urged to buy union-made products or products made in America). Only rarely, it seems, is a single target the focus of a buycott, such as a single brand and model of a product or a single manufacturer or retailer. While the reasons for this apparent difference in frequency of usage for the two types of buycotts are not altogether clear, two related factors may be influential. The first is that a consumer group may be reluctant to mount a campaign urging people to buy a single company's products or services because such a campaign might raise questions of propriety about the consumer group and its relationship to the benefiting firm. The second factor, which is more complex, stems from the observation that multiple-target buycotts (but not single-target buycotts) are sometimes multiple-target boycotts in disguise, with the accent, for public relations reasons, being on the positive rather than the negative. Thus, for example, a proposed consumer boycott by Americans of Japanese goods may be redefined as a consumer buycott of American goods; the change of emphasis from the negative to the positive reassures Americans that they are being asked to act patriotically rather than chauvinistically. Interestingly, single-target buycotts (such as a campaign to buy Coca-Cola) do not usually result from such a boycott-to-buycott transformational process since it is the rare multiple-target boycott that excludes all products, services, or firms except the one that would be the focus of a single-target buycott.

The foregoing analysis suggests that consumer buycotts are not likely to go beyond the simple assembling of "multiple-items-to-purchase lists," in that they seldom initiate campaigns (especially single-target campaigns) to serve the protest needs of consumer activist groups. As we have seen, one exception may be the case of a multiple target that cannot be boycotted due to public relations considerations, so a multiple-target buycott campaign is launched instead. Two other cases that constitute exceptions concern gay rights in Florida and viewer attachment to a national television show.

The Florida Gay Rights Buycott Campaign

This buycott was initiated by the Human Rights Task Force of Florida in early 1993, according to task force co-chair Todd Simmons, in reaction to Tampa's repeal of its Human Rights Ordinance, which had outlawed discrimination based on sexual orientation. The buycott's goal was "to identify and list businesses and organizations that have policies banning sexual-orientation-based discrimination, and to help businesses and organizations that do not have such policies consider and enact them" (Lyons, 1994, p. 14).

Why a buycott instead of a boycott? According to Simmons, even though Tampa's ordinance had been repealed, a human rights ordinance, although a weaker one, was still in effect for Tampa's Hillsborough County, so that opportunities were present for identifying and rewarding companies that were acting in accord with the ordinance's antidiscrimination principles. Also, according to Simmons, many local leaders denounced the repeal of the Tampa ordinance, leading the task force to believe that a buycott might be supported. And finally, the task force had been observing the reactions to the Colorado boycott called after a voter repeal of a state law banning sexual-orientation-based discrimination, and, according to Simmons, the task force believed that the boycott "was solidifying, rather than changing, public opinion."

The Florida buycott issued a *Buycott Handbook* in early 1993 with 104 local listings. Three printings later the handbook had increased its listings to more than 1,000, including state as well as national businesses and organizations. In addition to providing the handbook listings, the buycotters distributed buycott "thank you" cards to allow consumers to inform businesses that they were being patronized because of their antidiscrimination policies. One beneficial result of the buycott, according to Simmons, was that it helped secure nondiscriminatory changes in local business policies.

The *Twin Peaks* Buycott Campaign

About 10 years ago *Twin Peaks* was a successful offbeat television drama that appeared weekly on the ABC network. When the show's ratings dropped dramatically, the network decided not to renew it for another season.

Many of the show's loyal fans struck back in 1991 with a buycott of products advertised on the show. They hoped that their buying power and organizational skills could persuade advertisers to convince ABC to retain *Twin Peaks* for another season (Clary, 1991). The loyal fans formed COOP (Citizens Opposed to the Offing of *Peaks*) to reward the program's sponsors. COOP consisted of 10,000 members who spread the message through word of mouth, mailings, and computer bulletin board announcements. According to Clary (1991), COOP leaders urged its members to inform sponsors of their buycott actions through calls, letters, and proof-of-purchase receipts. Among the sponsors contacted were Burger King, Coors, Aqua Fresh, and Ultra Slim-Fast.

Despite special events, such as a planned nationwide buy-a-meal-at-Burger King day, the COOP campaign failed in that the show was canceled. According to one network executive, the show's low ratings did it in. "The economics aren't there," she said.

New Roles for Consumer Buycotts

Encouraged by these buycott campaigns, one might wish to consider special needs of consumer activist groups at the community and national levels that could be served by buycotts.

The Community Level

Local government often does a lot to help attract and retain for-profit companies, using such approaches as tax breaks, new access roads, rezoning, and free or low-cost parking for employees or customers. Sometimes, however, the appropriate initiative may have to come from outside government, with individual consumers coming together to help one or more for-profit companies survive and prosper. One such initiative that comes to mind at the community level considers campaigns to help selected retail businesses, such as special-niche bookstores, foreign restaurants, and other for-profit enhancers of "cultural diversity" or "ambiance" that are endangered by lack of patronage. A campaign by "Friends of . . ." to "Save . . ." may make a difference in the survival of such businesses and the special qualities their presence adds to a community. While such campaigns (as well as other fund-raisers) are common in the not-for-profit arena, they are relatively rare in the for-profit sector. One form such a campaign might take is promoting the sale of gift certificates for use at the threatened retail business. Just as annual campaigns in the not-for-profit arena, such as the United Way, have dollar-amount goals, so might a gift certificate campaign have an annual dollar goal to keep certain business off the "endangered status" list.

The National Level

At the national level, a similar rationale could be used to launch buycotts to reward for-profit companies, such as Ben & Jerry's and the Body Shop, that donate a substantial portion of their proceeds to charitable causes, although the "substantial" claim was recently questioned in the case of the Body Shop (Entine, 1994). Moreover, the Philanthropic Advisory Service, a Washington-based center that gathers data on charities, has warned that some companies suggest that they will increase donations to charities if consumers purchase more of their products when they in fact have already agreed to donate fixed dollar amounts (Elliott, 1992).

Consumer groups must also be sensitive to the possibility of backlashes. For example, a few years ago Sears, Roebuck & Company pledged to donate to the Humane Society 8 percent of the proceeds from sales of special stuffed animals in one of its annual consumer catalogs. When the National Rifle Association complained, according to Elliott (1992), Sears discontinued selling the toys.

Buycott Campaigns in Perspective

Buycott campaigns may represent a conceptual breakthrough for the consumer activist in that they look at for-profit companies through the same lens usually reserved for not-for-profits. Just as concerned consumers launch fund-raisers to reward deserving not-for-profit companies, so, the examples cited here suggest, they might also consider initiating buycotts to reward deserving for-profit organizations. For many businesses, and especially those associated with the arts and humanities, the distinction between for-profit and not-for-profit is disappearing as so-called for-profits find themselves increasingly vulnerable to economic pressures.

One important distinction that does, however, remain between the two is that the for-profit organization is more likely than its not-for-profit counterpart to offer a consumer commodity for sale in the marketplace. And, as we all know too well, the commodity can range in quality on a consumer economic scale from a "lemon" to a "best buy." While it may be reasonable in theory to employ buycott campaigns to reward businesses for their contributions to the community, most consumers would balk at participating in such campaigns if the commodities to be purchased are deficient from a consumer economic perspective. So consumer activists considering buycott campaigns should give thought to this perspective as well as others on which the target companies may be performing at a lower-than-desired level. (See the *Shopping for a Better World* publications of the Council on Economic Priorities for more information concerning corporate performance from various perspectives other than consumer economics.)

Some Research Questions

This brief analysis of consumer buycotts has raised far more questions than it has answered. Among the queries of interest to consumer researchers and practitioners are the following:

1. Why does the consumer buycott appear to be such a rarely used tactic among activist groups? Might a practical constraint be operating here in that relatively few opportunities emerge in the real world for activists to express their concerns through the promotion of selected consumer purchases (to reward firms for doing "good deeds")? Or, as suggested earlier, might it be a sociological constraint in that the opportunities may emerge but they are incompatible with the protest orientation of many activist groups, which appears to be far more in harmony with a consumer boycott approach?
2. Under what circumstances is a consumer buycott likely to be effective? Is effectiveness more likely for consumer economic campaigns (higher quality or lower price goods) or for campaigns in the political, ecological, and sociological arenas?
3. What success rate is likely to be associated with campaigns that combine a buycott *and* a boycott (a buoycott?)? Psycho-

logically speaking, this introduces approach and avoidance elements into the consumer's cognitive matrix; might some consumers find this message too complex or too contentious for comfort?

4. And finally, how does one ensure that consumer buycotts are not corrupted by the commercial interests that profit by selling buycotted goods? Might a high-sounding consumer buycott campaign be a sophisticated smokescreen for a retail sales promotion? To whom might consumers turn for guidance in such matters?

Concluding Comments

These findings, while modest in scope, offer some new questions and insights into consumer activism and some new possibilities for future campaigns. First, the findings suggest that true buycotts (those that go beyond simple calls for buycotts to include buycott campaigns) are relatively unusual. Second, some of those that do exist may really be boycotts in disguise (i.e., multiple-target boycotts that for public relations reasons have been billed as multiple-target buycotts). Moreover, given the protest character of many activist organizations, it is hardly surprising that they should favor boycotts over buycotts. However, this is not to say that no productive role exists for consumer buycotts; indeed, as we have seen, they would appear to offer a potentially effective tactic for rewarding deserving for-profit companies in somewhat the same way that fund-raisers have been used to reward deserving not-for-profit companies.

◆ 10 ◆
BOYCOTT ISSUES AND TACTICS IN HISTORICAL PERSPECTIVE

While many dimensions and types of boycotts have been identified in this book, two boycott distinctions have special importance as historical markers. The first distinction, which was alluded to previously, is between *marketplace-oriented boycotts* and *media-oriented boycotts*. Because this distinction deals with a boycott's primary orientation, a marketplace-oriented boycott may also be concerned with the media, and a media-oriented boycott may also be concerned with the marketplace.

The second distinction, between *surrogate boycotts* and *nonsurrogate boycotts*, derives from the observation that boycotts may be direct or indirect with regard to the actions they take against offending parties. If, as is usually the case, the offending party is an economic entity with consumer goods for sale to the public (e.g., a major food corporation), the boycotters can, of course, act upon it directly. If, on the other hand, the offending party is not accessible directly through the marketplace, an indirect action may be possible. This is what happens when a group is dissatisfied with the government policies of a city, state, or foreign nation, and acts upon its feelings by boycotting the businesses operating in the affected geographic area. Since their targets have a "stand-in" quality, we have referred to these indirect boycotts as surrogate boycotts, and we have referred to direct boycotts as nonsurrogate boycotts (Friedman, 1985).

In what follows we examine the two boycott distinctions in historical context.

Early Consumer Boycotts

At the turn of the century, consumer boycotts emerged as a major grassroots force to deal with economic issues. They were usually undertaken by the poor and powerless elements of society, often recent immigrants to America with few resources at their disposal. Not surprisingly, given the lowly position of these new Americans on the Maslow hierarchy of motives, their primary focus was on the acquisition of economic necessities—making a livable wage and securing basic consumer goods at affordable prices.

Given the minor role of the news media in the lives of Americans of the time, the early boycott efforts were marketplace oriented rather than media oriented. Moreover, almost all of the early boycotts were nonsurrogate (rather than surrogate) in that they attempted to directly affect the offending businesses at the cash register. Indeed, it was a loss of consumer sales that the boycott leaders believed to be the key to concessions by the targets. Some of the tactics used in an effort to secure these concessions are noted below.

Getting the Word Out

In the early marketplace-oriented boycotts it was essential for boycott leaders to inform consumers quickly and clearly that certain stores or goods were off-limits. The picket line has long been a dramatic and effective vehicle for communicating this message. The boycott picket line offers three psychological advantages over other tactics. First, as an unusual stimulus in the retail marketplace it gets the consumer's attention. Second, since it is experienced by consumers as they are about to enter a store, little memory loss of its message can be expected. And third, because crossing a picket line can be a highly intimidating action for the transgressor, consumers are motivated to comply with its message.

Other tactics used to get the boycott message out to consumers included word-of-mouth communications, public addresses, meetings in churches and union halls, and leafleting.

Selecting the Boycott Targets

Are some consumer goods and services better boycott targets than others? As Laidler (1913) noted, the early labor boycott leaders soon found that their actions were more likely to be effective if the boycotted goods were "common necessities and inexpensive luxuries purchased regularly by the mass of workers, such, for instance, as newspapers, cigars, hats and certain other articles of clothing, food and furniture" (p. 81). The early focus of consumer economic boycotts on meat (Piott, 1981) and later on other foodstuffs (Friedman, 1995a) is consistent with Laidler's observation.

Obstructionist Tactics

Since the objective of marketplace-oriented boycotts is to decrease sales of the targeted goods, it behooves boycott leaders to consider tactics that place obstacles in the way of consumers who are attempting to buy these goods. Over the years many creative forms of such obstructionist tactics have been used. They have their origins in the "stand-in," a tactic used by protesters in the 1880s to occupy auction halls they were boycotting. By crowding themselves into the halls they left no room for prospective customers to place their bids.

Other Direct Action Tactics

Economic boycott tactics have sometimes gone beyond the boundaries of propriety to assume the form of physical and verbal attacks (as well as the threats of such attacks) directed against uncooperative retail establishments and their customers. Such actions were frequently taken by boycotting immigrants at the turn of the century, and they occurred commonly during the Great Depression.

During this bleak economic period, unprecedented numbers of

urban blacks found themselves jobless, and many turned to the boycott tactic in an effort to create jobs for themselves in their neighborhood retail stores. The result was the "Don't Buy from Where You Can't Work Campaign" that swept across many American cities in the 1930s. The boycotters' attacks included acts of vandalism directed at neighborhood stores without black employees and acts of reprisals against the customers of these stores. Although intimidating tactics have sometimes been effective, often they have proved to be unproductive or counterproductive. Indeed, the immigrant boycotts at the turn of the century triggered a strong negative reaction on the part of the middle class and the establishment press.

Contemporary Consumer Boycotts

Dramatic changes have occurred with regard to the style and substance of consumer boycotts in the modern era. New boycott issues have emerged as have new approaches for conducting boycott campaigns.

New Boycott Issues

A century ago many consumer boycotts dealt with labor issues and consumer price issues. Boycotts relating to these two types of economic issues have largely faded from the scene, and for different reasons. With regard to consumer price issues, the last of the major boycotts addressing these issues occurred in the 1970s in response to rapid rises in prices for such basic food staples as coffee, meat, milk, and sugar. The deafening silence following these nationwide boycotts has been attributed to economic factors (principally a far lower rate of inflation) as well as noneconomic factors (Friedman, 1991). Included among the latter are the increasing unavailability of female homemakers for volunteer boycott activity, such as picketing, with many more now working outside the home; the decreasing role of food staples in the American diet with made-from-scratch meals being replaced by convenience foods and eating out; and the increasing appeal of other, more compelling issues to prospective boycott activists.

With regard to the last point, many activists apparently feel that price-increase issues are boring and unengaging, especially when compared to the currently popular animal rights issues and environmental issues. Moreover, the shift away from price issues may also relate to the financial rewards that women have derived from working outside the home. For many consumers this extra money has contributed substantially to their household incomes, and thus even a fairly large price increase for a favorite food item may have become a matter of no great urgency. Finally, and perhaps most importantly, it should be noted that the deafening silence of the 1980s and 1990s may simply reflect the poor track record of the 1970s. Boycotters cannot be expected to throw their energies into new campaigns when similar ones did not succeed in the past. In the 1970s, food prices dropped during the boycott periods, but typically they returned to their preboycott levels soon after the boycotts ended.

As for labor boycotts in the 1980s and 1990s, what has emerged is a far weaker labor movement and far fewer militant actions, be they strikes or boycotts. To illustrate, Greenhouse (1998) reports that the number of nationwide strikes in 1997 was lower than any year since World War II. As a result of these changes, labor unions are pressing their demands on management but less often on the picket lines through strikes and boycotts. Instead the two sides are more typically opting for the relative quiet of the corporate conference room where union and management leaders try to resolve issues through mediation and arbitration.

With labor and consumer price boycotts receding into the past, new boycott issues have assumed center-stage positions. Many relate to ethnic and racial groups, such as the African American tourism boycotts of Miami and Arizona. Others relate to special-focus groups, such as boycotts led by animal rights activists of cosmetic companies (e.g., Avon, Revlon, and Benetton) that test their products on animals; antiwar boycotts of manufacturers of military weapons (e.g., General Electric); and boycotts led by environmental groups against companies that import tropical timber from rain forests (e.g., Mitsubishi). The religious right has also been active with boycotts of corporate sponsors of network television programs it judges to be too sexually explicit or violent. Interestingly, unlike their historical counterparts, many of these newer issues are concerned not with economic necessities but with higher-order motives on the Maslow hierarchy, perhaps indicating that the comfortable standard of living enjoyed by many Americans is allowing them to go beyond survival concerns to wrestle with quality-of-life issues.

This higher-level concern is particularly evident with regard to the growing number of surrogate boycotts aimed at objectionable public policies at the local, state, and national levels. In the 1980s and 1990s surrogate boycotts have focused on states such as Alaska, Arizona, California, Colorado, Idaho, Iowa, Louisiana, Utah, and Wisconsin by groups representing such interests as animal rights, environmental rights, and gay rights, as well as the competing rights to life and to choose abortion. And, as indicated earlier, cities have not been excluded in that African Americans launched a tourism boycott of Miami in 1990 to protest the snubbing of Nelson Mandela by the city's Cuban American government officials when Mandela visited Miami. Moreover, national surrogate boycotts were called against China and Burma in the early 1990s to protest objectionable human rights practices and against France in the mid-1990s to protest its resumption of nuclear testing.

A New Strategic Approach

As some have noted (Friedman, 1991; Putnam & Muck, 1991), the marketplace-oriented boycotts of the turn of the century have been largely replaced by media-oriented boycotts in the 1980s and 1990s.

Why the change in strategy? Several reasons suggest themselves. The first, which was noted earlier, concerns the lack of foot soldiers to staff the boycott picket lines at the entrances to retail stores. Except for labor strikes, with their usually predominantly male participation, these foot soldiers have typically been middle-class female homemakers, and many of their 1990s counterparts have jobs outside the home.

A second reason stems from the new cognitive burdens on marketplace-oriented boycotters today as compared to yesterday. More and more of today's boycotts are directed at large national and international corporations with many subsidiaries marketing their own goods under a variety of brand names. A case in point was the consumer boycott of the Nestle Company, a major Swiss multinational corporation that sells a vast array of consumer products (including wines, cheeses, cosmetics, canned food, and frozen foods) and operates large chains of restaurants and hotels; since many of these items are not sold under the Nestle name, the cognitive demands on consumers wishing to honor the boycott become extremely onerous.

A third reason concerns the practical difficulties in turning consumers away from many boycotted products. With huge increases in recent years in advertising expenditures, many consumer products have now acquired strong customer loyalties that are not easy to break. To illustrate, many young African Americans may not have honored the Operation PUSH boycott of Nike athletic shoes, even though the youths were sympathetic with the boycott's objectives (one of which was placing more African Americans in executive positions at Nike) because honoring the boycott meant not buying and wearing articles of clothing representing a strong expression of their consumer values (values associated with the media images of such celebrated corporate spokespersons as superstar athlete Michael Jordan).

Quite apart from these difficulties in successfully executing marketplace-oriented boycotts, which make media-oriented campaigns a more viable option, there are compelling reasons for boycotters to embrace the news media as an instrument for aiding their campaigns. As suggested earlier, if one compares the role of the news media in America early vs. late in the century, it becomes apparent that a transformation of sea-change proportions has occurred, with today's news media having become one of the dominant forces in society. Boycott groups as well as other grassroots groups that ignore this obvious fact of life do so at their own peril, and most, of course, have decided to reorient their campaigns to take advantage of the extraordinary communication powers of today's news media.

New Boycott Tactics

In selecting tactics for a new era of media-oriented campaigns, boycott leaders have focused primarily on two concerns: the choice of corporate target and the steps to be taken to persuade the target to meet the boycott objectives. A third concern, which is sometimes overlooked, is the selection of consumer goods to boycott; even though media-oriented boycotts are primarily concerned with corporate image rather than corporate sales, a media-oriented boycott that targets goods that lend themselves to a marketplace-oriented boycott is likely to place additional pressure on the corporate target to yield to the boycott demands because hurting its image might well translate into hurting its corporate sales.

Let us look at these three concerns in turn.

The Choice of Boycott Targets

In choosing corporate targets for media-oriented campaigns, boycott leaders have typically looked for image-related weaknesses to exploit. Some are noted below.

1. *Visibility*. The preferred target is well known with one or more highly recognized brands; indeed, it is a leader, if not the leader, in its field.
2. *Reputation*. The preferred target has a reputation for social responsibility and trust, a reputation that might well be threatened by refusing to yield to the demands of a conscience-oriented boycott.
3. *Recent economic problems*. The preferred target has had a recent downturn in sales and/or profits that might make it willing to accede to a boycott group's demands if this is what it takes to get back to profitability expeditiously.
4. *Absence of a long-established position*. The preferred target is new in the area of concern to the boycotters, and thus more amenable to change than a competitor with a long-established position in the field.
5. *American-owned*. The preferred target is controlled by American interests and thus more amenable to pressure from American protest groups.
6. *A producer and retailer under the same name*. The preferred target is amenable to attack in not one but two ways: at its headquarters complex as part of a media-oriented boycott and at its retail stores (e.g., Mitsubishi or Benetton) as part of a marketplace-oriented boycott.

The Choice of Tactical Actions

Because the primary focus of the newer boycotts is on media image rather than marketplace sales, boycott leaders have had to make skillful uses of dramatic devices and techniques to secure media attention. Some are noted below.

1. *Using creative parodies of corporate names and slogans to advance the boycott cause.* For example, an animal rights boycott group claims that more than a million copies of its version of the familiar Avon door hanger were left on residential frontdoor knobs. Normally they say, "Avon calling," to indicate that a sales representative of the cosmetics firm recently dropped by. The boycott group's version said, "Avon killing," and went on to make a claim that Avon was killing animals in the process of testing its new cosmetics for safety.

2. *Calling for a national or international day of protest against the boycott target, with demonstrations planned in many cities.* National boycott groups have gained publicity for their causes with such dramatic measures.

3. *Involving children as activists.* Environmental groups have been particularly successful doing this in support of the tuna boycott and the tropical timber boycott. The human interest value of these stories of activist schoolchildren was clear to the news media, which gave the stories wide coverage.

4. *Committing acts of civil disobedience.* This tactic, which is commonly used by boycott groups, forces corporate targets to call in the police to arrest individual demonstrators. The presence of police exercising power over the demonstrators at the behest of large corporations is thought by activist groups to engender feelings of sympathy for the demonstrators and their cause.

5. *Advertising in the mass media.* What better way to embarrass a target than to use the same venue it uses to launch an attack upon it? Several religious right and environmental boycott groups have used this technique.

6. *Using graphic pictures to convey the boycott message.* Pictures, it turns out, may well be worth a thousand words or even more when it comes to dramatizing boycott issues. Animal rights groups have recognized this for years by their fre-

quent depictions of petlike furry animals in painful circumstances (e.g., rabbits and monkeys) to convey the need to stop animal testing.

The Choice of Goods to Boycott

As indicated earlier, boycott leaders launching media-oriented campaigns may also attempt to provide incentives for consumers to participate in the boycott. This may mean targeting companies that offer only a few product brands, most or all of which are easy to identify. It may also mean targeting companies with brands and models that are not unique in the retail marketplace, in that acceptable substitutes are readily available from competing firms at comparable prices.

The Effectiveness of the Various Boycott Tactics

Although the foregoing tactical approaches have logical or psychological bases that suggest they are likely to be effective, their effectiveness empirically is difficult to demonstrate. Indeed, an original objective of this book was to subject these tactics to empirical evaluation and to report the findings in the context of the instrumentality theory framework outlined in Chapter 2; we abandoned the task reluctantly when the methodological problems in conducting the evaluation proved too intractable to overcome.

As noted in Chapter 1, a major criterion problem concerned constructing a universally valid measure of boycott effectiveness. This proved to be a tough task for several reasons. To illustrate, success criteria are often vaguely stated and they may change over the course of a boycott campaign. Moreover, determining whether desired changes in a target's policy actually occurred was not always easy; even more difficult was determining whether the changes that did occur were due to the boycott initiative in general and to individual boycott tactics in particular. In most instances independent raters looking at the evidence arrived at "don't know" assessments of a causative link between boycott tactics and outcomes. Complicating the raters' task was the multitude of pressures placed on targets other than the boycott campaign. An additional complicating factor was separating the effects of a consumer boycott from that of a convention boycott or a retailer boycott. As we have seen in earlier chapters, many surrogate boycotts at the state and local levels have focused more on conventions scheduled by professional associations than on vacation visits made by individual consumers; and many labor boycotts, such as the UFW grape boycott, have concentrated more on getting retailers not to carry targeted products than on getting consumers not to buy them.

All this is not to say that there were no instances in which consumer boycott objectives were met and a causative connection clearly established between the realization of the objectives and the boycott campaign. Perhaps the tuna boycott of Heinz and the animal rights boycott of Benetton are the best examples of such a connection in that both corporations made the changes in policy sought by the boycotters and both corporations attributed their actions, at least in part, to the boycott campaigns. However, such clear cause-and-effect connections are the exception rather than the rule.

Ethical Issues Associated with Consumer Boycotts

As several authors have noted, no discussion of consumer boycotts would be complete without attention to their ethical implications (Garrett, 1986; Neier, 1982; Smith, 1990). For many ethicists the basic issue is whether the end sought by a boycott group justifies the means used to attain it.[1] Neier (1982) has proposed a simple model, based on the boycott focus, to help answer this question. He is most sympathetic to "boycotts against *practices* that are deemed objectionable," such as exploitation of farmworkers. He is least sympathetic to "black list" boycotts; these are actions that attempt to punish individuals or groups (often performing artists) simply because they hold points of view that are offensive to the boycotters.

Garrett (1986) has also contributed to the discussion of boycott ethics by identifying three parties that could be injured by boycott actions. One, of course, is the corporate target, and the ethical question looms large if it finds itself falsely accused, or if it finds that it is incapable of responding to the boycotters' demands. A second group identified by Garrett consists of the customers of the target, who, he believes, should not be forced by intimidating tactics to honor the boycott against their will.[2] Finally, a third group Garrett identifies consists of secondary parties (typically nonprincipals in the boycott struggle who find themselves caught in the crossfire, such as workers, suppliers, and distributors) whose economic fortunes could well be affected by the boycott outcome.

Surrogate Boycott Ethics

Ethical issues relating to boycotts are especially important in light of the growing popularity of surrogate boycotts. Needless to say, there are many nonprincipals in such boycott struggles who may be hurt by their outcomes. Perhaps the most publicized example of this problem surfaced in the late 1970s with the national boycott called by the National Organization for Women (NOW) to limit tourist and conventioneer travel to states whose legislatures had not ratified the proposed Equal Rights Amendment (ERA). As we saw in Chapter 6, NOW was hoping that the affected tourism industries in the targeted states would successfully lobby their state legislators to pass the ERA. An ethical concern noted at the time was that the owners and employees of restaurants and hotels in major cities in the boycotted states (e.g., Chicago, Miami, and St. Louis, since the Illinois, Florida, and Missouri legislatures had not ratified the ERA) might well become "innocent victims" of a successfully executed boycott in that it was not their behavior that was deemed objectionable by the boycotters, but the behavior of the state legislatures.

The problem is further exacerbated by instances in which the third parties are boycott supporters, resulting in a sort of peacetime version of victimization by "friendly fire." As we noted in Chapter 6, this is what happened in Colorado in the early 1990s when a statewide vote on a referendum restricted gay rights—an outcome that triggered a surrogate boycott campaign against the state that went beyond tourism to focus on all Colorado businesses. When the votes were tallied by city, it became apparent that many ski resort communities, such as Vail, had voted against the referendum; nonetheless, they were not excused for their "good behavior" by the boycotters, leading to a judgment at the time that the Colorado supporters of the gay rights position were likely to be one of the state's most injured parties economically as a result of the boycott (in light of their heavy dependence on visits from out-of-state tourists). Fortunately for these resort communities, the boycott was called off after the courts ruled that the offending referendum's provisions were unconstitutional.

Surrogate boycotters defend their positions with ends-justifying-means rationales, as do nonsurrogate boycotters. The problem, of course, is that typically many more "neutrals" or "friends" are affected or potentially affected adversely by a surrogate boycott than by a nonsurrogate boycott or by a buycott. And the problem is magnified by the recent increases in calls for surrogate boycotts.

Concluding Comments

This examination of American boycott actions from the 1880s to the present may suggest to some readers that consumer boycotts, like the poor, will always be with us. And while this may first appear a facile parallel, a moment's thought reveals that boycotts and the poor (or more aptly, the powerless or seemingly powerless) have been intimately linked throughout American history. Indeed, it was during the American Revolutionary period that the seemingly powerless early settlers boycotted British goods following the passage of the Stamp Act by Britain's Parliament in 1765. And some hundred years later in the 1880s, it was the seemingly powerless Knights of Labor, a ragtag collection of uneducated and largely unskilled immigrant workers, who strove to improve their lot by wielding the boycott weapon against their employers. Less than a hundred years later the pattern continued in Montgomery, Alabama in the 1950s, where the seemingly powerless black citizens of the city organized a yearlong bus boycott to protest the mistreatment of blacks on the city's segregated buses. Today, we find that consumer boycotts are often called and implemented on behalf of the seemingly powerless—volunteers serving such diverse causes as animal rights, gay rights, women's rights, and the environment.

As we have seen, these various grassroots groups, having typically lacked such organizational supports as a strong funding base and professional staffs, have had to seek and find a natural ally in the form of the boycott initiative with its direct action emphasis on denying consumer support to targeted corporations. Moreover, as the perspective of history has revealed, the boycott issues and tactics have not remained constant over the years. The tremendous strides made in raising the standard of living for millions of Americans has rendered economic survival issues less urgent as a boycott stimulus. These issues have been replaced by quality-of-life issues affecting the lives of boycott participants and, more altruistically, the lives of a host of others—Americans as well as foreigners, humans as well as nonhumans.

Furthermore, major advances in communication technologies and the American standard of living have largely obviated the need for the marketplace-oriented boycott campaigns of yesteryear, and they are being replaced by media-oriented campaigns aimed at embarrassing their targets by exposing their objectionable behaviors in the news media. These campaigns are using psychologically sophisticated tactics that present information in a dramatic and creative manner in order to capture the attention of the news media. While the boycott groups are not always effective, they seem to work best if and when their objectives can be reduced to simple messages with wide appeal to American consumers. Indeed, it would seem that boycott campaigns containing these cognitive and motivational features may constitute a success formula for the future.

Before closing, it might be well to look at the future and ask what it is likely to hold for boycotts. For example, will they take on new forms or engage new targets? As we stand on the doorstep of a new millennium, we find ourselves wondering if boycotts will assume a more humane "new age" perspective—one with a focus on conscience-oriented goals such as ecological sustainability and reward-oriented means such as consumer buycotts. Enthusiasts and critics of boycotts await the next chapter of the story with special interest.

THE 1966 CONSUMER PROTEST AS SEEN BY ITS LEADERS[1]

In the fall of 1966 a wave of consumer protests spread to communities across the United States in response to a sudden rise in supermarket prices. Consumers from all sections of the country exhibited their disturbance with higher prices through boycotts, demonstrations, and other direct actions. The protest received widespread coverage by the news media, although, as is often the case with such reporting, only a fragmentary picture emerged of the participants and their actions.

Many questions went unanswered. Who, for example, were the participants in this nationwide movement? Why did they get involved? What was the nature of their actions and what did these actions accomplish? And how did this experience affect the lives of the participants?

In an attempt to shed light on these questions, a mail survey was undertaken in August 1967 of the participants in the consumer protest of the previous fall. In what follows the survey procedures and results are presented and discussed in detail. The reader is referred back to the text of this book to see how this consumer economic protest compares with others in the postwar era.

Procedure

The survey instrument was an eight-page questionnaire consisting of structured items designed to explore the earlier posed questions. A preliminary draft of the questionnaire was circulated for comment to several staff members of the White House Office of Consumer Affairs. In addition, this draft form of the questionnaire was personally administered to the leaders of three protest groups in the greater Washington, D.C., area, who were instructed to evaluate the individual questionnaire items as well as the instrument as a whole. The suggestions from these various sources were carefully considered, and many were incorporated in the final version of the questionnaire.

Turning now to a consideration of the survey sample, we encounter an unusual methodological problem. In most social survey research studies, a target population of interest is identified and an appropriate sample selected; in the present study, however, no complete listing of protest participants was available to constitute the target population. Thus a necessarily incomplete list of participants had to be compiled from the many scattered bits and pieces of evidence that appeared during and since the time of the protest.

Three sources of names and addresses were explored. The first consisted of newspaper reports of the consumer protest. Letters were sent to the 150 American newspapers with the largest readership requesting the names of participants that had been cited in their news reports of the protest. In addition, news reports that appeared in the three newspapers for which indexes were provided (*Christian Science Monitor, New York Times*, and *Wall Street Journal*) were carefully searched for the names of protest participants. Once names were identified from these sources, telephone calls were placed to long distance information operators in the home communities of the participants in an effort to secure their addresses. The second source of participant names and addresses were 25 state organizations whose volunteer members work to advance the cause of the consumer. Letters were sent to each consumer organization requesting the names and addresses of protest participants residing in the state. The third source consisted of the respondents to the mail survey of protest participants. Each questionnaire requested its recipient to provide the names and addresses of protest participants residing in communities other than the recipient's.

From these several sources of information, complete names and addresses were identified for 211 participants representing 99 local protest groups. A questionnaire was mailed to each of these individuals along with a cover letter on university stationery that stressed the social scientific objectives of the study. To encourage a high response rate, as many as three reminder letters were sent to delinquent recipients.

Questionnaires were returned from 125 respondents representing 72 local protest groups. The questionnaire responses were analyzed to determine which of the participants had assumed leadership positions in their local protest efforts. The criteria employed in this analysis consisted of reported position in the local group, stated duties, and the total reported time devoted to the execution of these duties. After applying these criteria to the completed questionnaires, leaders were identified for 64 of the 72 local protest groups.

Results

Due to the small size of the respondent sample, the treatment of the survey results is limited to simple descriptive analyses.

Characteristics of the Local Group Leaders

What kind of individual donates time and energy to the leadership of a consumer protest effort? As Table A.1 indicates, all of the 64 respondents were women. As a group they were young (61 percent between the ages of 21 and 35), married (95 percent) homemakers (61 percent) who had attended college for one or more years (59 percent). Most were either very old or very new residents of their communities (42 percent in the first category and 41 percent in the second), and in either case, they tended to be joiners (61 percent reported belonging to two or more organizations). Most commonly reported organizations were social, civic, and educational groups, and for slightly over half of the affiliations cited (51 percent) the respondents stated that they held leadership positions.

**Table A.1 Characteristics of 64 Women Who Served
as Local Group Leaders**

Characteristic	Percent
Age	
21–25	13
26–35	48
36–45	28
46–55	6
56–65	3
No response	2
Marital status	
Single	2
Married	95
Divorced	3
Occupational status	
Homemaker	61
Employed fulltime outside home	34
No response	5
Highest educational level attained	
Less than 12 years of formal schooling	11
High school graduate	28
One or more years of college	36
College graduate	23
No response	2
Political party affiliation	
Democrat	47
Republican	28
Independent	14
Other	8
No response	3
Number of years lived in community in which protest occurred	
0–5	42
6–15	17
16 or more	41
Number of community organizational affiliations	
0	23
1–2	36
3–4	19
5 or more	16
No response	6
Prior participation in organized protest actions	
One or more protest actions	11
None	86
No response	3

Politically it would appear that most of the leaders could be considered in the mainstream of American opinion, with 75 percent reporting membership in one of the two major political parties. A further indication of a lack of politically extremist tendencies is their almost total lack of involvement in organized protest actions prior to the time of the consumer protest. Only 11 percent of the leaders had participated in actions of this kind, and, with one exception, all such protest efforts were directed at civil rights issues.

Family information for the 61 married respondents is summarized in Table A.2, inspection of which reveals husband's occupation and family income figures consistent with middle- and upper-middle-class membership for most of the group leaders. In one sense this is surprising, as are the home ownership figures (85 percent stated that they own their homes) and the relatively small number of unusually large families (10 percent reported having five or more children), in that it is the mother of a very large family with low income who would appear (on purely economic grounds) to be the most likely candidate to participate in a protest against rising food prices. As we shall see presently, other non-economic factors apparently played an important role in prompting the participation of these women in the protest effort.

Finally, it should be noted that the respondents as a group reported considerable familiarity with supermarket conditions as well as marketplace conditions in general (87 percent stated that they alone do the weekly marketing, and 69 percent reported having sole or joint responsibility for family financial matters).

Initial Involvement in the Local Consumer Protest

Countless thousands or perhaps even millions of women undoubtedly were disturbed by sharply rising food prices in the fall of 1966, yet only a fraction of their number took action, and an even smaller fraction assumed the burden of leadership for these actions. What prompted these women to devote themselves so vigorously to the cause?

Examination of Table A.3 suggests some answers. Apparently a major contributing factor was the opportunity for the respondents to ease the strain on their household budgets and the house-

Table A.2 Family Information for Local Group Leaders

Characteristic	Percent[a]
Number of children	
0	3
1	6
2	33
3	33
4	10
5 or more	10
No response	5
Occupation of spouse	
Unskilled or clerical	11
Skilled or lower management	43
Professional or upper management	33
Other	8
No response	5
Annual family income (in dollars)	
Less than 4,000	2
4,000–6,000	10
6,000–8,000	16
8,000–10,000	26
More than 10,000	41
No response	5
Relationship to resident dwelling	
Homeowner	85[b]
Renter	11
No response	3
Family member chiefly responsible for weekly marketing	
Respondent	87[b]
Husband	0
Both	10
Other	2
No response	2
Family member chiefly responsible for household financial matters	
Respondent	44
Husband	21
Both	25
Other	7
No response	3

[a] All percentages are based on a total of 61 married group leaders.

[b] Figures within this category do not add to 100 due to accumulated rounding error.

hold budgets of other members of the community as well. In addition, a majority of respondents (69 percent) perceived their actions as a response to unethical practices. In their view, a wrong had been committed that had to be righted.

Examination of Table A.3 also reveals that a number of intangible benefits commonly associated with personal participation in a mass movement were not considered to be important motivating factors by the respondents. The opportunities presented by the consumer protest to assert oneself as an individual, to associate oneself with an exciting issue, and to work with friends and respected members of the community were all rated as unimportant influences by a majority of the respondents. These findings do not lend themselves to a clear and simple interpretation. It is certainly possible that the respondents were completely candid in the always difficult task of self-assessment; on the other hand, it may be what Orne (1962) has called the "demand characteristics" of a testing situation influenced their judgments. In particular, it is not unlikely that protest leaders in general, and women leaders in particular (in light of the widely held stereotype of the

Table A.3 Factors That Prompted Local Group Leaders to Participate in Consumer Protest

Factor	Very Important	Important	Not Important	No Response	Sum
			Percent		
Ease strain on budget	52	30	12	6	100
Help poor in community	48	38	8	6	100
Help people at large	47	38	9	6	100
Assert self as individual	8	12	69	11	100
Associate self with exciting issue	2	20	67	11	100
Work with friends	2	22	62	14	100
Work with respected members of community	6	11	70	13	100
Be a force for right	41	28	20	11	100

emotional female), would be at least somewhat predisposed to deny to a scientific interrogator, and perhaps to themselves as well, that they were moved to action by nonrational as well as rational considerations.

Participants in the Local Protest Actions

All respondents were asked to report the number of key participants in their local group efforts and to provide background information for these individuals (Table A.4). The profile that emerges for these key participants is in substantial agreement with the protest leader findings presented in Table A.1, although

Table A.4 Characteristics of Key Participants in Local Group Protest Efforts as Estimated by Group Leaders

Characteristic	Groups Reporting	Estimated Number of Participants	Percent
Age			
Under 25		59	6
26–35		575	56
36–45		264	26
46–55		95	9
Over 55		34	3
Total	59	1027	100
Sex			
Female		935	90
Male		107	10
Total	59	1042	100
Marital status			
Married		968	95
Unmarried		54	5
Total	59	1022	100
Education			
Had attended college		343	36
Had not attended college		598	64
Total	57	941	100
Political party affiliation			
Democrat		350	50
Republican		350	50
Total	42	700	100

certain discrepancies appear. As a group, the key participants can be described as young married women who had not attended college and who were equally divided in their loyalties to the two major political parties.

Group Goals and Actions

In considering the goals and actions of the protest groups, we look first at what the local leaders perceived as the causes of the rapid rise in supermarket prices. Table A.5 presents their ratings of eight possible determinants. It is of interest to note that only two of the eight listed items were not considered to be important causes by a majority of the respondents and that these two (excessively high profits for farmers and excessively high wages for food industry workers) share in common a "little man" character. Of the remaining six items, all of which deal with private and public institutions, only one, the cost of extra supermarket services, was almost unanimously viewed as a very important cause of

Table A.5   Factors Responsible for Higher Supermarket Prices as Evaluated by Local Group Leaders

Factor	Very Important	Important	Not Important	No Response	Sum[a]
			Percent		
Excessively high profits for:					
farmers	0	5	87	8	100
supermarkets	34	34	27	5	100
wholesalers and distributors	45	31	14	9	99
Excessively high wages for food industry workers	6	12	77	5	100
Devaluation of dollar due to inflationary government spending	34	34	28	3	99
Advertising expenditures of food producers supermarkets	55	16	27	3	101
Cost of extra supermarket services	84	11	3	2	100

[a] Some values may differ from 100 due to accumulated rounding error.

higher prices. Advertising expenditures of food producers and of supermarkets were also singled out as key factors. A majority of the respondents considered these expenditures to be very important contributors to higher supermarket prices (55 percent and 58 percent, respectively).

Since the news reports of the consumer protest strongly suggested that protest leaders were highly critical of many extra supermarket features and services, items were incorporated in the questionnaire to explore this issue. Inspection of Table A.6 reveals that two items, trading stamps and games of chance, were considered very important contributors to high prices by about 4 out of 5 respondents (83 percent and 80 percent, respectively). No other issue elicited such a strong reaction although one item, premiums, was reported by many local leaders (62 percent) as a very important determinant. To sum up, the data of Table A.5 and A.6 point to extra supermarket features and services in general, and to trading stamps and games of chance in particular, as the key respondent-identified causes of high prices.

Turning now to a consideration of the actions taken by the local protest groups, we find that a full range of interest group practices was employed. These results are presented in Table A.7 along with an indication of what portion of group leaders who

Table A.6 Contribution of Extra Supermarket Features and Services to Higher Supermarket Prices as Evaluated by Local Group Leaders

Factor	Very Important	Important	Not Important	No Response	Sum[a]
			Percent		
Carry-out service	8	23	58	11	100
Check cashing	3	27	61	9	100
Credit	11	9	63	27	100
Delivery	9	6	63	22	100
Games of chance	80	8	5	8	101
Late hours	34	23	33	9	99
Music	14	19	58	9	100
Premiums	62	16	9	13	100
Trading stamps	83	11	2	5	101

[a] Some values may differ from 100 due to accumulated rounding error.

employed each action perceived it to be effective. Examination of the table reveals that almost all of the listed actions (10 of 13) were reported by more than half of the local protest groups. Cited most frequently were the issuance of press releases (95 percent), radio or television appearances (86 percent), and supermarket boycotts (81 percent).

Only three actions were considered to be effective by most of the group leaders who employed them. First and foremost here are supermarket boycotts (69 percent), followed by supermarket demonstrations (63 percent), and radio or television appearances (55 percent). The remaining 10 actions varied considerably in perceived effectiveness and one in particular—writing letters to members of Congress—received markedly fewer votes (19 percent) than the others. These findings, along with others presented in Table A.7, indicate that the traditional, moderate measures for advancing the cause of interest groups (letter writing, meetings and discussions) received few high marks for effectiveness by the group leaders; on the other hand the more militant measures

Table A.7 Group Actions and Their Effectiveness
as Estimated by Local Group Leaders

Action	Percentage of Leaders Reporting the Action for Local Groups	Percentage of the Group Leaders Reporting the Action Who Judged It to Be Effective
Appeared on radio or TV	86	55
Boycotted supermarket(s)	81	69
Circulated petition	69	48
Demonstrated at supermarket(s)	63	63
Distributed handouts	70	47
Held news conference(s)	77	49
Held rally in community	61	41
Issued press releases	95	44
Met with representatives of:		
community	33	38
farmers	36	43
government	41	42
supermarkets	77	39
Sent letters to congressmen or other governmental representatives	67	19

(boycotts and demonstrations) were viewed as highly productive of results.

Accomplishments of the Local Group Efforts

From a list of eight possibilities, each group leader was asked to identify the accomplishments of her local group's efforts. Lower food prices was the most frequently reported accomplishment, with about three fourths of the respondents (73 percent) checking this item (Table A.8). Next in frequency of response was the elimination of games and contests (55 percent), a supermarket service which, as we saw earlier, was widely believed to be a very important determinant of higher food prices. Elimination of trading stamps, the other almost universally cited contributor to higher prices, was not reported as a group accomplishment by many respondents (28 percent), however.

Since the respondent reports indicated that the vast majority of the local leaders achieved their single most important group objective, namely, lower food prices, one would think that most group leaders had viewed their overall efforts as a success. As Table A.9 indicates, two different evaluations are involved here, one relating to the short-term effects of the protest effort and the other to its long-term effects. Looking first at the short-term effects (during the time of the consumer protest), we find that

Table A.8 Group Accomplishments as Judged by Local Group Leaders

Accomplishment	Percentage of Group Leaders Reporting
Consumer representation established in local government	14
Elimination of games and contests	55
Elimination of trading stamps	28
Initiation of investigation of food prices by:	
federal government	34
local or state government	39
Local voluntary organization formed to:	
watch food prices	34
advance consumer cause in general	23
Lower food prices	73

**Table A.9 Effectiveness of Local Group Efforts
to Lower Supermarket Prices as Judged by Their Leaders**

Effectiveness by Time Periods	Percent
Short-term effectiveness (during the time of the consumer protest)	
A complete success	9
More successful than not	66
More unsuccessful than not	19
A complete failure	5
No response	2
Total	101ª
Long-term effectiveness (beyond the time of the consumer protest)	
A complete success	5
More successful than not	39
More unsuccessful than not	39
A complete failure	16
No response	2
Total	101ª

ª Does not add to 100 due to accumulated rounding error.

two thirds of the group leaders reported that their program of action, while not completely successful in lowering supermarket prices, was more successful than not. Turning to the long-term effects (beyond the time of the consumer protest), we find that many group leaders reported that the initial gains were short-lived. For this later time period, only 39 percent reported that their action programs were more successful than not, and coincidentally, a similar number reported that their efforts were more unsuccessful than not. Apparently, then, the protest leaders as a group perceived their efforts as having won the battle but not the war.

Aftermath of the Protest Experience

One year after the consumer protest, only 15 of the 64 local leaders reported that their groups were still active. Each of the remaining 49 leaders was asked to estimate the likelihood that her group would reestablish itself, should food prices once again rise sharply. The results of this inquiry, presented in Table A.10, are likely to disappoint the prophets of a new era of grassroots

Table A.10 Likelihood of Leader and Local Group Participation in Future Consumer Protest Efforts as Estimated by Local Group Leaders

Question	High	Low	Uncertain Response	No	Sum
			Percent		
What is the likelihood that your local group would re-form if food prices were once again to rise sharply? (asked of 49 groups no longer in operation)	29	45	18	8	100
What is the likelihood that you would participate in a local protest effort if food prices were once again to rise sharply? (asked of 64 local group leaders)	58	27	14	2	101ª

ª Does not add to 100 due to accumulated rounding error.

consumer activism. Only a minority of the leaders (29 percent) thought it highly likely that her group would reassemble in the event of another rapid rise in food prices. A rather different picture emerged, however, when the 64 group leaders were asked about the likelihood of their own participation in a local protest effort, should food prices rise sharply. A majority of the leaders (58 percent) thought it likely that they would participate under such conditions.

Discussion

The Generality of the Research Findings

Before a meaningful interpretation of the questionnaire responses can be made, we must ask if these findings for a limited sample of protest participants can be generalized to consumer protesters at large. Several considerations are of concern here. The first is whether the population of 64 identified protest leaders is representative of the total protest leadership. As stated earlier, we have no way of identifying this total nationwide population of protest leaders and consequently we have no way of rigorously assessing the representativeness of the subpopulation to whom questionnaires were mailed. However, it should be noted that three separate sources of names were explored, and this multiple approach may have compensated for deficiencies inherent in any one source. Thus the names of many local group leaders who were not identified in press reports were made known to us by state consumer organizations and by the survey respondents themselves.

Even if our list of protest leaders to whom questionnaires were sent was reasonably representative of the total population of such leaders, it is still possible that the resulting sample of respondents was not. About a fourth (27 percent) of the protest groups did not respond to our inquiry, and the local leaders for these groups, as well as the groups themselves, may have differed markedly from those who did respond. This suspicion is reinforced by the results of a mail survey study by Donald (1966) of members of the League of Women Voters, which found that nonrespondents were likely to be either nonparticipators or marginal participators in the activities of the organization. Although this finding suggests that many of our nonrespondents may have also had minimal involvement in the consumer protest effort, we have no data that speak to this point. However, the scanty evidence available to us, which is limited to the locations and populations of cities in which respondents and nonrespondents resided, is not suggestive of differences between the two groups.

A third consideration in evaluating the generality of the survey results is the nature of the measurement instrument. The methodological difficulties inherent in questionnaire studies, and particularly mail questionnaire studies, are well-known. Of particular concern to the present investigation are possible misinterpretations of questionnaire items and the possible adoption of artificial, test-appropriate response styles by the respondents.

Thus we find that several considerations (sample size, sample representativeness, and methodological weaknesses of the research instrument) all serve to question the generality of the research findings. They must accordingly be treated with caution, and in the discussion that follows they are viewed as yielding only a tentative description of the protest participants and their actions.

The Consumer Protest as a Social Movement

According to the sociologist Daniel Bell, for a social movement to arouse people it must do three things: "simplify ideas, establish a claim to truth, and, in the union of the two, demand a commitment to action" (1962, p. 401). Let us consider to what extent the consumer protest satisfied these several conditions. With regard to the first, the results suggest that the protesters rejected the notion that rising food prices resulted from a conglomeration of economic forces whose individual elements could be unraveled and evaluated only at the risk of oversimplification. They claimed instead that the determinants of higher prices could be identified and their individual contributions assessed. And in making this "claim to truth," they pointed to extra supermarket features and services in general, and to trading stamps and games of chance in particular, as the worst offenders. That the protesters apparently hit a sensitive nerve of public opinion in leveling this charge is indicated by the results of the Harris Poll alluded to earlier, which found that a majority of the public felt that trading stamps and cash prizes should be eliminated in order to reduce supermarket prices. Food industry advertising expenditures were also singled out as a leading contributor to higher prices, and interestingly, this judgment is also consistent with the findings of public opinion surveys. Greyser and Bauer (1966), after reviewing survey studies conducted over the last 30 years, concluded that throughout this period, a majority of Americans believed that advertising increases consumer prices. A third perceived cause of higher prices, excessively high profits for wholesalers and distributors, has also been subjected to public criticism over the years. Indeed, Riesman (1954) has found evidence for a harsh public view of the middleman in medieval thought and in American populism of the last century.

Thus it would appear that the protesters' diagnosis of the major determinants of high food prices was highly consistent with prevailing American public opinion, a circumstance that undoubtedly served to persuade many Americans to support their cause. However, a diagnosis that is consistent with public opinion is not necessarily consistent with the economic realities of the day. What does the evidence suggest here?

While this question is highly complex, there are indications that the protesters' focus upon two factors, the costs of advertising and the costs of trading stamps, was not without empirical support. For example, the Report of the National Commission on Food Marketing (1966) pointed out that advertising and sales promotion have contributed significantly to the considerable spread between farm and retail prices. According to the report, in 1964 alone, $2,172 million was spent by food corporations for advertising, and $680 million was spent by retailers for trading stamps. The report goes on to conclude that while these expenditures were not entirely wasted, in that consumers did receive premiums for trading stamps and other sales promotion devices, they are nonetheless added to the food bill and thus contribute to consumer costs.

Thus we find that the consumer protesters' "claim to truth" was supported subjectively by public opinion and objectively by a major government-sponsored study of the economics of food marketing. Under the circumstances it is perhaps not surprising that protest actions followed in some communities, but why direct action, and why on a nationwide scale? Several factors apparently played a role here.

First, in contradistinction to the static picture presented by the survey findings, the consumer protest is perhaps better viewed as a dynamic process—a social chain reaction that began in Denver, Colorado, and spread rapidly to many communities across the land. Support for this dynamic depiction of the nationwide protest comes from responses to two questionnaire items relating to the origins of the local protest efforts. When asked how they had heard about the protest actions around the country, only one respondent, a Denver leader of a direct action effort, claimed that these actions started with her group. Furthermore, a majority of the respondents (62 percent) reported coordinating their activities with other protest groups, and the Denver group was designated more frequently than any other as having played a coordinating role. Taken together, these findings suggest that one factor that contributed to the widespread use of direct action tactics by the local protest groups was the ready availability (through news media reports) of a model that employed such tactics successfully.

But an important question remains. The survey findings suggest that only a tiny fraction of consumers actually participated in the nationwide effort. Why did these women, and not others, see fit to involve themselves in the campaign to lower food prices?

To shed light on this question, let us briefly examine the findings of the study cited earlier of factors relating to the perceived legitimacy of social protest actions. Olsen (1968), in a survey of a limited sample of a middle-class urban community (Ann Arbor, Michigan), found education, income, and occupation all directly correlated with acceptance of protest actions, and an inverse relationship for age. His study also revealed that Democrats were more accepting of protest actions than Independents or Republicans. The findings for these five social factors are in agreement with our profile of the local consumer leaders and deviate markedly for the key participants only with regard to political party affiliation.[2]

While these five factors help account for respondent participation in the consumer protest effort, it would seem that other factors, more directly related to the specific issues underlying the consumer protest (e.g., family size and familiarity with supermarket conditions), may also have played a part.

The Success of the Consumer Protest

Before concluding this discussion of the questionnaire findings, let us look briefly at the respondents' assessments of the success of their efforts. We found earlier that while most of the respondents felt that their groups had succeeded in lowering prices during the time of the protest, only a minority saw any lasting effects. These assessments would appear to be in good correspondence with the objective realities of the situation. In an examination of the short-term effects of the consumer protest, DeGraff stated, "It was undoubtedly the impact of the boycotts that caused retail food prices on a national basis to decline one percent between October and December last fall" (1967, p. 27). Winter also reported that supermarkets lowered prices and, furthermore, that they attempted to maintain the lower levels despite rising wholesale prices and higher operating costs in 1967. Among the devices used to do this was the elimination of trading stamps. Allvine (1969) found a substantial decline in supermarket usage of stamps in 1967, and he cites the consumer protest as a responsible factor. The effects of the consumer protest are more dramatically apparent for supermarket games. According to Allvine, the incidence of game usage reached a peak in October 1966 (the month in which most of the protests began) and dropped 40 percent below this high level the following year.

That the respondents were also correct in judging that the gains realized by their efforts in 1966 were not maintained beyond this period is all too apparent from the rising retail prices in the next few years after the 1966 protest. DeGraff (1967), in assessing the long-term outlook for supermarket prices, felt that it could hardly have been otherwise. In his view, the trading stamps and games that served as focal points for the protest effort contributed so little to retail food costs that their elimination would have resulted in only a 2 percent reduction in supermarket prices. And he saw the elimination of food advertising (another concern of the protesters) as having a similarly small projected effect. Although a reduction in food prices of a few percentage points is not to be taken lightly, since it would have yielded a substantial savings for American families, DeGraff was undoubtedly correct in asserting that there were real limits to the long-term rewards to be expected from a campaign to eliminate supermarket advertising and extra services.

Summary

A mail survey of 64 local groups that participated in the consumer protest against rising supermarket prices in the fall of 1966 found that the leaders of these efforts tended to be young, well-educated, middle-class housemakers. Since these characteristics, along with their tendency to affiliate with the Democratic Party, have all been empirically associated with perceived legitimacy of social protest actions, it is not surprising that such direct action tactics as boycotts and demonstrations were employed by a majority of the local group. The findings indicate that these actions, along with others, were directed primarily at the elimination of trading stamps and games and the reduction of super-market advertising expenditures. Most of the local leader respondents reported that their efforts were successful in lowering prices during the time of the protest, but not beyond, and this assessment appears to be consistent with economic realities.

◆ APPENDIX B ◆

BOYCOTT OBSERVATIONS OVER TIME

What follows is a sample of notable boycott descriptions and opinions spanning more than 100 years. Taken together, the comments reveal the variety of views people have had of boycotts along with the emotional reactions that sometimes accompany these views.

"[Boycott] means that a peaceful subject of the Queen is denied food and drink, and that he is run down in his business; that his cattle are unsalable at fairs; that the smith will not shoe his horse nor the carpenter mend his cart; that old friends pass him by on the other side of the street, making the sign of the cross; that his children are hooted at the village school; that he sits apart, like an outcast, in his usual place of worship, all for doing nothing but that the law says that he has a perfect right to do." (*London Times*, 1885)

"The boycott is a foreign institution. . . . It is one of alien origin, and is set up here by persons who have not the faintest conception of what American citizenship is." (*New York Times*, 1886)

"[A boycott is a] hydra-headed monster, dragging its loathsome length across the continent, sucking the very life blood from our trade and commerce." (Turn-of-the-century grand jury description, according to Lott, 1997)

"There was no object so mean [as the boycott] and no person so exalted as to escape its power." (Wolman, 1914)

"[A boycott is] a withdrawal of enthusiasm." (A phrase used by Jesse Jackson's Operation PUSH in 1982 to avoid legal charges of engaging in boycotts)

"[Boycotts are] the weapon of the weak." (Scott, 1985)

"Boycotting, I think, is one of the glories of democracy—direct, principled political action that holds companies and other targets responsible for what they do." (Leo, 1992)

"Boycotts have been 'a very American tactic of social protest' since the early days of the republic, says the Stanford University historian Stewart Burns." (Wright, 1993)

NOTES

Chapter 1

1. Needless to say, there are almost as many definitions of boycotts and boycotting as there are students of the boycott practice. Two early definitions originated with Laidler (1913) and Wolman (1914). Laidler defined boycotting rather broadly as "an organized effort to induce others to withdraw from social or business relations with another" (p. 27). Wolman took a much narrower view by defining a boycott as "a combination formed for the purpose of restricting the markets of an individual or group of individuals" (p. 12). Later definitions include Wooton's (1978), with its emphasis on instrumentality, by referring to boycotting as "abstaining from using, buying from, selling to or otherwise dealing with a person or institution in order to exert influence" (p. 169).

   Still later, Garrett (1987) defined consumer boycotts as "the concerted but non-mandatory refusal by a group of actors (the agents) to conduct marketing transactions with one or more other actors (the targets) for the purpose of communicating displeasure with certain target policies and attempting to coerce the target to modify these policies" (p. 47). This last-noted definition may be too narrowly cast since boycotts sometimes target "neutral" parties who are asked to put pressure on other parties whose actions are deemed offensive by the boycotting groups. Thus a hotel chain in a certain state may be asked to lobby "uncooperative" state legislators to cast their votes on a particular issue in a manner consistent with the boycotters' position. As we shall see presently, such "surrogate" boycotts have become increasingly common in the United States. More recently, Smith (1990) has defined a consumer boycott as "the organized exercising of consumer sovereignty by abstaining from purchase of an offering in order to exert influence on a matter of concern to the customer and over the institution making the offering" (p. 140). This definition, which is closer to the author's, adds the element of "consumer sovereignty" but omits mention of the behavioral change effort often needed to persuade consumers to participate.

2. It can be argued that our working definition is incomplete because it does not consider the typically temporary nature of boycott actions. In particular, almost all boycotts occur for a limited time (which rarely extends beyond five years), while other campaigns not usually considered to be boycott actions, such as the Prohibition movement's urging of the federal government to outlaw the sale of alcoholic beverages, continued for decades. However, at the time a boycott is called, it is usually not clear that it will indeed be a temporary action. To illustrate, recently activated animal rights campaigns against animal testing of consumer products and services are likely to continue for many years, especially in the medical research area where, as is the case for prohibition, there is tremendous consumer resistance to its message. So while most boycotts are relatively short in duration, there is no inherent reason they have to be, and a few may indeed extend for considerable periods of time. (An important exception is punitive boycotts, which often specify the boycott duration in advance, just as a judge would announce a prison sentence as a punishment for a crime; these boycotts are defined and discussed later in this chapter.)

3. Taatgen (1992) argues that the boycott has played an important role in the "Irish civilizing process." As one indication of the boycott's place in early Irish history, Taatgen reminds us that almost 300 years ago Jonathan Swift (1720) referred to the practice ironically in his plea for the creation of an Irish clothing industry that would enable Irish consumers to boycott English-made clothing.

4. As we shall see in Chapter 3, secondary boycotts have had a long and complex legal history, with some varieties having been banned at federal and state levels. It is of particular interest to note that federal secondary boycott law is viewed by specialists as "notoriously dense and confusing" (Hager, 1991). The law makes a distinction between secondary boycotts aimed at offending products and secondary boycotts aimed at both offending and nonoffending products. While, as indicated above, the latter is illegal, the former is legal as long as the offending products do not constitute "so large a proportion of a secondary enterprise's business as to turn the offending product boycott into an enterprise boycott" (Hager, 1991, p. 793).

5. In light of the very small numbers of not-for-profit boycott targets, we generally refer to boycott targets in this book as businesses or firms.

Chapter 2

1. The problems noted relating to taste factors for commodity boycotts hardly constitute new insights into boycott behavior. A hundred years ago in Germany they were carefully considered by union groups who planned what has been called "The Great Berlin Boycott of 1894." The unions decided to strike out at some, rather than all, of the breweries so that some beer would be available to Berliners who wished to honor the boycott. In the words of the organizers:

   > During the warm season of the year, because of the greater importance of beer for the enjoyment and nourishment of the workers, we could not expect to have any success in imposing a general boycott. Such an action, based on the solidarity and energy of the workers, could certainly cause all breweries real losses, but certainly could not force them to surrender. Our energies would be spread too thin. However, by contrast a boycott of a few selected breweries would demonstrate the full might of our attack. Beer must be consumed, and boycotted beer can be more easily avoided when other beers are at our disposal. (Turk, 1982, p. 384)

Chapter 3

1. As Forbath (1991) has observed, the Knights were more than simply a boycott organization. They established labor parties, had candidates running for election in all but one of the nation's 35 states, and actually elected members to government office at city and state levels. They also established factory cooperatives and a variety of cultural organizations. All of this was intended to prepare the working classes for "republican self-rule," which members of the Knights took to mean using government power to curb the antilabor practices of corporations.

2. According to Laidler (1930), New York continued to be the center of boycott efforts with more than 1,300 boycotts being reported from 1885 to 1892 by the state labor bureau.

3. Ware (1929) has also made this point in the context of "labor solidarity" and "class consciousness"—a new social climate engendered by the Industrial Revolution. In his history of the labor movement he notes that there were two distinctly different sets of consumer goods at the time, one for the working classes and one for the middle and upper-classes. Goods designed for working classes were sold mainly in local working-class communities; these goods were marketed locally rather than nationally.

4. Gordon (1975) has claimed that the explanations put forth to account for the extensive usage and impressive success record for the labor boycott have ignored social factors. Most important here in his view is the fact that many of the labor boycotters were new immigrants to the United States. Gordon focuses on the New York experience:

> The boycott was conducted chiefly by immigrant workers in an industrializing society, and must be considered alongside other aspects of immigrant culture and labor's behavior in those years. It was an *adaptation*—not an *adoption*—of the Irish practice. An isolated tactic, the boycott was inseparably related to other traditional forms of popular immigrant protest (such as mass demonstrations, parades, and rallies), and patterns of organizing for protection, which were common to the European rural and urban worlds so many New York workers had known. (1975, pp. 186–187)

5. Wolman (1914) does suggest such an unusual circumstance. He notes that the products of the C.W. Post company, such as Postum, were allegedly consumed mostly by the middle class, "which has no sympathy with trade unionism." He claims that labor boycotts against this company were likely to be unproductive, or even counterproductive, due to the likelihood of increased patronage from the middle-class opponents of organized labor.

6. As Gordon (1975) has noted in the context of a fascinating story, the new and foreign status of the labor boycott was made dramatically apparent by a *New York Times* reaction to a labor boycott called by a local affiliate of the National Bakers Union against the Hudson Street Bakery in New York in 1886. The boycott was called after the proprietor declined to give the union assurances that her employees would be allowed to join the union and that she would maintain union working conditions in the bakery (e.g., a workday limit of 12 hours on weekdays and 14 hours on Saturdays). Union members picketed the bakery and distributed handbills. They also followed the bakery's delivery wagon on its daily route, made lists of the retail customers (e.g., local groceries), and urged them to discontinue buying from the boycotted bakery.

   The boycott story has several twists and turns, not the least of which is the newspaper reports of the boycotters' activities, which focused on their crudeness ("drunken and half-drunken men" who "insulted passers-by"); these reports apparently triggered a negative boycott or "buycott" by businesspeople in support of the bakery. During the first few weeks of the boycott, money came pouring in to the newspapers from their readers with instructions that it be spent to buy goods from the bakery for distribution to local charities. One millionaire contributor expressed the hope that the proprietor would "be sustained through this tyrannical attempt to dictate to you on the conduct of your business." Moreover, the boycotted bakery became an attraction for tourists visiting New York. It was even reported, "Men and women from fashionable neighborhoods used the boycott as an excuse for a Saturday outing, and journeyed to (the) shop where they bought pastries and gave them to workers' children in full view of the pickets" (Gordon, 1975, p. 220).

The *Times*, indignant at the actions of the immigrant boycotters ("ignorant Germans, who are unable to speak German intelligently"), called for American citizens to determine "whether this savage and un-American mode of welfare" is lawful. "The boycott is a foreign institution," noted the paper. "It is one of alien origin, and is set up here by persons who have not the faintest conception of what American citizenship is" (1975, p. 221).

7. The success of the UFWOC effort stimulated others to be called. Among the most notable was the boycott of Farah Manufacturing Company by the Amalgamated Clothing Workers of America, which started in 1971. Most of the Farah workforce in its Texas and New Mexico factories were Mexican American women. A 21-month-long strike and boycott enjoyed the support of Chicano organizations as well as the UFWOC and other segments of organized labor. The combined strike-and-boycott effort was successful, with a union contract signed with Farah in March 1974.

8. Greenhouse (1998) provides statistics to demonstrate labor's demise, in part by noting the decline of strikes, one indicator of union resolve. Federal labor officials reported that only 29 large-scale strikes ocurred in 1997. This total is half the number of a decade ago and one-eighth the number of two decades ago.

9. An interesting exception is a labor boycott that occurred in the early 1970s in an unnamed Midwestern city referred to by researchers as "Ericson" (Miller and Sturdivant, 1977). The researchers, testing the hypothesis that corporate misbehavior will be punished in the marketplace, collected data in the town after an acrimonious labor-management conflict arose. Sixty-eight workers at a local manufacturing plant contracted a severe illness due to unsafe working conditions that plant managers had known about but had not acted to remedy.

The company also had fast-food outlets in Ericson, and the union for the ill workers at the manufacturing plant called for local residents to boycott these outlets. The researchers compared sales for the boycotted fast-food outlets with others in the area. The study findings revealed a drop in sales at the company's local fast-food outlets and particularly at those that were the focus of the boycott.

Chapter 4

1. While consumer boycotts are a serious business for the boycotters and their targets, the phenomenon has not escaped the attention of humorists. Writing in 1902, the editor of the *Baltimore American*, in a prescient poem that looked at a future of continuing increases in beef prices, offered the following rhythmic recommendation:

> Mary had a little lamb,
>> With mintsauce on the side;
> When Mary saw the meat trust's bill,
>> It shocked her so she cried.
> Mary had a little veal,
>> A cutlet, nicely broiled;
> Her papa, to pay for that veal,
>> All morning sorely toiled.
> Mary had a little steak,
>> A porterhouse quite small;
> And when the bill came in, she sighed,
>> No dress for me next fall.
> Mary had a little roast,
>> As juicy as could be;
> And Mary's papa simply went,
>> Right into bankruptcy.
> Mary isn't eating meat,
>> She has a better plan;
> She vows it's ladylike to be
>> A vegetarian.

2. Tref meat is nonkosher, a taboo food item for the mainly Orthodox Jewish residents of New York City at the time of the boycott.
3. A more recent example considers boycotts called against Monsanto due to alleged health risks associated with two of its products, the artificial sweetener Nutrasweet and Bovine Growth Hormone (rBGH).

Chapter 5

1. According to Meier and Rudwick (1968–1969), there were precedents for the streetcar segregation and the boycotts it engendered. During the Reconstruction era following the Civil War there had been effective protests against Jim Crow horsecars by blacks in Charleston, Louisville, New Orleans, and Richmond, and a consumer boycott was reported in Savannah.
2. Some of the more important references are Abernathy (1989), Blumberg (1984), Branch (1988), Brooks (1974), Garrow (1987,

1989), Kennedy (1989), King (1958), Morris (1984), Powledge (1991), and Wright (1991).

3. The power of the media here was noted by local leader E. D. Nixon, who claimed that the news reports did "more to help bring people together in Montgomery, with reference to the bus boycott, than anything else." He added that the boycott planners "couldn't have paid for the publicity the white folks gave us free of charge" (Wright, 1991, p. 59).

4. According to some observers one factor that may have inadvertently contributed to this high figure was the decision by the city to mount a police presence throughout Montgomery on December 5 "to insure that black people were not restrained from riding the buses by those promoting the boycott" (Wright, 1991, p. 62). Police officers on motorcycles trailed the buses and others patrolled the principal bus stops. The presence of white police officers in segregated Montgomery of 1955 was hardly reassuring to the black working-class people who were the buses' largest group of riders. Indeed, some may well have seen it as a sign of intimidation. According to Wright,

> Seeing other police officers standing at the bus stops, many blacks refused to go to these waiting stations. They continued walking or took an alternative means of transportation to work. (1991, p. 62)

She concluded that the city's attempt to fight the boycott backfired.

5. Interestingly, the Montgomery Improvement Association also asked that black drivers be hired to operate buses on predominantly black routes; thus the boycott can be considered a labor protest as well as a consumer economic protest although it seems clear that the labor concerns were far lower in priority.

6. The street speakers and preachers were often masters at electrifying crowds with their colorful language. The following example from Hunter (1977) refers to a Southside Chicago boycott of a Woolworth store in 1930:

> Ladies and gentlemen, friends and fellow citizens, employment agents, private detectives, traitors, trap-setters, and stool pigeons. I am pleased to be with you tonight. If I were base enough to go into these Woolworth stores, I would deserve to be buried in a wilderness of worms, with rats for my relatives, lizards for my lodge members and bats for my beneficiaries. I would deserve a python for my pillow, funkweeds for flowers, maggots for mourners, polecats for pallbearers, a crocodile carcass for a casket and a cesspool for my cemetery. (p. 92)

7. The role of local newspapers as facilitators or combatants of consumer boycotts deserves study by journalism scholars. In New

York's Harlem and the Chicago Southside there is evidence to suggest that when two newspapers exist in a locale, one the establishment publication and the other the anti-establishment competition, the papers may adopt contrasting positions on a local consumer boycott, with the establishment paper being antiboycott and its competitor being proboycott. Both Hunter (1977) and Muraskin (1972) suggest that there may be more than a simple difference in philosophy involved here, since the stores being boycotted in Chicago and New York had frequently placed their advertisements in the establishment papers, so these publications may have had an economic incentive not to "bite the hand that feeds them."

8. As Moon (1966) has indicated, public utilities such as the non-competitive telephone, gas, and electricity companies were strong sources of irritation for blacks in the 1930s due to their monopolistic character and often hostile attitudes toward desegregating their workforces. To boycott such monopolies required creative approaches, and boycott leaders were often equal to the challenge. For example, Harlem boycotters of Consolidated Edison in 1938 organized a "blackout" against the company. Thousands of Harlem residents turned off their lights every Tuesday night and used candles instead. According to Hunter (1977), the campaign was so successful that Harlem merchants pleaded with Consolidated Edison to yield to its demands since the retailers were being criticized by the local community for leaving their lights on during Tuesday evening shopping hours.

9. The new wave of militancy received some welcome help from the federal government in the form of a 1938 Supreme Court ruling. Prior to the ruling picketed merchants had successfully sought injunctions against the black boycotters. These injunctions, granted in Baltimore, Cleveland, New York, and Washington, maintained that the right to picket was guaranteed (by the Norris-LaGuardia Anti-Injunction Act) to labor organizations engaged in labor conflicts, but not to nonlabor groups engaged in racial disputes. The landmark Supreme Court ruling, handed down on March 28, 1938, affirmed the right to picket a business to combat racial discrimination. The ruling held, "Race discrimination by an employer may reasonably be deemed more unfair and less excusable than discrimination against workers on the grounds of union affiliation" (Moon, 1966, p. 254).

10. The Port Gibson, Mississippi, boycott in 1969 was the most publicized of this group because of the judicial issues that grew out of it. The boycott had been called by the NAACP over several issues, including discrimination in hiring practices. The white merchants who were the boycott targets sued the NAACP for $3.5 million. A

Mississippi court found in favor of the merchants, forcing the NAACP to initiate an urgent national drive to raise $1.6 million to post bond and protect the organization's assets. In a landmark ruling in 1982 the U.S. Supreme Court overturned the state court decision, effectively reaffirming the right of groups to use the boycott as a protest tactic.

11. And due to space limitations our coverage of African American consumer boycotts is far from complete. Not noted are boycotts in the early 1960s of retail stores in such Southern cities as Birmingham and Nashville, to protest discrimination against African American consumers (Weens, 1998). Also not noted are a variety of media-related boycotts protesting the relative absence of African Americans in 1960s television advertising (Watson, 1990) as well as the demeaning quality of radio and television programs about African American life, such as *Amos 'n' Andy*, (Ely, 1991; Shankman, 1978).

Chapter 6

1. As Orbach (1982) points out, while the boycott began in response to the increasing anti-Jewish brutality of the Nazi regime, its roots are embedded in the World War I defeat of Germany. After the monarchy fell, the new democratic Weimar Republic was established, but it soon found itself overburdened by heavy reparations and the worldwide Depression of the late 1920s. During the Depression the then-small Nazi Party gained support, and in January 1933 its leader, Adolf Hitler, was appointed as the new chancellor of Germany. The successful March 5 election for the Nazis was an important step in consolidating their power and in making Hitler and his anti-Semitic policies a new and formidable presence in the Germany of the pre-World War II period.

2. Interestingly, this boycott was not limited to merchants in that "physicians and lawyers" were included as well (Gottlieb, 1967).

3. Orbach's (1982) article is interesting from a historical perspective because he makes comparisons between the anti-Nazi boycott of 1933–1941 and the Jewish boycott of Ancona in 1556. In the Ancona initiative Turkish Jews were led by Donna Gracia and Don Joseph Nasi, who attempted to boycott the merchants of Ancona in retaliation for the execution of 24 marranoes. This surrogate boycott, which failed due to faulty execution, is used by Orbach to draw interesting parallels between the two campaigns separated by almost 400 years. For example, he points out that opponents of both boycotts emphasized their dangers to the Jews in the target territories (Germany and Ancona). Also, in both instances, many

members of the rabbinate, often a traditional group in Jewish society, were not in favor of the boycotts, perhaps because of the "secular" quality of the boycott tactic.

4. Some opponents went further to refer to the boycott strategy as "fighting Hitlerism with Hitlerism." In this view Jews would be compromising their moral principles by boycotting, and "they could not very well scream rape when the Nazis boycotted German Jews" (Orbach, 1982, p. 157).

5. And the sleeping dragon, according to Dinnerstein (1994), appeared not to be sound asleep in the United States in the 1930s. He cites evidence that the fear of increasing domestic anti-Semitism was not without foundation.

6. The American Jewish Committee was the only major American Jewish defense organization that declined to support the boycott. In 1933 its president, Cyrus Adler, expressed the committee's position:

> The American Jewish Committee, in agreement with responsible Jewish organizations in Europe, declines to sanction a declaration of boycott against Germany. We will not make threats, but rather rely upon the moral forces of America and of other enlightened countries in the world. If these moral forces are dead, then civilized man will perish and brutes will rule. This is a question larger than Germany, even larger than the Jews. It should engage the attention of all nations who are still possessed of conscience. (Gottlieb, 1973, p. 223)

7. Untermeyer defined the boycott domain so broadly that it included a professional prizefight between an American, Jim Braddock, and a German, Max Schmeling. The fight was canceled, but, according to Evans (1982), not because of the anti-Nazi boycott.

8. According to Gottlieb, the Jewish War Veterans were the first boycott group to use picketing, a tactic he calls "the harshest and most problematic, but also the most effective measure in pressuring the boycott offender into submission" (1973, p. 202).

9. Indeed, Mexico had been a strong supporter of Israel in the United Nations from the time the UN voted to establish the new nation in 1947.

10. According to Montgomery (1989) the seven corporate sponsors of the two-part show withdrew support, leaving CBS with no commercials appearing in either episode. Moreover, 39 of the 198 CBS affiliates refused to air the two episodes. Finally, nothing further was heard about the planned punitive boycott of the seven corporate sponsors, which strongly suggests that it was a call for a boycott rather than a boycott campaign.

11. The description of the WAVAW actions that follows is drawn from

an unpublished interview in May 1991 of WAVAW spokeswoman Joan Howarth by Rita R. Robison. I thank Robison for the use of the interview.

12. According to Plagens (1991), Knopf was not the first publisher to consider *American Psycho*. The book was first under contract with Simon & Schuster, but once Ellis delivered the manuscript in December 1989, the negative in-house reaction was so strong that Simon & Schuster CEO Richard Snyder decided in November 1990 his company would not publish it. Ellis, however, was allowed to retain the sizable advance for the book ($300,000). Several days after the Simon & Schuster announcement, Knopf president Sonny Mehta decided to publish the book under the Vintage imprint. A few weeks later LA-NOW called for a boycott of Knopf.

13. This comment is from the Robison interview of Joan Howarth cited in note 11.

Chapter 7

1. Much of the description of the Legion of Decency campaign that follows is drawn from the detailed historical account provided by Inglis (1947). Other sources include Faccy (1945), Perlman (1936), Quigley (1937), and Seabury (1926).

2. Inglis (1947) notes that the industry focus on self-regulation seemed less concerned with expressing a sense of professional responsibility to the public and more concerned with responding to a fear of government intrusion.

3. According to Inglis (1947, p. 116) one interpretation of the rather vague "Don'ts and Be Carefuls" was "Don't forget to stop before you have gone too far" and "If you can't be good, be careful."

4. Also contributing to the discussion were the results of two special audience surveys, one commissioned by ABC and the other by NBC. Both surveys found, not surprisingly, that viewers were against excessive sex and violence on television, but both surveys also found that the so-called offensive programs were being watched on a regular basis by almost equal percentages of Moral Majority members and non-Moral Majority members (Schwartz, 1981).

5. Also dissociating herself from the planned boycott was Phyllis Schlafly, whose anti-ERA group had been part of the coalition.

6. One viewer expressed a sense of frustration with the advertisers and with Wildmon: "*Sister, Sister* is superb television, pointing the way to what television could be were it not for the spinelessness of the major advertisers who control the medium when confronted with pipsqueaks of the Wildmon variety" (Montgomery, 1989, p. 173).

7. Much of the description of ICCR that follows is based on the comprehension and timely account provided recently by Patricia O'Toole (1998) in her stimulating book, *Money and Morals in America.*

8. And at this writing, some 10 years later, the infant formula manufacturers have apparently still not complied with the WHO code. A study published by Taylor (1998) in the *British Medical Journal* looked at marketing practices in Bangladesh, Poland, South Africa, and Thailand. The study concluded that both the nature and number of violations found suggest the existence of "systematic contravention" of the WHO code.

Chapter 8

1. For descriptions of these and related organizations see Finsen & Finsen (1994), Jasper & Nelkin (1992), Scarce (1990), and Zakin (1993).

2. Cosmetics would appear to fall into this category, although some well-known brands of perfumes have distinctive odors that might reveal their identities to knowledgeable consumers.

3. For a full story of the glitches see Putnam (1992).

Chapter 9

1. See Chapters 3 and 5 for more detailed examples of boycotts by labor unions and black groups. Particularly relevant in Chapter 5 is the story of the effort to establish Housewives Leagues during the Great Depression, consisting of black women who agreed to make their consumer purchases in black-operated retail outlets.

2. See Chapter 6 for a fuller description of this campaign.

Chapter 10

1. Mills (1996) has recently raised other ethical questions about the circumstances that justify the termination of a consumer boycott. Her provocative comments are discussed and analyzed in Friedman (in press).

2. Obstructionist boycotts, discussed very briefly earlier in this chapter and more fully in Chapter 1, would appear to be what Garrett has in mind in that they are initiatives that pressure consumers into complying unwillingly with a "don't-buy" demand.

Appendix A

1. This is an abridged and edited version of an article with the same title that appeared in the summer 1971 issue of the *Journal of Consumer Affairs.* The study reported here was undertaken in 1967 when I was a Congressional Fellow of the American Political Sci-

ence Association. At the time I was working in Washington, D.C., as a staff member in the office of U.S. Congressman Lester Wolff of New York. I would like to thank Mr. Wolff for his interest and encouragement during the research planning and execution stages of the study.

2. How much significance should be attributed to this departure is not clear. It will be recalled that the data for the key participants derive from estimates offered by the protest leader respondents, and while figures for such physical characteristics as age and sex can be expected to be fairly reliable, greater uncertainties are to be anticipated in judging the less readily accessible political party information.

REFERENCES

Abernathy, R. D. (1989). *And the walls came tumbling down*. New York: Harper & Row.

Adams, T. (1991). *Grass roots: Ordinary people changing America*. New York: Citadel Press.

Alinsky, S. (1972). *Rules for Radicals*. New York: Vintage.

Allvine, F. C. (1969). The future for trading stamps and games. *Journal of Marketing, 33*, 45–52.

Anderson, S. (1993, Jan. 9). Why Colorado is being boycotted. *Denver Post*, p. A12.

Anonymous. (1991, Feb.). Civil rights activists try an old proven tactic: the resurgence of boycotts. *Emerge*, p. 52.

Bandura, A. (1969). *Principles of behavior modification*. New York: Holt, Rinehart & Winston.

Bandura, A. (1987). Self-regulation of motivation and action through goal systems. In V. Hamilton & N. H. Fryda (Eds.), *Cognition, motivation, and affect: A cognitive science view*. Dordrecht, The Netherlands: Martinus Nijhoff.

Barnes, C. (1983). *Journey from Jim Crow: The desegregation of Southern transit*. New York: Columbia University Press.

Baxandall, R., Gordon, L., & Reverby, S. (Eds.). (1976). *America's working women: A documentary history, 1600 to the present*. New York: Random House.

Bell, D. (1962). *The end of ideology*. New York: Collier Books.

Berry, J. (1977). *Lobbying for the people: The political behavior of public interest groups*. Princeton, NJ: Princeton University Press.

Berry, M. F. (1988). *Why ERA failed: Politics, women's rights, and the amending process of the Constitution*. Bloomington: Indiana University Press.

Bird, N., & Robinson, J. (1972). The effectiveness of the union label and "buy union" campaigns. *Industrial and Labor Relations Review, 25*, 512–523.

Blumberg, R. L. (1984). *Civil rights: The 1960s freedom struggle*. Boston: Twayne.

Boulding, K. E. (1968). Reflections on protest. *Bulletin of the Atomic Scientists, 24*, 18–20.

Boycott, anti-Nazi (all countries). (1971). *Encyclopedia Judaica, 4*, 1280–1282.

Branch, T. (1988). *Parting the waters: America in the King years.* New York: Simon & Schuster.

Brier, S. (Ed.). (1992). *Who built America? The nation's economy, politics, culture, and society.* New York: Pantheon.

Brobeck, S. (1991). *The modern consumer movement.* Boston: G. K. Hall.

Brobeck, S. (Ed.). (1997). *Encyclopedia of the consumer movement.* Santa Barbara, CA: ABC-CLIO, Inc.

Brockway, G. (1975). *The effects of an economic boycott on retail strategic and tactical decision making.* Ann Arbor, MI: University Microfilms International.

Brooks, T. R. (1974). *Walls come tumbling down: A history of the civil rights movement, 1940–1970.* New Jersey: Prentice Hall.

Brown, J. (1972). *The United Farm Workers' grape strike and boycott, 1965–1970: An evaluation of the culture of poverty theory.* Unpublished doctoral dissertation, Cornell University, Ithaca, NY.

Brown, W. (1978, June 26). Boycott: Black protest in Tupelo stirs Klan-led backlash. *Washington Post,* pp. 1–2.

Capeci, D. J., Jr. (1980). From Harlem to Montgomery: The bus boycotts and leadership of Adam Clayton Powell, Jr., and Martin Luther King, Jr. *The Historian, 41*(4), 721–737.

Cassidy, R. (1974). Jesse Jackson: Will push come to shove? *Business and Society Review/Innovation, 10*, 55–63.

Caudron, Shari (1993, March 1). The Colorado Boycott: A Wake-up Call to All Businesses? *Industry Week,* p. 48.

Chase, S., & Schlink, F. (1927). *Your money's worth.* New York: Macmillan.

Chetley, A. (1986). *The politics of baby foods: Successful challenges to an international marketing strategy.* London: Frances Pinter.

Clarkson, F. (1984). The taming of Nestle: A boycott success story. *Multinational Monitor, 5*, 1–3.

Clary, M. (1991, April 29). Save *Twin Peaks! Adweek's Marketing Week,* p. 17.

Coles, J. V. (1938). *The consumer-buyer and the market.* New York: Wiley.

Commanding Officer, 70th Precinct, New York City Police Department. (1990). *Chronology of events surrounding Haitian demonstration on Church Avenue.* New York: Author.

Conner, P. (1990, June 17). The conversion of StarKist. *This World,* pp. 7–11.

Cunningham, M. (1992, May/June). If you're queer and you're not angry in 1992, you're not paying attention. *Mother Jones,* pp. 60–68.

Davidson, W., Worrell, D., & El-Jelly, A. (1995). Influencing managers to change unpopular corporate behavior through boycotts and divestitures: A stock market test. *Business and Society, 34*(2), 171–186.

Davis, J. (1991). *Greening business: Managing for sustainable development.* Oxford: Basil Blackwell.

DeGraff, H. (1967). Rising food prices: Implications to the food industry. In *Rising food prices: Causes and consequences.* Ithaca: New York State College of Agriculture.

DeSimone, B. (1981, Aug. 1). Don't vacation in Florida, ERA campaigner says here. *Ann Arbor News,* p. 3.

Dinnerstein, L. (1994). *Antisemitism in America.* New York: Oxford University Press.

Donald, M. H. (1966). Implications of nonresponse for the interpretation of mail questionnaire data. *Public Opinion Quarterly, 24,* 99–114.

Dunne, J. G. (1971). *Delano.* New York: Farrar, Straus & Giroux.

Elliott, S. (1992, April 18). When products are tied to causes. *New York Times,* p. 17.

Ely, M. P. (1991). *The adventures of Amos 'n' Andy.* New York: Free Press.

Entine, J. (1994). Shattered image. *Business Ethics, 8,* 23–29.

Ettinger, W. (1996). Headline sickens. *Boycott Quarterly, 3*(4), 4.

Evans, A. (1982). The Jim Braddock-Max Schmeling affair: An assessment of a Jewish boycott of a professional prizefight. *Journal of Sport and Social Issues, 6,* 1–12.

Facey, P. W. (1945). *The Legion of Decency.* Unpublished doctoral dissertation, Fordham University, New York, NY.

Feder, B. J. (1989, November 26). Pressuring Perdue. *New York Times Magazine,* p. 32.

Finsen, L., & Finsen, S. (1994). *The animal rights movement in America.* New York: Twayne.

Foner, P. S. (1955). *History of the labor movement in the United States.* New York: International Publishers.

Forbath, W. E. (1991). *Law and the shaping of the American labor movement.* Massachusetts and London: Harvard University Press.

Forbes, J. D. (1985). Organizational and political dimensions of consumer pressure groups. *Journal of Consumer Policy, 8,* 289–302.

Ford, D., & Vezeridis, B. (1978). Ecological pressures on the firm: Cases and conclusions. *Cranfield Management Review, 2.*

Fowler, G. (1984, Sept. 20). Rights groups sign pact with Coors. *New York Times,* p. 17.

Friedman, M. (1968). Local consumer organizations: Problems, prospects and a proposal. *Journal of Consumer Affairs, 2,* 205–211.

Friedman, M. (1971). The 1966 consumer protest as seen by its leaders. *Journal of Consumer Affairs, 5,* 1–23.

Friedman, M. (1985). Consumer boycotts in the United States,

1970–1980: Contemporary events in historical perspective. *Journal of Consumer Affairs, 12,* 96–117.

Friedman, M. (1991). Consumer boycotts: A conceptual framework and research agenda. *Journal of Social Issues, 47,* 149–168.

Friedman, M. (1995a). American consumer boycotts in response to rising food prices: Housewives' protests at the grassroots level. *Journal of Consumer Policy, 18,* 55–72.

Friedman, M. (1995b). On promoting a sustainable future through consumer activism. *Journal of Social Issues, 51,* 197–215.

Friedman, M. (1996a). Grassroots groups confront the corporation: Contemporary strategies in historical perspective. *Journal of Social Issues, 52,* 153–167.

Friedman, M. (1996b). A positive approach to organized consumer action: The "buycott" as an alternative to the boycott. *Journal of Consumer Policy, 19,* 439–451.

Friedman, M. (1997). Consumer boycotts. In Brobeck, S. (Ed.), *The encyclopedia of the consumer movement* (pp. 67–68). New York: ABC-CLIO Publishing, Inc.

Friedman, M. (in press). Ethical dilemmas associated with consumer boycotts. *Journal of Social Philosophy.*

Fusfeld, D. R. (1980). *The rise and repression of radical labor in the United States, 1877–1918.* Chicago: Charles H. Kerr Publishing Company.

Garman, E. T. (1993). *Consumer economic issues in America* (2nd ed.). Houston: Dame Publications.

Garrett, D. E. (1986). Consumer boycotts: Are targets always the bad guys? *Business and Society Review, 58,* 17–21.

Garrett, D. E. (1987). The effectiveness of marketing policy boycotts: Environmental opposition to marketing. *Journal of Marketing, 51,* 46–57.

Garrow, D. (Ed.). (1987). *The Montgomery bus boycott and the women who started it: The memoir of Jo Ann Gibson Robinson.* Knoxville: University of Tennessee Press.

Garrow, D. (Ed.). (1989). *The walking city: The Montgomery bus boycott: 1955–1956.* Brooklyn, NY: Carlson.

Gitlin, T. (1981, Oct.). The new crusades: How the fundamentalists tied up the networks. *American Film.*

Gitlin, T. (1983). *Inside prime time.* New York: Pantheon.

Goodstein, L. (1998, June 14). Look who's leading the country. *New York Times,* p. WK4.

Gordon, M. A. (1975). The labor boycott in New York City, 1880–1886. *Labor History, 16*(2), 184–229.

Gottlieb, M. (1967). *The anti-Nazi boycott movement in the American Jewish community.* Doctoral dissertation, University Microfilms, Inc., Ann Arbor, MI.

Gottlieb, M. (1968). The first of April boycott and the reaction of the

American Jewish community. *American Jewish Historical Quarterly*, *57*, 516–556.

Gottlieb, M. (1973). The anti-Nazi boycott movement in the United States: An ideological and sociological appreciation. *Jewish Social Studies*, *35*, 198–227.

Gottlieb, M. (1983). Reactions of American Jewish defense organizations to the liquidation of the B'nai B'rith in Nazi Germany. *Jewish Social Studies*, *45*, 287–310.

Gould, J. (1961, March 26). Disturbing pact: Compromise on "Untouchables" holds dangers for well-being of TV. *New York Times*, p. 17.

Graen, G. (1969). Instrumentality theory of work motivation. *Journal of Applied Psychology*, *53*, 206–212.

Green, H. (1990). *On strike at Hormel*. Philadelphia: Temple University Press.

Greenhouse, L. (1995, Feb. 22). High Court to Rule on Colorado Law Barring Protection of Homosexuals Against Bias. *New York Times*, p. A17.

Greenhouse, S. (1998, July 12). Labor unrest masks peaceful trend. *New York Times*, p. WK4.

Greyser, S. A., & Bauer, R. A. (1966). Americans and advertising: Thirty years of public opinion. *Public Opinion Quarterly*, *30*, 69–78.

Gutman, H. (1973). Work, culture, and society in industrializing America, 1815–1919. *American Historical Review*, *78*(3), 576–577.

Hager, M. M. (1991). Farm workers, boycotts, and free speech. *Labor Law Journal*, *42*(12), 792–799.

Hay, R., & Napier, H. S. (1973). Political effects of the Marianna black economic boycott: A preliminary statement. *Arkansas Business Review*, *6*(4), 3–6.

Herrmann, R. (1970). Consumerism: Its goals, organizations and future. *Journal of Marketing*, *34*(4), 55–60.

Herrmann, R. (1991). Participation and leadership in consumer movement organizations. *Journal of Social Issues*, *47*, 119–133.

Herrmann, R., & Mayer, R. (1997). The U.S. consumer movement: History and dynamics. In Brobeck, S. (Ed.), *Encyclopedia of the consumer movement*. Santa Barbara, CA: ABC- CLIO, Inc.

Herrmann, R., Walsh, E., & Warland, R. (1988). The organizations of the consumer movement: A comparative perspective. In E. S. Maynes & ACCI Research Committee (Eds.), *The frontier of research in the consumer interest* (pp. 470–494). Columbia, MO: American Council on Consumer Interests.

Hicks, J. P. (1985, July 25). Coors mends minority fences. *New York Times*, pp. D1, D5.

Hinds, M. D. (1989, April 15). Value of car crash test is contested. *New York Times*, p. 52.

Hirschman, A. (1970). *Exit, voice and loyalty*. Cambridge, MA: Harvard University Press.

Hunter, G. J. (1977). *"Don't buy from where you can't work"*: Black urban boycott movements during the Depression, 1929–1941. Doctoral dissertation, University of Michigan, Ann Arbor.

Hyman, P. (1980). Immigrant women and consumer protest: The New York City Kosher meat boycott of 1902. *American Jewish History,* 70, 91–105.

Inglis, R. A. (1947). *Freedom of the movies.* Chicago: University of Chicago Press.

Jackson, J. (1971). Two black boycotts: A contrast of success and failure. *Afro-American Studies,* 2, 87–94.

Jackson, J. (1974). The guiding principle. *Business and Society Review/Innovation,* 10, 61.

Jasper, J., & Nelkin, D. (1992). *The animal rights crusade.* New York: Free Press.

Jones, B. (1977, August 17). Consumers find coffee only as good as next price drop. *New York Times,* pp. 29–30.

Jordon, L. (1973). Meat boycott galvanizes consumers. *Voice of the Virginia Consumer,* May, p. 1.

Kandel, B. (1991, Jan. 4). Tensions ease year after NYC grocery boycott. *USA Today,* p. 8A.

Kennedy, R. (1989). Martin Luther King's constitution: A legal history of the Montgomery bus boycott. *Yale Law Journal,* 98(6), 999–1067.

Kilborn, P. T. (1992, April 9). Gay rights groups take aim at restaurant chain that's hot on Wall Street. *New York Times,* p. A8.

King, M. L., Jr. (1958). *Stride toward freedom: The Montgomery story.* New York: Harper & Row.

Klapper, Z. (1978). A boycott list to not buy by. *Business and Society Review,* 27, 33–37.

Kotler, P. (1972, May-June). What consumerism means for marketers. *Harvard Business Review,* 50, 48–57.

Kraft, J. (1973, April 3). Meat boycott: A lesson in public opinion. *Washington Post,* p. A19.

Krieger, D. (1971). The "another mother for peace" consumer campaign—a campaign that failed. *Journal of Peace Research,* 8.

Kushner, S. (1975). *Long road to Delano.* New York: International Publishers.

Laidler, H. (1913). *Boycotts and the labor struggle.* New York: Russell and Russell.

Laidler, H. (1930). Boycott. In R. A. Seligman (Ed.) *Encyclopedia of the Social Sciences* (pp. 662–666). New York: Macmillan.

Lawler, E. E. (1971). *Pay and organizational effectiveness: A psychological review.* New York: McGraw-Hill.

Lawler, E. E. (1973). *Motivation in work organizations.* Monterey, CA: Brooks/Cole.

Leo, J. (1992, Dec. 21). When in doubt, boycott. *U.S. News & World Report,* p. 35.

London, J., & Anderson, H. (1970). *So shall ye reap*. New York: Thomas Y. Crowell.

Lohr, S. (1993, Jan. 23). New appeals to pocketbook patriots. *New York Times*, p. 17.

Lott, J. (1997, Winter). The unintended legacy of Capt. Charles Boycott. *Boycott Quarterly, 13*, 16.

Lyons, Z. (1991, July). Marlboro cigarettes, Miller beer. *Boycott Monthly*, pp. 1–2.

Lyons, Z. (1994, Fall). Boycott reports. *Boycott Quarterly, 2*, 14–17.

Lyons, Z. (1995). Crazy Horse malt liquor: Custer in a can. *Boycott Quarterly, 2*, 29–30.

Lyons, Z. (1996, Summer). Anti-Queer boycott listing reprehensible. *Boycott Quarterly, 3*, 5–6.

Lyons, Z. (1998a, Spring). Ongoing boycotts. *Boycott Quarterly, 15*, 34.

Lyons, Z. (1998b, Spring). News and updates. *Boycott Quarterly, 15*, 26.

Mahoney, J. (1976). The relation of anticipated effectiveness, alienation and value structure to planned participation in a national meat boycott. *Psychology, 13*, 39–47.

Mann, E. (1986, Fall). Keeping GM Van Nuys open. *Labor Research Review*, pp. 35–45.

The Martin Luther King Jr. companion. (1991). New York: St. Martin's.

Mayer, R. (1989). *The consumer movement: Guardians of the market place*. Boston: Twayne.

McCarthy, J., & Zald, M. (1973). *The trend of social movements in America*. Morristown, NJ: General Learning Press.

McCarthy, J., & Zald, M. (1977). Resource mobilization and social movements: A partial theory. *American Journal of Sociology, 82*, 1212–1240.

McNulty, T. (1978, Aug. 11). Race fears resurface in Mississippi: Black protest, KKK's reaction, a echo of the '60s. *Chicago Tribune*, pp. 4–5.

Meier, A., & Rudwick, E. (1968–1969). The boycott movement against Jim Crow streetcars in the South, 1900–1906. *Journal of American History, 55*, 756–775.

Meier, B. (1998, Jan. 15). Files of R. J. Reynolds Tobacco show effort on youths. *New York Times*, p. A10.

Meisler, M. (1975, Dec. 14). Mexico trying to mollify U.S. Jews in boycott. *Los Angeles Times*, p. 1.

Meister, D., & Loftis, A. (1977). *A long time coming*. New York: MacMillan.

Miller, K. E., & Sturdivant, F. D. (1977). Consumer responses to socially questionable corporate behavior: An empirical test. *Journal of Consumer Research, 4*(1).

Mills, C. (1996). Should we boycott boycotts? *Journal of Social Philosophy, 27*, 136–148.

Mishel, L. (1985, Fall). Strengths & limits of non-workplace strategies. *Labor Research Review*, 69–79.

Montgomery bus boycott. (1981). *Southern Exposure*, 9(1), 12–21.

Montgomery, K. C. (1989). *Target: Prime time*. New York: Oxford University Press.

Moon, H. L. (1966, May). The black boycott. *The Crisis*, pp. 249–254, 278.

Morgan, E. S., & H. M. (1962). *The Stamp Act crisis*. New York: Collier Books.

Morris, A. D. (1984). *The origins of the civil rights movement*. New York: Free Press.

Morris, R. B. (Ed.). (1983). *A history of the American worker*. Princeton, NJ: Princeton University Press.

Mouat, L. (1977, Jan. 7). National boycott on coffee cools. *Christian Science Monitor*, p. 4.

Muraskin, W. (1972). The Harlem boycott of 1934: Black nationalism and the rise of labor-union consciousness. *Labor History*, 13(1), 361–373.

Nadel, M. (1971). *The politics of consumer protection*. Indianapolis: Bobbs-Merrill.

Naylor, J. C., Pritchard, R. D., & Ilgen, D. R. (1980). *A theory of behavior in organizations*. New York: Academic Press.

Neier, A. (1982, May 29). On boycotts. *The Nation*, pp. 642–643.

Nelson, W., & Prittie, T. (1977). *The economic war against the Jews*. New York: Random House.

Nemy, E. (1979, April 24). Chinese-Americans join other groups in campaign against Opium perfume. *New York Times*, p. C13.

New York City Mayor's Committee. (1990). *Report of the Mayor's Committee investigating the protest against two Korean-owned groceries on Church Ave. in Brooklyn*. New York: Author.

Noble, K. (1997, Feb. 15). NAACP is optimistic but has questions about new chief. *New York Times*, p. 9.

Norrell, R. J. (1985). *Reaping the whirlwind: The civil rights movement in Tuskegee*. New York: Alfred A. Knopf.

O'Guinn, T., & Faber, R. (1989).Compulsive buying. *Journal of Consumer Research, 16*, 147–157.

Olsen, M. T. (1968). Perceived legitimacy of social protest actions. *Social Problems, 15*, 297–309.

O'Neil, C. (1990, Aug. 1). Six activists storm Helms' office. *Outweek*, pp. 12, 32.

Orbach, W. (1982). Shattering the shackles of powerlessness: The debate surrounding the anti-Nazi boycott of 1933–41. *Modern Judaism, 2*, 149–169.

Orne, M. T. (1962). On the social psychology of the psychological experiment: With particular reference to demand characteristics and their implications. *American Psychologist, 17*, 776–783.

O'Toole, P. (1998). *Money and morals in America*. New York: Clarkson Potter Publishers.

Pagan, R. D. (1982, July 15). Carrying the fight to the critics of multinational capitalism: Think and act politically. *Vital Speeches of the Day, 48,* 19.

Perlman, W. J. (Ed.). (1936). *The movies on trial*. New York: Macmillan.

Peterson, E. (1995). *Restless: the memoirs of labor and consumer activist Esther Peterson*. Washington, D.C.: Caring Publishing.

Phillips, W., Jr. (1961). The boycott: A Negro community in conflict. *Phylon, 22,* 24–30.

Pinder, C. C. (1991). Valence-instrumentality-expectancy theory. In R. M. Steers & L. W. Porter (Eds.), *Motivation and work*. New York: McGraw-Hill.

Piott, S. L. (1981). Missouri and the beef trust: Consumer action and investigation. *Missouri Historical Review, 76,* 31–52.

Plagens, P. (1991, March 4). Confessions of a serial killer. *Newsweek,* pp. 58–59.

Porter, L. W., & Lawler, E. E. (1986). *Managerial attitudes and performance*. Homewood, IL: Dorsey.

Post, J. (1985). Assessing the Nestle boycott: Corporate accountability and human rights. *California Management Review, 27,* 113–131.

Powledge, F. (1991). *Free at last?* London: Little, Brown.

Prud'homme, A. (1990, July). The new face of Coors. *Business Month,* pp. 47–50.

Pruitt, S., & Friedman, M. (1986). Determining the effectiveness of consumer boycotts: A stock price analysis of their impact on corporate targets. *Journal of Consumer Policy, 9,* 375–387.

Putnam, T. (1992, Spring/Summer). Tuna boycott victory. *National Boycott News,* pp. 13–21.

Putnam, T. (1993a, Spring). Arizona Tourism. *National Boycott News.*

Putnam, T. (1993b, Spring). Boycotts are busting out all over. *Business and Society Review, 85,* 47–51.

Putnam, T. (1994, Summer). Boycott report: Warner-Lambert. *Boycott Quarterly,* pp. 42–44.

Putnam, T. (Ed.). (1990s). *National Boycott News*. Various issues.

Putnam, T., & Muck, T. (1991). Wielding the boycott weapon for social change. *Business and Society Review, 48,* 5–8.

Quigley, M. (1937). *Decency in motion pictures*. New York: Macmillan.

Rafferty, T. (1992, March 23). The current cinema. *New Yorker,* pp. 88–90.

Rea, S. (1974). The economics of a consumer boycott. *Journal of Economics and Business, 27,* 89–92.

Redpath, J. (1881). Talks of Ireland. *Magazine of Western History, 5,* 214–215.

Remer, C. (1933). *A study of Chinese boycotts: With special reference to their economic effectiveness.* Baltimore: Johns Hopkins Press.

Report of the National Commission on Food Marketing. (1966). Washington, D.C.: U.S. Government Printing Office.

Riesman, D. (1954). *Individualism reconsidered.* Garden City, NY: Doubleday.

Roberts, A. (1975). Do economic boycotts ever work? *New Society, 11.*

Rogers, R. (1981, Summer). How to confront corporations. *Business & Society Review,* pp. 60–64.

Sahagun, Louis (1995, Oct. 9). Gays weigh alternatives to boycott. *Los Angeles Times,* p. 14.

Savan, L. (1989, June 6). Where the boycotts are. *Village Voice,* pp. 47–48.

Scarce, R. (1990). *The eco-warriors.* Chicago: Noble Press.

Schwab, D., Olian-Gottlieb, J., & Henemen, H. (1979). Between subjects expectancy theory research. *Psychological Bulletin, 86,* 139–147.

Schwartz, T. (1981, June 19). Studies by 2 networks dispute Moral Majority. *New York Times.*

Scott, J. (1985). *Weapons of the weak: Everyday forms of peasant resistance.* New Haven, CT: Yale University Press.

Seabury, W. M. (1926). *The public and the motion picture industry.* New York: Macmillan.

Sen, S. (1996). Marketing and minority civil rights: The case of Amendment 2 and the Colorado boycott. *Journal of Public Policy and Marketing, 15,* 311–318.

Sentry Insurance Co. (1977). *Consumerism at the crossroads* (a national opinion survey conducted for Sentry by Louis Harris & Associates, Inc. and Marketing Science Institute). Stevens Point, WI: Author.

Shankman, A. (1978). Black pride and protest. *Journal of Popular Culture, 12,* 236–252.

Sharp, G. (1972). *The politics of nonviolent action.* Boston: Porter Sargent.

Sims, C. (1990, May 17). Black shoppers and Korean grocers: Ties of need and mistrust. *New York Times,* p. A15.

Sims, C. (1993, Aug. 31). NAACP revises the prize. *New York Times,* pp. B1, C2.

Skotnes, A. (1994). "Buy where you can work": Boycotting for jobs in African-American Baltimore, 1933–1934. *Journal of Social History, 27,* 735–762.

Smith, G. (1982). *The consumer interest.* London: John Martin.

Smith, N. C. (1990). *Morality and the market.* London: Routledge.

Smith, T. (1996, Nov. 1). Message from executive director Timothy Smith. *The Corporate Examiner, 25*(5), 3–4.

Stahl, M. J., & Harrell, A. M. (1981). Efforts decisions with behavioral decisions theory. *Organizational Behavior and Human Performance, 27,* 303–325.

Stein, A. (1975). Post-war consumer boycotts. *Radical America, 9,* 156–161.

Stencel, M. (1991). The growing influence of boycotts. *Editorial Research Reports, 3*(1), 2–13.

Sterling, C., & Kittross, J. M. (1978). *Stay tuned: A concise history of American broadcasting.* Belmont, CA: Wadsworth.

Stuart, E. (1992, April 18). When products are tied to causes. *New York Times,* p. 17.

Swift, J. (1720). *A proposal for the universal use of Irish manufacture in cloaths and furniture of houses, etc. utterly rejecting and renouncing every thing wearable that comes from England.* Dublin: E. Waters Publisher.

Taatgen, H. (1992). The boycott in the Irish civilizing process. *Anthropological Quarterly, 65,* 163–176.

Taylor, A. (1998, Apr. 11). Violations of the international code of marketing of breast milk substitutes: Prevalence in four countries. *The British Medical Journal, 316* (7138), 1117–1122.

Taylor, R. B. (1975). *Chavez and the farm workers.* Boston: Beacon Press.

Terry, B. (1972, Feb. 14). Marianna—a town torn by race. *Washington Post,* p. 3.

Thompson, D. (1989, Dec. 25). What's the cure for burnout? *Time,* p. 68.

Thompson, E. P. (1971). The moral economy of the English crowd in the eighteenth century. *Past and Present, 50,* 116.

Thorelli, H. B. (1955). *The federal antitrust policy.* Baltimore: Johns Hopkins Press.

Tilly, C. (1978). *From mobilization to revolution.* Reading, MA: Addison-Wesley.

Toro, M. (1992). [Labor boycotts; Letter]. Unpublished raw data.

Tulsky, F. (1978). Southern issues and organizing: Standing up to fear in Mississippi. *Southern Exposure, 6*(3), 68–72.

Turk, E. L. (1982). The great Berlin beer boycott of 1894. *Central European History, 15*(4), 377–397.

United States Commission on Civil Rights. (1992). *Civil rights issues facing Asian Americans in the 1990s.* Washington, D.C.: Author.

Vogel, D. (1970). *Lobbying the corporation.* New York: Basic Books.

Vroom, V. H. (1964). *Work and motivation.* New York: Wiley.

Ware, N. (1929). *The labor movement in the United States: 1860–1895.* New York: Appleton.

Watson, M. A. (1990). *The expanding vista.* New York: Oxford University Press.

Weems, R.E. (1998). *Desegregating the* dollar. New York: New York University Press.

Weisbord, R. G., & Stein, A. (1970). *Bittersweet encounter: The Afro-American and the American Jew.* Westport, CT: Negro Universities Press.

Weisman, J. (1979, March 17). He's counting every jiggle and cuss-word. *TV Guide*, pp. 12–14.

Welles, B. (1976, June 27). Travel power: The story behind the Mexico boycott. *New York Times*, Section 10, p. 1.

Welsh, H. (1990). *Animal testing and consumer products*. Washington, D.C.: Investor Responsibility Research Center Inc.

Whitney, S. (1984). *The Equal Rights Amendment: The history and its movement*. New York: Franklin Watts Publishers.

Winter, R.C. (1967, June 26). Supermarkets attempt to placate house-wives as higher prices loom. *Wall Street Journal*, p. 1.

Wohl, L. (1974, March). Phyllis Schlafly: The sweetheart of the silent majority. *Ms.*, pp. 55–56.

Wolman, L. (1914). *The boycott in American trade unions*. Baltimore: Johns Hopkins Press.

Wooton, G. O. (1978). *Pressure politics in contemporary Britain*. Lexington, MA: Lexington Books.

Wright, M. (1993, October). Avoidance tactics. *Atlantic Monthly*, pp. 44–48.

Wright, R. H. (1991). *The birth of the Montgomery bus boycott*. Southfield, MI: Charro Press.

Zakin, S. (1993). *Coyotes and town dogs: Earth First! and the environmental movement*. New York: Viking.

Zorc, A. (1991, Summer). Cracker Barrel. *Boycott Action News*, p. 14.

PERMISSIONS

INDEX